the series on school reform

Patricia A. Wasley
Coalition of
Essential Schools

Ann Lieberman
NCREST

SERIES EDITORS

Joseph P. McDonald
Annenberg Institute
for School Reform

This series also incorporates earlier titles in the
Professional Development and Practice Series

Assessing Student Learning

From GRADING to UNDERSTANDING

David Allen Editor

Foreword by Howard Gardner

Teachers College
Columbia University
New York and London

Published by Teachers College Press, 1234 Amsterdam Avenue, New York, NY 10027

Library of Congress Cataloging-in-Publication Data

Assessing student learning : from grading to understanding / edited by
    David Allen ; foreword by Howard Gardner.
        p.   cm. — (The series on school reform)
    Includes bibliographical references and index.
    ISBN 0-8077-3754-2 (cloth). — ISBN 0-8077-3753-4 (pbk.)
    1. Grading and marking (Students)—United States. 2. Educational
tests and measurements—United States. 3. Portfolios in education—
United States.   I. Allen, David, 1961–   . II. Series.
LB3051.A7664   1998
371.27—dc21   98-16982

ISBN 0-8077-3753-4 (paper)
ISBN 0-8077-3754-2 (cloth)

Printed on acid-free paper

Manufactured in the United States of America

05   04   03   02   01   00   99   8   7   6   5   4   3   2

Contents

PART III: CONTEXTS THAT WORK

Foreword

HOWARD GARDNER

Despite the conflicts that roil every profession, a broad consensus usually exists about viable means of training students. In medicine, it is assumed that students will attend case conferences where patients will be presented and discussed by the hospital staff. In the law, students ponder precedent-making cases, are trained in Socratic dialogue, and learn to write briefs. Graduate training in the arts and sciences features a close apprenticeship with a master disciplinarian and culminates in the authoring of a dissertation.

These training regimens all focus on the work that the future professional will carry out. The novice sees instances of quality work from the first, becomes cognizant of the standards that are applied in the profession, is drawn as rapidly as possible into productive work, and ultimately makes the transition to a full-blown professional. Whatever the imperfections, few critics would challenge these basic rules of operation.

Such training should ensure two outcomes. First of all, the new professional should be prepared to carry out the work that is central to that profession, whether it be the diagnosis and treatment of patients or the preparation and argument of cases in the courtroom. Second, the work of the new professional should display the skills that are valued today by leading members of the profession. Moreover, to the extent that the profession itself changes, it is expected—and opportunities are accordingly provided—that professionals will retool and become current with the most innovating thinking and practices.

Doubtless this picture is idealized to some extent; the grass is always greener in other professional pastures. Nonetheless, it is patent that teaching in the United States deviates to a distressing degree from this portrait of professional training. Much of teacher education still consists of listening to lectures by individuals who themselves have not been in front of a precollegiate classroom in many years; and many, perhaps most, of our teachers have little if any first-hand experience with the practices and innovations endorsed by leading educators—ranging from personalized pedagogy, to alternative forms of assessment, to effective learning in groups. To be sure, inservice training and summer institutes are more common now than in the past; yet even they do not substitute for the intensive practice, with tailored feedback, that characterizes training in our most rewarded professions.

As a result of this state of affairs, the kind of work that is respected by educated adults is only infrequently central in the lives of young children. From the point of view of most children—and, reluctantly I must add, of many teachers, parents, and legislators—school is seen as a series of lockstepped phases: Learn to decode; become literate in basic skills; read and spit back the facts (and, in more challenging schools, the concepts) in texts; listen to and recall the facts (and concepts) in lectures; take lots of tests; if you do well, go to a good college; if you don't do well, try to "play the system" so you can still graduate and secure some kind of postsecondary education.

Most of the current ferment in what might loosely be called "neo-progressive education" calls into question this lockstepped scenario. No one claims that skills and concepts are unimportant; but many ask why the visible parts of education are so remote from what is—or ought to be—valued in the broader community. One could easily pass through the educational system in this country with little sense of what it means to use one's mind well and little familiarity with individuals who are involved in productive scholarly work within and across the disciplines.

From my perspective, any educational system should have as a primary mission the enhancement of student understanding, within and across the disciplines. As a result of their education, students should secure a better understanding of the physical and biological world, the social world, the world of the arts, the world of self. Though rewarding in itself, such understanding is not pursued only for its own sake—rather, it should allow students to become productive adult workers, thinkers, and members of their community. But such understanding will never come about through the piling on of facts. It can only emerge if students have the opportunity to tackle authentic problems; to use their skills appropriately in plausible settings; to create projects, alone and in cooperation; to receive feedback on these endeavors; and, ultimately, to become willing, productive thinkers.

A few students will proceed along the path to understanding on their own or with a smidgen of guidance from parents, teachers, and/or peers. However, if we are to give all the students the opportunities to obtain a better understanding of the world and of themselves, we must consider new approaches to teaching, to learning, and to demonstrating what has been understood.

Here is where the book in your hands can be of help—providing both intellectual stimulation and powerful practical suggestions. The authors represent, collectively, several of the most important "neo-progressive" educational enterprises underway today in the United States. In these efforts they are pioneers—conducting Collaborative Assessment Conferences, applying a Tuning Protocol, using the Primary Language Record, constructing Digital Portfolios.

The authors share a strong conviction. In their collective view, the approaches being developed cannot be created in one locus and shipped or delivered to another. There is no kit—not even a kaboddle! Rather, such approaches need to be built up together by communities of teachers—individuals who are willing to put their own understandings at risk, to construct new practices, to try them out, to receive feedback from friendly critics and critical friends, and to try again.

It is intriguing to realize that the work being done by such communities bears a significant resemblance to the work that teachers are—and will be—asking students to do. The work is driven by problems and pressures that are real; it involves constant experimentation, revision, and reflection; it requires a comfortable surrounding where one can speak one's mind without feeling threatened and without threatening others; it features the honing of skills, the devising of high standards, that can be put to productive use within the community. Whatever their own earlier education, these groups of teachers are developing modes of professional practice, ones that in due course should influence the scholarly "habits of mind" of their students. They are understanding student learning and, in the process, helping students to enhance their own understandings.

The work that these teachers (and researchers) are espousing is not easy to carry out, especially in the current climate of "back to basics," "testing and more testing," and "uniform standards." The very margin that is needed for experimentation is being threatened by insistent calls for accountability, with accountability usually being defined as "higher scores" on the very instruments whose legitimacy has been strongly challenged by the pioneers.

The work described in these pages is still preliminary, and the question arises as to how best to ensure that it can be allowed to grow and prosper. Here I have three suggestions.

First of all, it is important that those involved in the new focus on student work be in close touch with one another and, whenever possible, make common cause. Networks such as the Coalition of Essential Schools and the Network of Progressive Educators provide indispensable guidance and necessary running room for those who are involved in often-lonely efforts at reform.

Second, it is important to share with the relevant publics multiple examples of student work, as well as the most useful kinds of feedback on that work. Though talk of exhibitions, portfolios, and performance-based examinations is already "old hat" to readers of the educational literature, it remains frankly mysterious, if not threatening, to the vast majority of the American public. When citizens come to see that exhibitions are not a New Age plot, but rather a time-honored, sensible way of observing students as they demonstrate their knowledge, skills, and understandings, much of their skepticism dissolves; and on some occasions, one even secures an enthusiastic convert.

My third suggestion is addressed to the authors of the book. It is important to develop ways of looking at work, and of comparing student work, that go beyond the individual school building. Parents have a right to know not only the views of teachers in a building but how student performances and under-standings stack up against others in comparable communities, with comparable objectives. This is not a call for a single standard; I feel that, however laudable or lamentable that goal might be in the abstract, it is simply not feasible in the America of today. Rather, it is a call for collections of educators from different sites to develop together methods of assessment that are valid and that actually demonstrate to a broader public what diverse students understand and can do.

The authors of this book have not yet arrived at this point, and it is perhaps unrealistic to think that they should be. Indeed, given the enormity of the task and the short period of time of these experiments, they and their colleagues are proceeding in the right way and at the proper speed. Nonetheless, I feel that "standards beyond the individual classroom and the individual building" is a necessary goal if these promising new approaches are to have a chance to sur-vive over the long haul. I hope that the authors agree with me. If they do, I have confidence that they can accomplish the next two steps toward two vital and integrally related missions: helping precollegiate educators to become re-spected professionals in this country and helping their students to achieve and exhibit genuine understandings.

Acknowledgments

The editor would like to acknowledge the unique and invaluable contributions to this work of Helen Featherstone, Howard Gardner, and Joseph McDonald. Colleagues at the Annenberg Institute for School Reform and the Coalition of Essential Schools, both at Brown University, and from the ATLAS Seminar generously contributed their insight and guidance. The Annenberg Institute supported the work throughout the project.

The editor would also like to acknowledge the fine work and perseverance of all the chapter authors. Brian Ellerbeck and the staff at Teachers College Press and Carrie Peterson and Sara Lightner at the Annenberg Institute patiently and expertly kept things moving ahead.

Finally, the editor would like to thank and commend the teachers, students, parents, administrators, and others whose work is described in these pages.

Assessing Student Learning

From GRADING to UNDERSTANDING

Introduction

Learning from Students' Work

DAVID ALLEN

What happens to all the book reports, stories, posters, models, dioramas, and other pieces of students' work once they've been turned in, graded, and passed back? A glance at the grade. A slow settling to the bottom of the bookbag or a quick trip to the bottom of the trash can. Occasionally, for younger children's work, a place of honor on the refrigerator door. Is there another life beyond the grade?

Of course, some teachers have always done more with the students' work than just assign and grade it; for example, posting exemplary pieces as models for other students; collecting student writing in books that take their place in the classroom library; asking students to collect work in portfolios to demonstrate growth; and encouraging students to develop a piece of work for an audience outside school—by entering a science fair or submitting an editorial to the local newspaper.

This book explores another dimension of that "afterlife" and seeks to move students' work to a more central and valued place in teachers' own practice. It describes the work of educators who have developed processes for "group reflection on particular children, materials, ideas and patterns" (Perrone, 1991, p. 86).

In the view of these educators, to better understand student learning—and improve teachers' capacity to support it—is to examine and reflect on the ideas and patterns in the actual work that children create in school, rather than the approximations of learning that grades and test scores offer.

Patricia Carini (1979) writes, "Reflection is thinking which gathers, keeps and preserves by finding the pattern of relationships among seemingly disparate events" (p. 30). One may strive to find such patterns alone or with others; the emphasis in this book is on reflection through collaboration—primarily, but not exclusively, with other teachers.

The first section describes processes and methods for observing and describing young children's work. The second section considers "protocols" for examining and providing feedback to teachers on students' work and the instructional context for the work. The third section explores some of the important contexts and resources that support collaborative inquiry and reflection, including the school, the district, and university–school partnerships, as well as technology as a resource.

The focus here is on how *teachers* use, adapt, and create processes for examining students' work that support their own reflection and understanding. Often, the processes involve the perspectives of "critical friends," including teacher educators, parents, and representatives from the community, but it is the teachers' learning that is most directly related to improving conditions for student learning.

The samples of students' work that provide the focus for the processes take many forms: essays, poems, and stories; visual and three-dimensional products, including drawings, posters, bulletin boards, maps, and working models; audio- and videotapes of oral presentations, debates, skits, and plays; and observational records kept by teachers on students at work. The media in which students' work is presented are probably limited only by the imagination; in Chapter 9, for example, Niguidula describes how students' work may be presented in computer-based and multimedia formats.

Students' work may be *product-* or *process-*oriented—a lively classroom discussion or a student's one-on-one conference with a teacher may provide a sample of a student's work, in other words, the student at work. Of course, any piece of student work can support teacher inquiry and learning, but the nature of the work determines the quality of the inquiry. Products of tasks that are complex, that involve problem-solving skills, that are meaningful to students, and that call for sustained work (Duckworth, 1996; Newmann, Secada, & Wehlage, 1995; Resnick, 1987) will provide more grist for observation and discussion.

As King and Campbell-Allan describe in Chapter 7, portfolios provide teachers with a wealth of students' work for examination, discussion, and reflection (Darling-Hammond, Ancess, & Falk, 1995; Jervis, 1996; Wolf, 1989). With portfolios, as with all students' work, selection of the piece or pieces to examine is an important consideration. The Collaborative Assessment Conference (Chapter 1) and Descriptive Review processes (Chapter 3) demonstrate that there is often value in describing a single piece of work, a drawing or fragment of writing.

COMMON PRINCIPLES . . .

There are many purposes for examining students' work described in this book. They range from understanding an individual child as a learner and creator to establishing standards for student performance. While the processes differ in purpose and approach, they share these principles:

- They involve collaboration, bringing multiple perspectives to bear in a focused inquiry.
- They move beyond grading and evaluation of the work to discussion that contributes to teachers' understandings of students' learning and their own instructional practice.
- Participants agree upon structure and norms for the inquiry.

Educators who choose to take part in these processes share a belief that through the description, questioning, feedback, and reflection integral to the processes they can become more effective teachers. It often seems that in looking at students' work samples teachers are really looking—as in double exposure—at their own work.

An interesting dynamic often occurs when teachers engage in these processes. While, typically, only one teacher (or team of teachers) presents students' work and receives feedback, observations, and questions on it, "nonpresenting" participants find that the experience provokes powerful self-reflection on their own practice.

Of course, educators are not the only ones who learn from looking at students' work. Chapters on the Primary Language Record (Chapter 2) and Roundtables at University Heights High School (Chapter 6) demonstrate how looking at students' work—and students at work—can strengthen the connection between home and school.

. . . And Different Approaches

In considering which process may be appropriate for their purposes, it may help readers to differentiate among them on several points: (1) scope, (2) territory, and (3) place of judgment.

Scope. The processes range from a focus strictly on the child's work and/ or the child as creator to one that includes the context for the work. In the Descriptive Review of Children's Work (Prospect Archives and Center for Education and Research, 1986), a facilitator continually refocuses the group on observing and describing what is present in the child's work, not on describing or speculating on contextual variables (about the child or the classroom). The Descriptive Review of a Child (see Chapter 3) begins with a focus on the whole child.

In contrast, in the Tuning Protocol and California Protocol models, the context for the students' work—along with samples of the work itself—is often presented. These contextual artifacts include assignment sheets and scoring rubrics, as well as the teacher's verbal description of the assessment process.

Territory. Another difference among the processes is the quantity of work examined and period of time in which it was completed. In the Collaborative Assessment Conference (Chapter 1), for example, an individual piece of work is the centerpiece for a discussion of the child's intentions and interests; in the Roundtables at University Heights High School, staff, students, parents, and critical friends from outside the school consider multiple samples of a student's work, collected in portfolios and completed over a period of as long as 3 years.

Judgment. Perhaps the most important theoretical difference among the processes is the role of judging. While all the processes help teachers develop *judgment* about children and their work, not all advocate *judging*, that is, evaluating, students' work. The Collaborative Assessment Conference and Descriptive Review processes, as well the portfolio development process at Carrie E. Tompkins Elementary School (Chapter 7), ask participants to "withhold judgment" and emphasize description of the children's work. The Tuning Protocol, California Protocol, and the Roundtable process at University Heights High School (Chapter 6) make a place for judging, or providing critical feedback on, students' work. They do so not to grade or score the work—though feedback may, at times, contribute to scoring—but to address the presenting teachers' (or presenting students', at University Heights) questions and contribute to their understanding of the work and to improvement of the instructional context.

CONVERGING INFLUENCES

Processes develop and evolve; each one described in this book reflects many influences. The Collaborative Assessment Conference and the Tuning Protocol were influenced in their development by the Prospect Center's Descriptive Review processes. The California Protocol, in turn, drew upon the Tuning Protocol in its development (see Chapter 5).

There are many sources for the processes described in this book, including the work of individual schools, such as Central Park East Secondary School in East Harlem (Darling-Hammond et al., 1995; Meier, 1995; Schwarz, 1994), and colleges, such as Alverno College (1985). Below, I touch briefly on three broader and converging areas of influence: developments in the teaching of writing, new forms of assessment drawing on the visual arts, and the work of Patricia Carini and the Prospect Center.

Teaching Writing in the Open Field

The movement among English teachers to help students appreciate the process of writing has had a profound influence on curriculum, instruction, and assessment in language arts and across the curriculum. Students no longer see writing as a direct linear progression from assignment to grade, but rather as a complex multistage process from prewriting activities to producing—and sometimes "publishing"—a final draft. Teachers have helped students to see their works as inherently meaningful and valuable, not simply means to a grade.

Writing teachers have also been instrumental in helping teachers appreciate that "reading" students' work can be part of a much more complex and educative process than simply grading. In developing the Tuning Protocol, for example, McDonald (1996) and his colleagues drew on the work of writing theorist Peter Elbow (1981) and the National Writing Project. New ways of examining and reflecting on students' work have derived in part from a new appreciation of what teachers can learn from careful examination of student writing samples.

In *Errors and Expectations*, Mina Shaughnessy (1977) helped reorient composition teachers in how they look at student writers' mistakes in grammar, spelling, and syntax. As the City University of New York embarked on a new policy of admitting any New York City resident with a high school diploma *regardless of other entrance requirements*, Shaughnessy and her colleagues were called upon to teach adult student writers "who appeared by college standards to be illiterate" (p. 3).

While the book has become a resource and textbook for teaching composition, it has also had a profound impact on educators' thinking about how we gain information to guide practice. It has helped to shift the focus from the assignment to the pieces students actually produce. Shaughnessy shows us how educators analyze samples of students' work to guide their teaching of individual students and to guide their teaching of writing more generally.

> Not only do basic writing students produce essays that are full of points but the points they make are often the same ones that more advanced writers make when writing on the subject. The differences lie in the style and extent of elaboration. Once we have identified some of these differences, we should find it easier to decide what the content of instruction ought to be when the student moves from the sentence into the open field of discourse. (pp. 226–227)

Nearly a decade later, in a very different place and level of schooling, Lucy McCormick Calkins, a classroom teacher working with Donald Graves, began a unique research project. She decided to follow a group of 16 first-graders through fourth grade in a small New Hampshire school, "building a tentative map of children's growth in writing" (1983, p. 7). While the study continued to document the learning of the class from year to year, Calkins found herself narrowing her focus even more than she had expected—to one child.

Lessons from a Child tells the story of Suzie's learning from year to year. Throughout the book Calkins incorporates and analyzes pieces of Suzie's writing, allowing the reader to share with Calkins in reflecting on the growth demonstrated in the work. Calkins begins to rethink her own understanding of how children learn to write—constantly holding up theories from outside, including the work of Graves and others, against what she is encountering in Suzie's development.

Like Shaughnessy, Calkins is aware that focusing on the individual student teaches lessons that apply more generally. She argues, however, that we need to resist generalization in favor of seeking to understand each child's unique "pathway": "More than anything I hope this study highlights the need to learn from other young writers at work in their classrooms. My hope is that through closely observing one child's growth in writing, we'll learn to watch for and to respect each child's growth in writing" (p. 7).

Kathe Jervis and Ann Weiner (1991) offer another view. In their study of one child's transition from elementary to middle school, they selected at random a "low-profile" child, one who might have "remained an invisible presence in the school had she not been the subject of our teacher research project" (p. 114). In looking closely, over the course of a year, at Keshana and her work, they "gained insight into her school persona, and by implication, understood more about other preadolescent girls who similarly distance themselves from school adults" (p. 124).

The observation protocols, including the Primary Language Record (Chapter 2), and reflective processes described in this book help teachers deepen their understanding of both the individual child as a learner and children's learning more generally.

Learning from the Arts: Portfolios

In the 1980s, while process writing was taking off in classrooms across the country, a smaller group of teachers and researchers were exploring a radically different approach to assessing students, one that led away from the time-honored mechanisms like quizzes, tests, and single letter or number grades and instead drew on models from the visual arts.

Dennie Palmer Wolf (1988) worked with teachers from the Pittsburgh public schools and staff from the Educational Testing Service to explore how educators can learn from the arts in assessing student learning in a way that answers the "lack of powerful qualitative information" (p. 24) provided by traditional assessment methods.

"The arts are more than another academic subject; they have some unique properties that make them provocative context for rethinking how we assess student learning" (p. 26). The image of the art student with a large portfolio of sketches, paintings, and photographs comes to mind. Wolf and her colleagues looked deeper to consider not just how students' work is selected and presented in portfolios, but also how it is produced and what happens with the portfolios once they exist.

For Wolf, chief among the properties the arts bring to assessment are: (1) an emphasis on long-term projects that engage students in a "search for individual meaning"; (2) the use of portfolios to "see the processes that underlie long-term development"; and (3) reflective interviews that encourage students to judge their own work and themselves as learners (pp. 27–28).

These three properties have had a powerful influence on American education in the last decade, and all three have implications for students' work and how it is assessed and discussed. The last property, reflective interviews, has frequently been left off. In reflective interviews, students and their teachers look at the work, collected in portfolios, to "form a picture of what has developed, how it came into being, where difficulties remain, and directions for future work" (p. 28).

The reflective interviews Wolf and her colleagues engaged in share many traits with the processes described in this book, and several chapters here explicitly consider how portfolios provide samples of students' work for teachers' reflective discussions (see Chapters 6, 7, and 9).

The Power of Collective Thought

One of the strongest influences on the development of the processes described in the chapters that follow is the work of Patricia Carini and the Prospect Archive and Center for Education and Research in Bennington, Vermont. The Center includes a number of components: the independent Prospect School (founded in 1965); an archive of hundreds of individual children's work; and teacher education programs. In addition to recognizing the research value of archiving students' work, the Center has developed a number of approaches for observation of children and description of the work. Over the years, the Center has become a professional development "academy," training teachers in close observation and description of children's work.[1]

For Carini, observing and describing is prized above judging, a choice that goes against the grain of American educational practice. Also valued is collaboration among teachers; the Prospect Center's descriptive processes—including, among others, the Descriptive Review of a Child and the Descriptive Review of Work—*must* be undertaken as a collaborative endeavor (see Chapter 3).

The processes seek to identify and emphasize children's strengths and potential as the basis for their continued education. For Carini (1982), the processes of observation and description are strengthened by the "power of collective thought"; in other words, by bringing educators together to observe, describe, reflect, and discuss:

> The primary purpose of the Staff Review of a Child [later the Descriptive Review of a Child] is to bring varied perspectives to bear in order to describe a child's experience within the school setting. On the basis of this description and discussion of its implications, the staff comes to recommendations for supporting and deepening the child's school experiences, and, according to need, offers ways for supporting and deepening the child's strengths and interests and to support ways to structure the classroom in order to facilitate those strengths. (pp. 112–113)

The Descriptive Review processes—in which a facilitator guides a group through a series of "rounds" of description—have influenced directly or indirectly many of the processes in the book. Like these later processes, Descriptive Review recognizes that observation and description require a frame or structure to bring them out and keep them focused.

Carini and other educators, in particular other members of the North Dakota Study Group on Evaluation,[2] have led us away from making judgments about the quality of a child's work to describing the multiple *qualities* that inhere in every product of human effort. In describing what they see in children's work, teachers have discovered that they are learning much about themselves and their own work—not only how they might alter their instruction for one child, the child whose work has been described, but how they plan and conduct instruction for all students. To do so, without losing sight of the individual, is just one of the challenges of teaching.

WHY IS IT SO DIFFICULT?

Why haven't more teachers created—or tried to create—a "professional learning community" (Talbert & McLaughlin, 1994) characterized by "civil discourse" and "rigorous analysis" (Wasley, Hampel, & Clark, 1997), as well as "reflective practice" (Schön, 1983), exemplified by collaborative processes for examining students' work?

The processes we describe in this book counteract four tendencies of traditional schooling: (1) school community's avoidance of controversy, (2) teachers' autonomy in making decisions about their students, (3) the "shining example" phenomenon, and (4) mistaking the plan for the product.

Avoiding Controversy

Schools often behave like dysfunctional families. Important issues and conflicts simmer below the surface, but a visitor would never know it from how school people interact. Often, a tacit agreement not to discuss the most essential—and potentially the most divisive—problems reigns. "Raising fundamental questions by necessity generates uncertainty, ambiguity, confusion, passion, and sometimes anger. Too many schools are characterized by a denial of conflict and an absence of tools for unearthing and dealing with conflict. Schools undertaking deep, intentful change use specific, agreed upon tools and processes that facilitate the unearthing and airing of deeply held beliefs and feelings" (Szabo, 1996, p. 87).

Autonomy

The need for "tools" and facilitation to approach issues of teaching and learning is enhanced by the virtual isolation of adults from one another in the school. Teachers are trained to work alone, that is, as the one adult among children. Supervision after preservice training is typically cursory, if it occurs at all. "Rather than work collectively on their problems, everyone must struggle alone" (Lieberman, Saxl, & Miles, 1988, p. 151). The "culture of the staffroom" prevents teachers from raising questions about their practice (Educational Extension Service, 1996) or about their students' work. Little encouragement is provided to teachers to observe one another's classes, let alone to engage in substantive discussion about teaching and learning.

As Linda Darling-Hammond (1996) reminds us, "investments in professional development for teachers are extremely small, and inside-the-school supports for collegial experimentation are rare" (p. 9). Consequently, teachers are rarely used to, or comfortable with, the idea of someone else commenting on their students' work or their own.

Shining Examples

The norms and habits of the profession have led teachers to guard the actual products of students' work, limiting them to the transaction between student and teacher, occasionally involving the parents. Except for "shining examples," which tend to reflect well on student and teacher alike, samples of students' work are rarely if ever seen by anybody besides the teacher, the student, and perhaps the parent; a teacher's next-door colleague may be the least likely to see the work.

Teachers recognize that in "exposing" students' work, they are exposing their own work of planning, instructing, and grading to scrutiny, praise, or critique. Along with managing the classroom, teachers' abilities to carry out these tasks are central to their professional self-identity. Questions and comments that might contain useful feedback are often construed as criticism of the teacher or teachers, as described by Kammer (Chapter 5). The education of teachers and the culture of schooling have not provided opportunities to gainfully explore the difference between the two.

Similarly, teachers must learn to consider both the "glimmers" and the "benchmarks" (Wolf, 1996) in students' work, the pieces that represent a student's struggle as well as the victories.

Mistaking the Plan for the Product

When teachers are asked to demonstrate evidence of their work—a rare enough occurrence—they frequently produce the worksheets or unit plans they have developed absent any students' work. This is natural enough, since these are unmistakably products of the teachers' creation or selection. Presenting samples of students' work is much less common and a more risky affair. After all, what the students do with an assignment is beyond the teacher's absolute control—is it fair for teachers to be evaluated on it? The collaborative processes in this book help teachers move away from a conception of assessment as ranking (of teachers, as well as students) and toward a conception of assessment as surfacing more and better information about their students and their own practice.

Even when we do adopt processes to examine students' work, we are pulled by old habits of looking at the "inputs" and losing focus on the child as learner and the work as a demonstration of learning. As it gains wider currency, the phrase "looking at students' work" is already in danger of becoming a new label for old practices. A continual "refocusing" needs to occur, and is built into some of the processes through facilitators' questions and "debriefing" of the process.

PROFESSIONAL CHALLENGES

The processes described in this book, in their effort to reach for better information, may strike some readers as artificial, even constraining. Why can't "they" (meaning those teachers) just put the work on the table and let us "take our best shot." Those who propose such an approach might do well to consider what happens in other professions.

Processes of inquiry that deal with human subjects tend to adhere to protocols and prize confidentiality. The teacher–student relationship has something in common with that of doctor–patient or lawyer–client. A natural, even praiseworthy, protectiveness of the students and, consequently, one's own practice comes to the surface when a teacher is called upon to produce documents of that relationship. Grades and test scores have become accepted as the semi-public results of the teacher–student interaction.

Teaching must develop and practice some of the forms and protocols for professional exchange—consultations, rounds, case reviews—that allow for professional learning and growth and for the training of clinical judgment. These forms must focus on actual cases and artifacts—including samples of student work—from teachers' daily professional lives. Some will provide necessary peer review (Darling-Hammond, 1988); others, like the ones in this book, will emphasize collaborative reflection.

"De-privatization of practice" represents one of the five "critical elements" of strong professional communities identified by Kruse, Louis, and Bryk (1994). The others are collaboration, reflective dialogue, shared norms and values, and collective focus on student learning. Collaborative processes for examining student work represent one key set of practices in building and sustaining such communities.

Building a strong professional community based on collaboration, inquiry, and reflection becomes even more important in light of the challenges faced by today's teachers, some of which are summarized by Devaney and Sykes (1988, p. 19):

- Helping students make complex constructions of knowledge
- Requiring students to tackle ill-structured problems
- Preparing students to organize and monitor their own learning
- Stoking problem-solving with highly specific prior knowledge
- Emphasizing collaborative and situation-specific learning
- Setting students to work on tasks that incorporate skills.

In addition to these formidable challenges, many teachers work with highly diverse student populations and students from socially and economically disenfranchised groups. "The assessment of diverse students is best accomplished through a diversity of assessment, involving multiple definitions of competence and evaluation methods" (McLeod, 1994, p. 26). As important as multiple *methods*, the authors in this book contend, are multiple *perspectives*.

Increasingly, we understand that learning is social as well as cognitive, dependent on the learner's family, cultural, and linguistic contexts as well as individual differences (Gardner, 1983; Ogbu, 1991; Romaine, 1995; Vygotsky, 1962). Few teachers feel equipped to understand all these contexts alone.

Teachers at schools such as University Heights (Chapter 6), which use the actual evidence of students' work and involve the perspectives of teachers, family, peers, and "critical friends" from outside the school in discussing it, are better able to respond to issues of diversity within their classrooms because they create a place for perspectives that other schools do not.

The processes in this book have the potential to draw upon diverse perspectives, experiences, and knowledge in seeking to understand individual learners. In Chapter 2, for example, Falk considers how the Primary Language Record has helped teachers to recognize and build on the strengths of children from diverse cultural and linguistic backgrounds.

Standards and Understanding

Teachers who understand assessment as identifying and promoting children's strengths, as well as addressing their needs, face the onslaught of the "standards movement." From the president on down come calls for "world-class standards" and tough tests to show which children meet them and which do not. Holding schools and teachers accountable has come to be equated with students' performance on standardized tests.

Good standards, like good assessment instruments, provide resources for teachers and contribute to their understanding of teaching and learning, as well as of their disciplines. In Chapter 7, for example, King and Campbell-Allan describe how involvement in the New Standards Project helped the faculty of Carrie E. Tompkins Elementary School develop its portfolio system. But many standards documents, and the rhetoric that surrounds them, threaten to reduce teaching to the mechanical delivery of information and assessment to the even more mechanical activity of filling in ovals on a standardized multiple-choice test.

The processes described in this book are not one more school reform initiative. Nor do they come packaged with a whole new set of standards for curriculum content or student performance, or even for teachers' practice. Rather, they represent a *standard of practice* for schools and teachers engaged in meaningful, principled education reform and school restructuring.

Some, such as the School Quality Review Process (Chapter 8) and the Digital Portfolio (Chapter 9), help teachers and others to understand how standards—a school's or a state's—relate to the day-to-day work students and teachers do. Others, such as the Roundtables at University Heights (Chapter 6) or the Tuning Protocol (Chapter 4), help stakeholders—including parents, community members, business partners, and even policy makers—appreciate and support teaching and learning that reaches for deeper understanding.

Standards may provide one entry point to more powerful teaching and learning. If they are used this way, the school will benefit from a careful process that allows the full community "to look at the student work actually going on in the school" (Mitchell, 1996, p. 27).

WHEN DO WE MEET AGAIN?

Engaging in any one of these processes is a serious undertaking—a bit like putting on a play, although the dialogue is mainly improvisational. While the willingness to bring students' work to a group for examination and reflection is the crucial ingredient, other concerns quickly follow. The processes described in this book require a commitment of time and careful consideration of questions of who participates and facilitates, as well as how the process will relate to other functions of the school.

Time is a key consideration. Some of the processes described in the book—the Tuning Protocol, Collaborative Assessment Conference, and the California Protocol—are designed to work within an hour or an hour and a half of staff development time. Some, like the Descriptive Review of a Child, take somewhat longer. Too much time is a rarity; too little time robs the process of the benefits it can offer.

Getting people together to engage in a process once is hard enough; trying to bring the group together regularly over time so that the collaborative work can deepen is a tall order. Some schools have tried to do so by using staff or team planning time, release days, or after-school meetings. Teachers using the Primary Language Record often engage in regular meetings with others outside of school hours, sometimes as part of a college course.

Who participates often relates to the goals for looking at students' work in the first place. Within a school, if goals are schoolwide clarification of standards or curriculum development, bringing together people from different departments and levels of schooling is important. For every purpose, it is valuable to consider how including "critical friends" from inside and outside the school—parents, community members, local college professors, and others—can add valuable perspectives to the process.

Some of the processes described here, especially the Roundtables at University Heights High School, show us effective ways to meaningfully involve parents, students, and other critical friends in the school's work. It is important to remember that teachers often feel more comfortable with the language, or jargon, of schooling than those outside the profession. Parents and others need more clarification of roles and practices to actively participate. If students are involved, how will they understand their role? Writing has proved useful in bringing out the voices of those hesitant to speak up, even within the "safety zone" established by the process.

Another important consideration is *facilitation*. Skilled facilitation plays an important role in most of these processes. In many cases, facilitators come into schools and groups of schools from organizations such as the Coalition of Essential Schools, Harvard Project Zero, and the Prospect Center. It is sometimes difficult for teachers to facilitate a group of peers from their own school, perhaps because they're too closely identified as a participant to be seen in a new, neutral role. But in some schools, such as Piner High School (Chapter 5), teachers have taken on the role of facilitation successfully and found ways to share the responsibility and the benefits. Facilitation itself can be a powerful professional development experience.

To build and sustain a professional community, structural supports "must be grounded in the system, not added on" (Comer, 1996). The recognition that teachers need time and authority to work together has resulted in a range of strategies, including critical friends groups, study groups, and inquiry groups, as well as committees engaged in school-site-based management.

Ultimately, to succeed, this kind of collaborative work must be supported not just by the school but also by the larger systems for education. Policies and allocation of resources must support "within school professional development" (Darling-Hammond & McLaughlin, 1996, p. 211). King and Campbell-Allan (Chapter 7) consider some of the elements of leadership necessary to begin and sustain a purposeful examination of students' work across a school or district. In Chapter 8, Smith and Ruff describe how a school–university partnership provides resources for student-centered, school-based inquiry and reflection.

FROM GRADING TO UNDERSTANDING

Behind all of the processes developed here is the belief that the individual process should be a part of a culture in which students' work and performance is valued, examined, and discussed. The processes are developed and used in the hope and belief that what happens in the formal setting increasingly happens informally—just as teachers hope that students who practice reading and discussing books in a class will do so on their own.

Paul Allison, an author in this book, points out that the formal processes, like Tuning Protocol or Collaborative Assessment Conference, may be most useful as "examples for inspiration, not emulation" as teachers develop processes that address their own purposes (personal communication, January, 1996).

At Fannie Lou Hamer Freedom High School in the Bronx, for example, teachers and other professional staff read the portfolios of five or six students twice a year—by design, not those of their own students—and respond to the students in letters. Then they meet as a faculty to look at and discuss sample portfolios and sample letters. They have created their own ongoing process for looking at their students' work and reflecting on it as they develop the school's graduation by portfolio system and, more generally, build a "portfolio culture" (Wolf, Bixby, & Gardner, 1991) across the school.

Schools and teachers use multiple ways of examining and reflecting on students' work within and across their classrooms and school communities. Some are described in this book; others are developed by the teachers "as they go along." None produce anything so clear-cut as a numerical score, but each has the invaluable potential to add layers of understanding about children, their learning, and teaching.

NOTES

1. The Prospect Archive and Center for Education and Research is a membership network of educators from across the country. It publishes a *Review* and occasional papers, does ongoing consulting work in schools, and sponsors annual teacher institutes. The Center can be contacted by writing to: Prospect Center, Box 326, North Bennington, VT 05257.

2. The North Dakota Study Group on Evaluation began in November 1972, bringing educators from across the United States to the University of North Dakota to discuss common concerns about the predominance of testing in schools and classrooms, and alternative means to document and assess children's learning.

REFERENCES

Alverno College. (1985). *Assessment at Alverno*. Milwaukee, WI: Author.

Calkins, L. (1983). *Lessons from a child: On the teaching and learning of writing*. Portsmouth, NH: Heinemann.

Carini, P. (1979). *The art of seeing and the visibility of the person*. Grand Forks: North Dakota Study Group on Evaluation.

Carini, P. (1982). *The lives of seven children*. Grand Forks: North Dakota Study Group on Evaluation.

Comer, J. (1996, February). Panel discussion, ATLAS Seminar meeting, Cambridge, MA.

Darling-Hammond, L. (1988). Policy and professionalism. In A. Lieberman (Ed.), *Building a professional culture in schools* (pp. 55–77). New York: Teachers College Press.

Darling-Hammond, L. (1996). The right to learn and the advancement of teaching: Research, policy, and practice for democratic education. *Educational Researcher*, 25(6), 5–17.

Darling-Hammond, L., Ancess, J., & Falk, B. (1995). *Authentic assessment in action: Studies of schools and students at work*. New York: Teachers College Press.

Darling-Hammond, L., & McLaughlin, M. (1996). Policies that support professional development in an era of reform. In M. McLaughlin & I. Oberman (Eds.), *Teacher learning: New policies, new practices* (pp. 202–218). New York: Teachers College Press.

Devaney, K., & Sykes, G. (1988). Making the case for professionalism. In A. Lieberman (Ed.), *Building a professional culture in schools* (pp. 3–22). New York: Teachers College Press.

Duckworth, E. (1996). *The having of wonderful ideas and other essays on teaching and learning.* New York: Teachers College Press.

Educational Extension Service. (1996). *Changing minds.* Michigan State University, Bulletin 12.

Elbow, P. (1981). *Writing with power: Techniques for mastering the writing process.* Oxford, UK: Oxford University Press.

Gardner, H. (1983). *Frames of mind.* New York: Basic Books.

Jervis, K. (1996). *Eyes on the child: Three portfolio stories.* New York: Teachers College Press.

Jervis, K., & Weiner, A. (1991). Looking at a child's work. In K. Jervis & G. Montag (Eds.), *Progressive education for the 1990s: Transforming practice* (pp. 114–123). New York: Teachers College Press.

Kruse, S., Louis, K. S., & Bryk, A. (1994, Spring). Building professional community in schools. In *Issues in Restructuring Schools* (Report No. 6; pp. 3–6). Madison: Center on Organization and Restructuring of Schools, University of Wisconsin–Madison.

Lieberman, A., Saxl, E., & Miles, M. (1988). Teacher leadership: Ideology and practice. In A. Lieberman (Ed.), *Building a professional culture in schools* (pp. 148–166). New York: Teachers College Press.

McDonald, J. (1996). *Redesigning school: Lessons for the 21st century.* San Francisco: Jossey-Bass.

McLeod, B. (1994). *Language and learning: Educating linguistically diverse students.* Albany: State University of New York Press.

Meier, D. (1995). *The power of their ideas.* Boston: Beacon.

Mitchell, R. (1996). *Front-end alignment: Using standards to steer educational change.* Washington, DC: The Education Trust.

Newmann, F., Secada, W., & Wehlage, G. (1995). *A guide to authentic instruction and assessment: Vision, standards, and scoring.* Madison: Wisconsin Center for Education Research.

Ogbu, J. (1991). Immigrant and involuntary minorities in comparative perspective. In M. Gibson & J. Ogbu (Eds.), *Minority status and schooling: A comparative study of immigrant and involuntary minorities* (pp. 3–33). New York: Garland.

Perrone, V. (1991). *A letter to teachers: Reflections on schooling and the art of teaching.* San Francisco: Jossey-Bass.

Prospect Archive and Center for Education and Research. (1986). *The Prospect Center documentary processes.* North Bennington, VT: Author.

Resnick, L. (1987). *Education and learning to think.* Washington, DC: National Academy Press.

Romaine, S. (1995). *Bilingualism.* Oxford, UK: Blackwell.

Schön, D. (1983). *The reflective practitioner: How professionals think in action.* New York: Basic Books.

Schwarz, P. (1994, November 23). Needed: School-set standards. *Education Week*, pp. 34, 44.

Shaughnessy, M. (1977). *Errors and expectations: A guide for the teacher of basic writing*. Oxford, UK: Oxford University Press.

Szabo, M. (1996). Rethinking instruction: Building habits of effective inquiry. In M. McLaughlin & I. Oberman (Eds.), *Teacher learning: New policies, new practices* (pp. 73–91). New York: Teachers College Press.

Talbert, J., & McLaughlin, M. (1994). Teacher professionalism in local school contexts. *American Journal of Education, 102*(2), 123–153.

Vygotsky, L. (1962). *Thought and language*. Cambridge, MA: MIT Press.

Wasley, P., Hampel, R., & Clark, R. (1997). The puzzle of whole school change. *Phi Delta Kappan, 78*(9), 690–697.

Wolf, D. P. (1988, December/January). Opening up assessment. *Educational Leadership*, pp. 24–29.

Wolf, D. P. (1989). Portfolio assessment: Sampling students' work. *Educational Leadership, 46*(7), 35–39.

Wolf, D. P. (1996, April). *Performance assessment collaboratives for education (PACE)— A multidistrict effort*. Paper presented at the annual meeting of the American Education Research Association, New York.

Wolf, D. P., Bixby, J., & Gardner, H. (1991). To use their minds well: Investigating new forms of student assessment. In G. Grant (Ed.), *Review of research in education, 17*. Washington, DC: American Educational Research Association.

PART I

Describing Children's Work

In an elementary school library in Gloucester, Massachusetts, a group of teachers discuss a second-grader's drawing and poem. In the discussion, which takes place over several hours, Jessica's work is treated with the seriousness and respect of literary scholars approaching a work by Dante or Toni Morrison.

In New York City, a first-grade teacher meets with the mother and grandmother of one of his bilingual students. What he learns from them about Carla as a reader, writer, and learner—along with observational notes and samples of her work—contributes valuable information to the learning record he compiles and draws on over the course of the year.

In a teacher's home in Philadelphia, elementary teachers from schools across the district listen to one teacher's detailed description of Matthew, a 7-year-old, about whose reading development she is concerned. Based on this "Descriptive Review," the group shares questions and observations to help her address her questions—and help each other learn about children, teaching, and learning.

While teachers have always considered their children's work, the scenarios above, each from a chapter in this section, demonstrate a profound shift in why and how they do it.

Instead of looking at the work in order to grade it, they are examining it in order to describe it, and so to learn from it—about the child, about learning, and about their own practice.

Instead of looking at the work alone—between classes or at home at night—they are examining it with colleagues, other educators, and, in some cases, with children and their families.

Instead of trying to get through stacks of children's work, they are focusing on small samples—individual pieces of work and individual children at work.

Instead of sporadic and rushed conversations in teachers' rooms or between classes, they are making time and following established processes for careful and purposeful examination of—and reflection on—the work.

The methods teachers use to examine student work differ from one another in many regards, from the size and composition of the group to the particular process—or *protocol*—they follow in examining the children's work. The authors of these chapters, along with the growing number of teachers engaged in examining children's work, share the conviction that, as educators, we have much to gain in the process—and much to learn about doing it well.

1

Wondering to Be Done

The Collaborative Assessment Conference

STEVE SEIDEL

I remember meditating on these attached objects . . . (feet and hands, especially, but also chest, knees, stomach) . . . looking at them, touching them, feeling them from the outside and from the inside, wondering about them because there was wondering to be done, not because there were answers to be found.

—Jane Smiley, *A Thousand Acres*

In 1993, I conducted a series of workshops with 10 teachers from the Fuller School in Gloucester, Massachusetts.[1] When the final session was over, our meeting room cleaned up, and our goodbyes spoken, I began a long period of wondering about the value of the work we'd just completed. We'd had the pleasure and the leisure to meet for five 4-hour sessions over a period of 3 months. Our purpose had been to explore the difficulties and the benefits of working with a protocol for examining children's work called Collaborative Assessment Conferences. In so many ways, things had gone well. We'd enjoyed ourselves and remained engaged in looking at and talking at great length about pieces of student writing. Final evaluations were very positive, pointing to many lessons and benefits for the participating teachers.

So why was I uncertain about the value of these sessions? In part it was that I kept hearing Elizabeth Parillo, one of the teachers in the workshop, asking how this would translate into something positive for her students. Liz raised this question several times in the course of the meetings, both orally and in her reflections. I always felt quite inadequate trying to provide an answer to her question. The truth was that I didn't know if sitting together for these many hours talking about specific pieces of writing would, in fact, translate into something positive for her students. Of course, how could I answer that question? I didn't know Liz, or any of the other participants, very well. I knew little of what they actually did in their classrooms. And I had little idea what meaning they would make of these workshops.

However, I did notice that, as the sessions progressed, though Liz continued to ask the same question, she also became very involved with our discussions and wrote at one point about one effect these sessions were having on her.

> [It may be] off the subject, but I'm aware of how alive I feel when I am part of a conversation [or] discussion about *language*—I like to be reminded about possibilities and options—offering the child options—seeing possibilities in writing. There doesn't have to be a definitive answer—*so* different from when I *was* a student. (emphasis in original)

It seemed to me she was torn between her sense of responsibility to her students—specifically, her feeling that if she was not in class with them, she should be doing something that would clearly benefit them—and her enjoyment of these conversations.

In retrospect, now several years later, I suspect that in the high-stakes, outcome-based world of education and professional development, I heard Liz's very real and very serious question (How will my students benefit from this?) and felt insecure about what I really believed. I shared my thoughts with that group, but I was not confident. Having spent the intervening years engaging many more teachers in regular sessions devoted to looking collaboratively at pieces of student work, I've become more clear about the value of that activity and the protocol we've used. In short, I've come to believe that the protocol encourages a sense of wonder—about children, writing, teaching, curriculum, assessment, and more. And, like Jane Smiley's narrator in *A Thousand Acres*, I've found value in "wondering . . . because there was wondering to be done, not because there were answers to be found."

During those hours sitting around a long table in a conference room at the Fuller School, we had looked at and talked about 10 pieces of student writing. Each of the teachers from this K–5 program shared a piece of writing from one of their students, and we followed the Collaborative Assessment Conference structure. Each conference took about an hour. The conference protocol called for extensive examination and description of the work under consideration. Questions were noted. Speculations were made about "what the child is working on." The presenting teachers shared their perspectives on the work and the child as well as their questions. The group considered possible next steps to take in working with the child and next steps they might take in exploring issues raised during the conference.

Our experience was luxurious. Four hours at a time just to look at and talk about student work. There were no placement decisions to make. No scores to decide on. No remedial plans to hammer out. It was a situation so out of character from the ways professional time is spent in most schools that virtually everyone participating was, at times and especially in the beginning, somewhat ill at ease. In time, though, some very interesting things began to happen.

Even in the first session, I observed an interesting phenomenon. Reflecting on the first conference, Julie Carter noted the effect of describing the work collaboratively. "It made me see a lot more than I would just sitting alone. And the more you looked, the more you saw." This seemed true to me, as I had noticed that their first hesitant observations led slowly but surely into a long sequence of more and more specific descriptions. It wasn't, however, until the sessions were completed that the consequences of this phenomenon began to become clear to me.

As I reviewed what had gone on in the workshop, I noticed certain patterns in our conversations. It seemed that the more the teachers saw in a piece of student writing, the more they recognized the complexity of the child's effort and accomplishments. As they grappled with the complexity of the work, they became even more interested in the child who had created it. The more interested they became in the child, the more they wanted to meet and talk with him or her. They had questions that only that young author could answer. They wanted those answers and they wanted to get to know the child.

This process of teachers looking carefully together at pieces of student work had made them curious about the children who made them, in awe of the complexity of the act of writing, and ever more respectful of the work of writing. This chapter is about that process of looking at student work and how it generated this curiosity, this awe, and this respect.

COLLABORATIVE ASSESSMENT CONFERENCE: STEPS OF THE PROTOCOL

The Collaborative Assessment Conference protocol has a series of distinct sections and some basic guidelines. Briefly, the protocol has the following structure.

1. *Reading the text.* In silence, everyone reads a student text that has been brought to the session by a participant who has agreed to be the "presenting" teacher for the conference.
2. *Observation and description.* All other participants discuss the work, focusing first, as strictly as possible, on a description of the piece.
3. *Raising questions.* Description is followed by articulation of questions about the text, the author, or the context of the writing
4. *What is the child working on?* Finally, these readers speculate on what they think the child was working on as he or she created this text.
5. *The presenting teacher responds.* Throughout this discussion, the presenting teacher has been silent. At this point, though, the presenting teacher adds any observations he or she has of the text and answers as many of the questions as possible.
6. *Teaching moves and pedagogical responses.* Together, the readers and presenting teacher consider possible teaching moves the teacher could make to encourage and challenge this writer.
7. *Reflection.* When all of this is done, the entire group, including the facilitator, reflect on the conference, considering its satisfactions, frustrations, confusions, and ways to improve the next conference.

In addition to prescribing when the presenting teacher should speak and when to listen, the protocol has two major guidelines or rules. First, participants are asked to withhold their judgments of the work under consideration, including expressions of taste ("I like or don't like this about the work . . . ") or of quality ("This is good but this isn't . . . "). Second, the initial phases of the conference are conducted with as little information revealed as possible about the writer and the context of the writing (assignment, grade, gender, materials provided, etc.). These guidelines, which I consider later in the chapter, make Collaborative Assessment Conferences quite different from most forms of assessment regularly practiced by teachers.

Furthermore, most teachers rarely experience any form of structured and regular professional conversation about specific pieces of children's work. It is hardly ever part of regular staff discussion, inservice programs, or most teacher training courses. In this light, the Gloucester workshops, focused and structured as they were, were an extraordinary professional experience for these teachers. Without making specific claims for their value, it is reasonable to suggest that the focus and structure of these workshops were a radical departure from the ordinary.

A CONFERENCE IN ACTION

What follows is an account of one of the 10 discussions of a single piece of student work we had during the Gloucester workshops. This is certainly

FIGURE 1.1. "May Is"

> May is
>
> flowers rainbows With red blue yellow gree.
> bees in flowers birds in the sky butterfiys
> dancing in the sky dogs walking flowers
> that are blue and red Two lips

briefer than a full transcript, but it does represent the flow and focus of the session. This account is of the first of two conversations about works in our fourth workshop session. This was the eighth piece we were to discuss together.

After we settled in from the break, Julie and Pam handed out copies of "May is" for everyone to read. (See Figure 1.1. *Please note:* Reading it carefully, even aloud, before reading further will help you follow the discussion described below.) Julie had agreed to take the role of the facilitator for this conference, and Pam was the presenting teacher. Julie gave people several minutes to read and reread this text and to dwell on the picture.

Julie called for observations and descriptions. The ambiguity of the author's meaning was noted first. Ellen had said that "to me it [the text] is a child brainstorming the world going on around them or feelings about the month of May which is 'bees in flowers' and 'birds in the sky.'" And Alyce jumped in, "Or 'sky dogs walking flowers!' That's what I see."

It didn't take long for the issue of punctuation—or the lack of it—to come up. Cherylann was first to point to the lack of punctuation. "I don't see any punctuation, and I see an interesting choice of word placement that sometimes doesn't reflect whether the child has sentence structure—such as the whole idea of 'butterflies dancing in the sky dogs walking flowers . . . ' or is it 'dogs walking. flowers that are blue and red.' There isn't a real finite way of knowing where things stop and start."

Throughout this conference, the "no punctuation" issue and the subsequent ambiguity of the phrasing in the piece came up time and again, through and around observations, questions, and speculations. There was talk of the relationship of the text to the picture and the process through which this work came to be. There was comment on the child's spelling and questions about the ending. (The child appears to have written and erased "thats the end" after "two lips" in line 4. This is difficult to make out on the photocopy but much clearer on the original.) There was extensive discussion about whether or not this was a poem. But the dominant concern was over how to read the meaning of these words and phrases without any punctuation to guide the way.

Annette: I want to know why the writer stopped at "two lips." It seems like
there should be more to this. Unless . . .
Cherylann: Maybe the dogs are blue and red.
Annette: The dogs are walking flowers that are blue and red tulips.

And a short time later, Margaret came back to the final phrases of the piece. "I have a meaning question. Is it 'flowers that are blue and red, tulips' or 'flowers that are blue and red tulips'? And if you put an exclamation point on it, it would make a meaning to the whole poem."

Annette: If you are interpreting it by the picture, it looks like she is saying
"flowers that are blue and red" and "tulips" is another thought.
Liz: Is the tulip made of red and blue?
Annette: No, it's purple.

Later, someone questioned how the child could mean "in the sky dogs walking flowers," and Cherylann said that it made sense to her. On reading those lines, she had imagined looking up at a sky full of clouds and seeing "dogs walking flowers" in the ever-changing cloud formations. Alyce wanted to see "all of us put in the punctuation we think should go in here. We'd come up with seven or nine different pieces."

Since Julie seemed to be handling the role of the facilitator quite comfortably, I decided I could participate in this conference as a reader. I had been quiet for some time but then, in examining the poem, made a discovery that startled me. It had been noted earlier that the child had written "thats the end" in line 4 after "two lips" and then erased it. Somehow this observation and my own confusion over why this child had broken the lines where she did had led me to count the syllables in each line. "I noticed . . . I did this quickly counting on my fingers. There are four lines. I didn't have to use my fingers for that, but there are 10 syllables in lines 1, 3, and 4, if you count 'that's the end,' which the writer has taken out, and 11 [syllables] in line 2."

This observation was striking to others as well and immediately raised questions about whether this was an accident or intentional and, further, what implications this had for whether or not this was a poem. Could this young child have actually counted the syllables? Could she have known that syllabification is an established way in which many poets determine where to break the lines of their poems? Could she have "invented" this poetic form? Or was this simply an accident? As usual, there were no clear conclusions. The discussion proceeded and explored questions about the nature of the assignment. (Could the child have been told to go outside and observe nature on a recent May day?) The group jumped back and forth between observations and thoughts about the feeling of the piece and its structural components (e.g., punctuation, line breaks, use of conjunctions).

Finally, it was Pam's turn to speak, and she was quick to note that in September this child had been writing complete sentences with punctuation. "As a matter of fact, the poetry piece I had her do before last time was much more sentence-oriented. Less free-flowing. It was interesting to me that she broke out of that mold." Julie asked Pam to say more about this. "She was very much into a prose mold. Here's my complete thought and this is the ending. This strikes me as atypical of her work."

Pam added that "two lips" was, indeed, meant to be tulips and that the last line should be read as "flowers that are red and blue [pause] tulips." Pam reported that she had heard Jessica, the writer, read this poem aloud, and her reading of the final line had made clear where the pause should be.

Teaching Moves and Responses

Julie decided, after considerable conversation about the child and her relationship to this piece of work, to writing in general, and to Pam, that it was time to move on to a discussion of teaching moves and responses. I include here a significant portion of the transcript of that part of the conference since it touches on so many issues that seem central to where the group had come by this point, in the next to last, of these five sessions.

Julie: Pam, what did you do or might you do in relation to this?

Pam: With this particular piece of work, I'm not sure because where it wasn't an assignment [it was done during free-choice time], I don't know that she should touch it. Perhaps I'd have her work on commas.

Steve: To me the question is to think back to what did I say? What was my response?

Pam: Thinking back, I wonder if she wanted to share it with the class. I could go back and offer her a chance to do that.

Nancy: I would think the very last thing you would want to do is punctuate [this piece].

Pam: No. I don't want to touch this. But I do want to talk about the use of commas in future work. No, I wouldn't touch this.

Liz: You might show her some poetry and how it is put in lines. She might want to put this in more standard form of poetic lines.

Steve: Except I think . . .

Liz: It might help with the meaning. There is still some confusion for me.

Cherylann: But the various meanings were really interesting.

Liz: Well, what is the problem then? The value is in the meaning for us or is the value in the meaning they want to have?

Steve: Well, would that be a response? To say, hey, I can read this in two different ways. I can read this and it means "dogs walking flowers" and that makes me laugh or as "dogs walking [pause] flowers that are blue." Just to let her know that when you write poetry this way it has an ambiguity that is playful.

Liz: I like that approach better than the way . . . my approach was more clinical.

In the midst of this interchange, Liz posed a question that I take as central to this whole enterprise. In essence, she asked: Whose meaning matters? The writer's or the reader's? During the discussion of "Beautiful Butterfly," another piece, in the third session, Cherylann had talked about the writer's voice and the reader's voice, naming this issue but not really pushing the question. Liz spoke of "value" in raising her question. Whose meaning has more importance? The problem is complicated for these teachers. If the job of a writing teacher is to help children communicate clearly and effectively what *they* mean to say, how might the teacher attend to both the child's intent and the meaning the teacher makes from the text? This question is further complicated by recognizing, as we were, the remarkable variety of meanings that could be drawn from a single text.

In retrospect, it is no surprise that Liz raised this question when we were talking about teaching moves. Just a bit later, Margaret picked up on this issue of multiple meanings. "If you are to read it aloud and say there are lots of ways of looking at this, it opens up for a writer a different way of looking at their work. It would be interesting to see if the child saw other ways."

Talking About the Conversation

The last step in the protocol is to conclude the discussion of teaching moves, thank the presenting teacher for sharing the work with the group, and make sure everyone is prepared to move from talking about the work in question to talking about the conversation about the work. Julie felt it was time to move on, checked on her hunch with the group, and, getting consent, moved into the reflection on the conference.

"All I can say is whatever you are doing, you are doing a great job because when she [Pam's student, Jessica] left me at the end of last year, she couldn't do this. Bits of it, maybe, but not all of this. So I applaud you," said Alyce, starting off the reflection.

With that spoken, Pam took a turn to talk about her experience of the discussion, and frustration was the first thing she expressed. "That was really hard not to talk and I felt a lot of time was wasted on 'tulips' and if I could have just said, 'this is how she meant it!' The tulip conversation was OK that it went that way but at the time it seemed like wasted time. And I just wanted to say, 'flowers that are red and blue [pause] tulips!' And get on to the next thing!"

Pam's comments were followed by some silence, so Julie, since she was still facilitating, asked if there were any other thoughts about the process. I felt obliged to defend, or at least explain, why I tolerate and even encourage this "wasted time." I had talked before about this kind of conference as a practice, something that might be done regularly if not frequently as a part of keeping one's clinical eye focused and keen. "You are practicing your ability to wonder about children's work. It is an exercise in living with the idea that there isn't one right answer and [in] entertaining the [multiple] possibilities. I think there is some value in that even if, in the end, you tell us what the child meant and we accept that."

Annette responded by commenting on how the child's reason for writing might affect the way the teacher chooses to respond to the ambiguity or lack of clarity in the writing. The rest of the conversation picked up and pursued these themes.

Cherylann: But in terms of the process, if Pam had clarified the question and we'd never had the conversation about what to say to that child about the ambiguity . . . And what I take away from this conversation is that the next time a child comes to me with a poem, I may say, "Hey, this is really ambiguous. Did you mean that? Do you mean it to be this way?" Talking about the process, if you had clarified it beforehand we never would have discussed the issue of ambiguity.

Margaret: I agree. And I think one of the most wonderful things you can say to a child about their work is, "I thought about this. And in my thinking I can see all different kinds of meanings." And that ambiguity is part of the richness. That it can mean one thing to the person who wrote it and something equally rich and equally meaningful to someone else. Isn't that wonderful? That kind of richness of experience.

Steve: Why do you think that's wonderful?

Margaret: I think that's wonderful because it is telling the person that wrote it that there are more things in heaven and earth than they can see. Something that they have written has more meanings than they meant. It also has meanings for others that might be different. Their experience has made it one meaning and my experience has made it another meaning. And that's not to say that my meaning is right. A piece is very rich when there are lots of meanings. Language is very flexible.

Cherylann: But it also carries into other forms. Right now I'm concentrating on the science fair. If a child came up with ambiguous language in that, there would be a problem. Sometimes ambiguity is appropriate and fine, but not in science writing. Sometimes you need concise, precise language.

Julie: What I think is important about going back to the child and saying that I've been thinking about your work is the message that you matter to me. And your work matters and you are on my mind and you exist in my mind when you are not with me.

Liz: And I respect you . . .

Julie: And I respect you enough to think about you or your problem or your work . . .

Margaret: That's why I think your immediate reaction may just be, "Oh, that's very interesting." But if you come back with, "There are a lot of meanings here and I wonder what you meant . . . "

Liz: It shows you are really interested in their learning.

I include this rather lengthy account of a Collaborative Assessment Conference to provide an example of how questions emerge in the course of these conversations and the way in which a genuine interest in the child writer can grow from an examination of the meaning of the text. Questions, in this case, are both an expression of interest and a means by which to explore one's curiosity. It may be useful to examine how the protocol encourages the discovery of questions and what kinds of questions seem to emerge during these conferences.

WHERE DO QUESTIONS COME FROM?

Questions come from becoming curious about something that has engaged one's attention. It is a curious phenomenon that one often has difficulty staying interested in things one believes one knows everything or nothing about. To become engaged with something, it helps to have some but not too much familiarity with it. Like works of art, the things children make can be highly engaging. They can captivate, confuse, charm, and alarm the viewer/reader. But if we think we know everything about children, their work, this kid in particular, and so on, we won't watch with such care. The protocol is a trick, then, to focus the attention and encourage engagement.

Questions, then, come from engagement and from having one's perceptions challenged. I believe three elements of the Collaborative Assessment Conference protocol combine to encourage engagement:

1. Withholding context
2. Withholding judgments
3. Hearing your colleagues describe what they see on the page (and saying what you see)

Withholding Context

Perhaps the most fundamental belief underlying the structure of the Collaborative Assessment Conferences is that the work children produce is worthy of serious consideration and analysis and that in that work can be seen much about the child and his or her interaction with the environment in which the work has been produced (the classroom, the school, the family, the community). Most readers, given information about the child and the context for producing a piece of writing, will view that child's work through the lens of that information rather than letting a picture of the child emerge from the work itself. Experience had indicated to me that teachers often adjust their expectations of the work based on their associations to the bits of information they have about the child (usually such things as age, gender, grouping in school, neighborhood, native language, socioeconomic background).

There is nothing surprising about this. Taking small clues about people and making assumptions about who they are is one of the ways in which all of us negotiate our way through our complex worlds. The problem for teachers is that our associations often mislead us in our perceptions of individual children and might actually blind us to important aspects of a child's personality and learning.

In describing group examinations of children's writing at the Bread Loaf School of English, Armstrong (1992) addressed this issue of the effect of knowing the context of the writing on a reader's investigation of the text:

> So we begin by immersing ourselves in the text. It doesn't always pay at first to know too much about the child who wrote it or the circumstances of its composition. As Geoff Keith said in our class the other day, the trouble with concentrating on the child rather than the story is that "it allows you to marginalize the text." . . . All the time we're trying to concentrate our whole attention on the significance of the words on the page. (1992, p. 3)

One of the central goals of this protocol is to encourage direct engagement between teachers and student texts with little context about the child or the assignment provided. As one of the Gloucester teachers said, we were focusing on "the actual writing itself." Of course, much of this contextual information is revealed in the course of the conference, but the initial reading and discussion, as noted, are conducted in as decontextualized a fashion as possible. In general, everyone knows the presenting teacher and what grade she teaches, so there are some strong clues about the context of the work that cannot be hidden.

In every one of these workshops, the challenge of looking at children's work in this decontextualized manner was considered confusing, difficult, and frustrating. Over the five sessions, though, the group made slow and steady peace with this aspect of the protocol. The most conciliatory comments about it were not made until the end of the last session and in the follow-up interviews and questionnaires.

On the whole, though, working with the texts in this decontextualized manner created a conflict for people. Liz questioned this practice a number of times. In the third session, she declared, "I find so much energy goes to figuring out who the child is and that feels very artificial. I mean, when do we ever read work without knowing who the child is?" On this occasion, I responded, "Well, certainly, in your classroom, you always know who the child is. So why do I do that?" But then, instead of offering a direct answer, perhaps unsure of what I really thought, I asked a question. "Is there anything gained in *not knowing* the identity of the child when you first encounter the work?"

A bit later, Liz came back to this issue. "To me the essence of writing is to make an 'I am' statement. The person—and this came up last week—the person's voice and the energy in the writing are an 'I am' statement. And that's part of why some kids have trouble with writing and then to totally deny the identity of the person . . . " This seemed to me a rather harsh description of the protocol. I responded, "Well, the question, Liz, is that if the child is really present in the work, are we really denying them or are we just looking for them in a particular way within the work?"

Responding to this interchange, Annette offered her perspective.

I felt a lot like Liz that a lot of valuable time was wasted because we didn't know the identity of the child because we were almost making up reasons for things that would be completely simplified if we just knew who it was. And yet, especially when I was choosing some of the other work, I was really glad that people wouldn't know who the child was because I really wanted to hear a real reaction to the writing and not to the personality of the child. I don't even know how to explain why, but some of the selections I picked, if people knew who the writer was, there would be a strong reaction because the children's personalities are so strong. But I think there are some really interesting pieces of writing there just to respond to. And it really does provide more objectivity and insight.

Withholding Judgments

In Collaborative Assessment Conferences, teachers are asked explicitly to keep their opinions of the work to themselves. The structure leaves essentially no room for statements about personal taste (likes and dislikes), judgments of quality ("this was really good!"), or judgments of developmental level ("this is excellent for a kindergartner!"). As facilitator, I often chose to allow some judgmental statements, especially in the first conferences. I simply didn't want to cut people off as they did what is habitual—making quick judgments. As participants came to see reasons for withholding judgments in these conferences, I became more diligent in actually stopping people when they made judgmental comments.

This practice is wholly different from scoring sessions in which pieces or collections of student work are judged in relation to a set of criteria by teams of independent readers. Scorings by independent readers are also largely decontextualized, although the prompt, or assignment, will be known to the reader/scorer. Little information may be provided about the writer or the circumstance of the writing, but the purpose and premise of the reading are entirely different from those in Collaborative Assessment Conferences. In scoring sessions, readers are making judgments immediately and, in most cases, without benefit of conversation with other readers. They usually can, but are not required to, provide evidence from the texts for their judgments.

In these conferences, the purpose of the reading is to investigate the meaning of the writing and the child's intent—what he or she was trying to say and do in the piece—in order to bring the reader closer to the child through becoming familiar with the text. This purpose presents difficulties for many participants. Meaning is subjective and a teacher's grasp of a child's intent is speculative. Sometimes there is considerable evidence and other times there is very little. In these sessions, teachers' concerns about the subjective nature of this practice were almost as constant as those expressed about our decontextualized readings of the works.

These two aspects of the protocol—the decontextualized nature of our readings of the student work and the nonjudgmental character of the discussion—are based on a belief that was, I believe, deeply unsettling for most of the teachers. Simply put, in relation to children's writing, there are no absolute or "right" answers about meaning or quality! Not only that, the structure demands questions more than answers. It encourages speculations based on evidence, and it requires thinking about how to teach writing based on reasonable but uncertain ideas about what children are working on and interested in. To some people, finding a compelling question is a more important moment in the learning process than finding an answer. However, while that is not a belief at the heart of our educational system, it is a belief at the heart of this practice, and it seemed to be quite disconcerting for many of the participants.

I also suspect, however paradoxical it may seem, that it is this belief and the way it is embedded in the protocol that was deeply exciting to these teachers. Margaret was often most vocal about the delight she felt at times in this work. At the end of the final session, she spoke about how these meetings had "made me very humble." The repeated process of thinking she knew what was going on in a piece of work and then hearing something surprising from one of her colleagues and needing to rethink her whole interpretation delighted her. "[I would] think, 'well, this and this and this' and somebody would come along and say something that would open up a whole new world for me." She suggested that simply looking at a work with a colleague "and saying, 'what do you see?' and 'this is what I see!' [would be] immensely fruitful."

What I came to see is that this kind of careful examination of "the actual work itself" can be a bit like stepping through Alice's looking glass into a room at first familiar, but one in which further exploration reveals remarkable surprises. In this case, looking at the object not only allowed us to see the child presented in a unique fashion but also provided unusual views of the classroom. Typically, we begin learning about classrooms from observation, teachers' experiences, stated goals, and so on; and at least sometimes, we move to looking at student work. By reversing this order, we ensure that we will first attend to these products of student and teacher work, and then move backward to look at materials, ideas, pedagogy, and so on.

Questions Raised

Raising questions about the work did not seem especially difficult for the Gloucester teachers. In all of the conferences there were at least half a dozen questions raised, and most conferences generated many more. I have noticed that there are at least three significant kinds of questions that came up in these sessions. The first are questions that one could ask of any piece of student writing and concern the context of the work. The second are those that could only be asked of a particular piece of writing. Some common examples of the first variety seek to establish the nature of the assignment, the age and gender of the author, and whether the child worked alone or received help from the teacher.

The second variety of questions grows more directly out of the specific description of the particular piece. The specificity of the questions raised may well be an indication of the depth of engagement the readers have had with the text. The deeper the reading, which I take to be, in turn, an indicator of the rigor and success of this collaborative assessment process, the more text-specific the questions. In the discussion of "May is," for example, there were many text-specific questions. One that intrigued a number of us had to do with why Jessica erased "thats the end" from the last line.

Further analysis of all the other questions that emerged in the course of the ten Collaborative Assessment Conferences revealed a third type of question that in turn fell into three major categories: teaching, curriculum, and assessment; the nature of writing in different genres; and children as writers. These categories are significant because they provide insight into both the participants' concerns and interests and what aspects of a child's work can and are likely to be explored through use of the protocol. In working with numerous other groups of teachers and the protocol, I've found these categories to be consistently useful for parsing the questions raised. What I find significant about these categories is that they represent a range of concerns that cover many aspects of serious professional development in the realm of teaching writing. In other words, through the practice of conducting Collaborative Assessment Conferences, teachers are likely to articulate issues and concerns that are both important to them and significant to the field.

The first category is questions about teaching, curriculum, and assessment. In the conversation about "May is," for example, participants talked at length about the relationship between the lack of punctuation and the meaning communicated in the poem. This gave rise to questions about when and how to approach the problem of "teaching" punctuation. Should Jessica's poem be "corrected" for punctuation? Can punctuation be discussed in the context of exploring what meaning Jessica wants to communicate? What could Pam do to help Jessica as a writer at this point? These kinds of questions may come up at any time in the conference, but they are most likely to emerge during the discussion of teaching moves. Other questions in this category explore the relationship between the assignment and what the child hands in; in particular, they explore how children make sense of teachers' instructions and what kinds of assignments encourage creativity and expressiveness.

The second category is questions about writing in particular genres. In our conversations, given the nature of the pieces we read, most questions centered around story writing, poetry, and writing with illustrations. Through the discussions of several poems, many questions emerged about the nature of poetry. Just what makes a poem a poem? Can a piece of writing be a poem simply because a child declares it to be a poem? These are obviously not trivial questions, and, while there may be no absolute answers to them, how deeply teachers have considered them and their complexity will have significance for how they structure their assignments and how they consider their responses to the writing their students produce.

A third category of questions raised in these sessions concerned children as writers and sought a developmental perspective. Here are just three of the many questions I noted from the ten conferences.

1. Do children imagine an audience when they are writing? If so, what audiences do they imagine? Peers, teachers, parents, others?
2. How is children's writing influenced by the things they have read or have been read to them? Are those influences observable?
3. Is there a point in young children's development as writers when they begin to desire standards, criteria, or rules for good writing?

Taken together, these kinds of questions represent a sample of sincere and genuine teacher concerns. If noted and pursued, they could easily provide the basis for compelling professional discourse.

WONDER (THE VERB)

There is an interesting paradox in considering the meaning of *wonder*. My dictionary offers two definitions of *wonder* as a verb.

1. a. To have a feeling of awe or admiration; marvel.
   b. To have a feeling of surprise.
2. To be filled with curiosity or doubt. (*American Heritage Dictionary*, 1993)

It is with both of these meanings in mind that I identify the act of wondering as a goal of participation in the protocol. Both have been discussed in this chapter. The poem itself inspired admiration, and we marveled at the complexity of the images and meanings in the text. We further admired Jessica as a writer and illustrator of seriousness and playfulness. Jessica's efforts reminded us of the challenge of becoming a writer, a goal we ask all of our students to accept and embrace but one that takes years and enormous persistence to achieve.

We were also filled with surprise and doubt. Did Jessica intend this ambiguity? Were our own interpretations of the text reasonable? Why did others read this poem so differently from me? What, as a writing teacher, can I or should I do to help this child at this point in her development?

The combination of awe and doubt is a particularly potent mixture. It has a way of opening us up to learning. We become engaged with this object of our awe, this text or this child, or, usually, both. We become humble because of the complexity of the challenge of becoming a writer, the desire and seriousness of the child that leads her to accept the challenge, and the uncertainty we feel as teachers, for we also face a remarkable challenge. We doubt our own capacities to meet the challenge, but we are inspired by our students. We redouble our efforts.

But we are slow to learn and must return to this state time and again. The paradox I find in my dictionary's definition of *wonder* as a verb is that, I believe, "to wonder" is not always as passive as this definition suggests. It is not simply "being filled . . . " and it is not always spontaneous or magical. Wondering can be an active effort to "be filled." We travel great distances to be filled with wonder in museums and in nature, for example. Of course, we don't always have to travel. The plant on the windowsill can inspire wonder, as can the children in a classroom. But wondering takes time, attention, and effort. It is not unlike prayer.

Liz's Question, Again

I'd left the last session of the Gloucester workshops with considerable uncertainty that Liz or I or the others had an answer to Liz's question. She wanted to know how her students, or any of the children in the school, would benefit from their teachers' taking hours at a time to leave the classroom, sit in a room together, and talk about single pieces of student work. This question sat on my shoulder during the countless hours I've studied the transcripts of those sessions. I wanted to see if any clues to Liz's question could be found in what actually transpired during those sessions. In time, I found some clues.

Let's return to a piece of the conversation shared earlier in this essay. Julie, Liz, and Margaret were talking in the reflection on the conference about "May is"

Julie: What I think is important about going back to the child and saying that I've been thinking about your work is the message that you matter to me. And your work matters and you are on my mind and you exist in my mind when you are not with me.
Liz: And I respect you . . .

Julie: And I respect you enough to think about you or your problem or your
work . . .

Margaret: That's why I think your immediate reaction may just be, "Oh,
that's very interesting." But if you come back with, "There are a lot of
meanings here and I wonder what you meant . . . "

Liz: It shows you are really interested in their learning.

Why is this conversation so important? If teaching and learning are an
interaction, surely the feelings between teacher and student will determine much
about the success of that interaction. Arguably, respect is the critical feeling for
a mutually beneficial relationship. But it cannot be respect built entirely on role
or some other general quality ("authority figure" or "older person"). The stresses
of classroom life are too great to sustain respect built on such an abstract foundation. It must rest solidly on the particulars of the specific people involved.
Teacher and student (and for that matter, teachers and their colleagues) must
come to know, appreciate, and respect the passions, curiosities, experiences,
efforts, and accomplishments of each other. This doesn't happen quickly. When
it develops, it builds, I suspect, from genuine interest in each other as individuals. That interest has to come from some interaction that makes one take notice
of another.

It seems easy to talk about respecting children and their work. Many of us
in education do this kind of talking all the time. I worry, though, that we often
like the idea of respecting children more than we actually experience the feeling
deeply enough to inform and guide our behavior. I worry about this because so
much of what I've seen in schools—from the condition of buildings and learning
materials to many of the daily interactions between adults and children—seems
to disregard and disrespect the very seriousness of intent and complexity of
thought that we saw demonstrated over and over in the 10 texts we examined.
Real respect is not a simple thing to build, and I suspect it rests best on particulars and poorly on generalities.

Over 3 months, these 10 teachers left their classrooms to sit around a table
and read and discuss children's writing. In our 18 hours together in the superintendent's meeting room and the school library, our examinations of these texts
followed the pattern established by the protocol. We started by looking, and we
dwelled on what we saw. As we looked more, we saw more, and, in turn, we
became more interested. Interest kept us looking, and, as even more was revealed to us, we became amazed. Through all of this we deepened our appreciation of the complexity of the tasks undertaken by these children and the significance of their accomplishments. In short, we felt respect.

All of this made us want to meet these children, to get to know them, to
ask them our questions and hear their answers, to tell them what confused us
and delighted us, what their work made us wonder about. We wanted to learn

from them and to help them in their learning. We wanted to look at the work of other children, too.

Much was unresolved when the last session was finished. Significant questions had been raised but not answered. Few of the teachers knew yet how this work would really influence their teaching. None knew if they would ever use the protocol again or sit again with their colleagues in similar sessions. Still, when we left the table at the end of our last session together, all of this looking and wonder and respect made a fine foundation, I thought, for going back into the classroom the next morning.

NOTE

1. Thanks to the Lilly Endowment, the Pew Charitable Trusts, and the Rockefeller Foundation for support of the research discussed in this chapter. Grateful acknowledgment, also, of the teachers and administrators at the Fuller Elementary School in Gloucester, Massachusetts, who supported and participated in this work: Bill Bruns, Julie Carter, Pamela Card, Ellen Sibley, Margaret Wilmot, Alyce McMenimen, Elizabeth Parillo, Nancy Rhodes, Cherylann Parker, Ron Eckel, Sheila Callahan-Young, and Annette Boothroyd. Also, thanks to Jessica Brennan and her family for permission to use her poem and illustration.

REFERENCES

Armstrong, M. (1992). Children's stories as literature: An interview with Michael Armstrong. *Bread Loaf News, 5*(1), 2–4. [Middlebury College].
Smiley, J. (1991). *A thousand acres.* New York: Knopf.

2

Looking at Students and Their Work

Supporting Diverse Learners with the Primary Language Record

BEVERLY FALK

As our nation's rapidly changing demographics make classrooms a meeting place for multiple cultures, the important and difficult task of improving literacy learning for *all* children becomes an increasingly complex challenge. Teachers are called on to find ways of ensuring that children from a diversity of backgrounds are able to achieve the same high standards. Meeting this challenge requires that teachers not only understand their students' vastly different experiences and understandings, but also be able to use this knowledge to provide educational experiences responsive to diverse needs.

Observing and recording children's behavior and work has long been a strategy that teachers of young children have used to provide information that is supportive of these goals (Cohen, Stern, & Balaban, 1997; *National Association for the Education of Young Children*, 1988, 1991). More recently, teachers of students from all age groups have come to appreciate how looking at students and their work can inform day-to-day teaching in classrooms (Darling-Hammond, Ancess, & Falk, 1995).

The Primary Language Record (PLR) (Barrs, Ellis, Hester, & Thomas, 1988), developed in England and increasingly used in the United States, is one way of examining student work that helps teachers understand students and their learning and better support their literacy development. The PLR is an assessment instrument for documenting classroom events and samples of work; recommending strategies for addressing needs and building on talents; and discussing ideas and perceptions with students, their parents, and other faculty.

By offering a way to examine student work in natural contexts over extended periods of time, the Primary Language Record reveals many types of student skills and understandings demonstrated in a variety of ways. Such information not only helps teachers to keep track of what students know and can do; it also reveals much about students' different approaches to and strategies for learning.

This chapter describes the Primary Language Record, how it operates in practice, and how it provides information that can be used to support the literacy growth and achievement of diverse learners. Drawn from a series of studies of the PLR as it is used in New York City public elementary schools (Falk & Darling-Hammond, 1993; Falk, MacMurdy, & Darling-Hammond, 1995; Falk & New York Assessment Network, 1995) and informed by studies conducted in California (Barr & Cheong, 1993; Barr & Syverson, 1994; Center for Language in Learning, 1995; Miserlis, 1993; Wilson & Adams, 1992) and the United Kingdom (Centre for Language in Primary Education, 1990, 1995; Feeney & Hann, 1991; O'Sullivan, 1995), the chapter takes a close-up look at several very different learners as revealed through the evidence in their Primary Language Records. It describes, too, how teachers take what they learn through assessment to envision and use students' differences in positive ways.

A FRAMEWORK FOR RECORDING LITERACY PROGRESS

The Primary Language Record was conceived in 1985 by educators in England who were searching for a better means of recording children's literacy progress. It is a framework for documenting evidence about students and their learning through a variety of mechanisms in different contexts: focused interviews with students and their families that inform teachers about students' cultures, languages, past experiences, and interests; systematically recorded teacher observations of students; samples of student work that provide an evidence base of students' strategies and approaches to the learning process; and developmental rating scales describing the continuum of progress in literacy learning (see Appendix).

By virtue of what it asks teachers to observe and record, the PLR offers a coherent view of what constitutes progress and development in language and literacy learning. It is grounded in the philosophy that literacy acquisition develops through immersion in meaningful and purposeful activities that take place in diverse contexts spanning the curriculum. Its format helps teachers note the strategies and behaviors that are part of successful reading, identify children's strengths, regard errors as information useful to teaching, and analyze growth patterns in a constructive way.

The Primary Language Record represents a shift in thinking about the purposes and uses of assessment (Darling-Hammond, 1989, 1991; Edelsky & Harman, 1988; Garcia & Pearson, 1994; Medina & Neill, 1988; Wiggins, 1989). Rather than measuring student performance in decontextualized, snapshot-like testing situations, it captures authentic demonstrations of learning in natural contexts over time. It includes a variety of perspectives—those of teachers, families, and students themselves—in the assessment of students' growth and achievement, drawing on multiple forms of evidence of many types of student skills and understandings.

The purpose of the Primary Language Record is not to rank and sort students, as norm-referenced standardized tests are designed to do, but rather to provide a variety of audiences, including families and other teachers, with a holistic picture of individual students' progress. It provides a basis for collegial discussions about individual children and the teaching strategies that can best support learning.

This shift in the use and purpose of assessment represented by the Primary Language Record reflects a distinct stance about the learning process. The PLR is based on the premise that good teaching comes not only from knowledge of curriculum and teaching methodologies but also from teachers' knowledge of students. It is grounded in the assumptions that teachers need to know their students well—the strategies they use, their approaches to learning, and their particular strengths, problems, and needs—and that when teachers are equipped with this kind of knowledge, they can shape effective teaching strategies that help them to support student learning. Within this general way of thinking about teaching lie answers to how to teach toward diversity. Learning about students through their work helps teachers to find appropriate entry points for students' learning. It gives teachers a sense of the experiences and understandings students bring to their learning, heightening the probability that the educational environment teachers provide will be responsive to students' needs.

CARLA'S STORY: THE PRIMARY LANGUAGE RECORD IN USE

The format of the Primary Language Record can be understood by looking at how Mark, a first-grade teacher, used it to follow his student Carla's[1] progress.

In the fall Mark interviewed both Carla and her mother to complete the initial section of the PLR—a teacher–parent interview and a student–teacher conference focused on language and literacy issues. The purpose of these meetings was to encourage communication and to establish a partnership between Carla's home and the school.

At the parent conference, Carla's mother and grandmother shared knowledge about Carla as a learner. They informed Mark that primarily Spanish is spoken in their home. They told him about the kinds of things that Carla reads, writes, and talks about with them—that she is in love with books and will read with anyone who will sit with her for that purpose. They described Carla's increased ability to communicate in both English and Spanish since she began attending school. And they discussed their concerns, hopes, and expectations for Carla's academic progress. All of this information helped Mark to better understand the context of Carla's home and community. It was recorded in Part A of Carla's Primary Language Record.

The conference that Mark convened with Carla (also recorded in Part A of the PLR) provided her with an opportunity to tell him about the things she liked in school, the strategies she used in her learning, and ways she felt he could help her learn. She told him about some of her favorite books, explained how she loved to look at illustrations, and demonstrated how he could help her during reading by pointing to the words one by one and by translating them into Spanish when needed.

For Mark, the conference was useful in that it revealed Carla's interests and preferences for different learning styles and contexts. It also provided him with insights into the ways in which Carla's languages were developing and how each language could be used to support her learning. The conference gave Mark and Carla a chance to develop a joint working plan for the school year, allowing her, the student, to assume an active role in shaping the course of her learning.

At the same time that Mark was gathering background information about Carla through the conferences, he also began documenting observations of her during classroom time and systematically collecting samples of her work. This helped him construct a portrait of Carla's literacy growth and development over the year. His notecards documented things that Carla could do and were correlated to specific pieces of her work. For example, from several pieces collected in October, Mark learned that Carla knew the difference between pictures and print (see Figure 2.1), that she did not yet understand the concept of directionality, and that she was aware of uses of print in her environment (see Figure 2.2). From a running record[2] (Goodman, 1979) made during Carla's reading of *Whistle for Willie* (Keats, 1964) in February, Mark noted that her reading strategies relied heavily on pictures and the meaning of the text. He also noted that she showed an awareness of letters, showed an interest in print, and was aware of the skills and competencies that she did not have (see Figure 2.3).

Mark used this and other evidence he had collected throughout the year to

FIGURE 2.1. Carla's Drawing

FIGURE 2.2. Carla's Page of Words

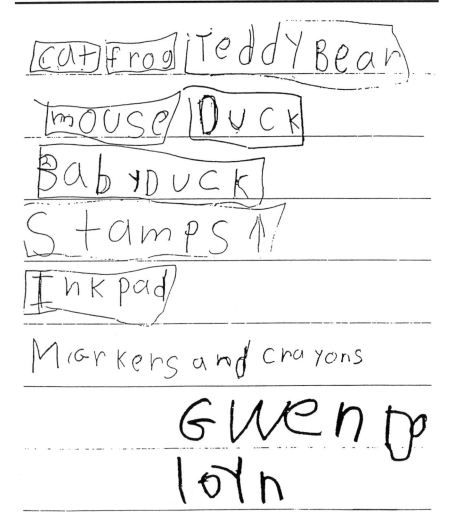

cat frog Teddy Bear

mouse Duck

BabyDUCK

Stamps

Inkpad

Markers and crayons

GWen D

loYn

FIGURE 2.3. A Running Record of Carla's Reading

WHISTLE FOR WILLIE

~~Willie~~ Willie ✓ ✓ Can ✓
Oh, how Peter wished he could whistle!

His friend is ✓ ~ ~ and he turned himself around and around
He saw a boy playing with his dog. Whenever the boy whistled, the dog ran straight to him.
in circles

And ✓ ✓ turned
Peter tried and tried to whistle, but he couldn't. So instead he began to turn himself around-

around and around he whirled...faster and faster....

forwards?
(Then he went ✓ ✓ ✓ ✓ ✓ back and forth) and
When he stopped everything turned down...and up...and up...and down... and around and

around.

This, he had, There was a box on the street
Peter saw his dog, Willie, coming. Quick as a wink, he hid in an empty carton lying on the

sidewalk. "Wouldn't it be funny if I whistled?" Peter thought. "Willie would stop and look
And he ✓ ✓ ✓ ✓
all around to see who it was." Peter tried to whistle - but still he couldn't. So Willie just

walked on. And the dog kept on walking
he ~ ? ~
haltingly

Peter got out of the carton and started home. On the way he took some colored chalks out of
So he made ✓ ✓ ✓ (excitedly)
his pocket and drew a long, long line.

right up to his door. He stood there and tried to whistle again. He blew till his cheeks were ||
V

tired. But nothing happened.

✓ ✓
He went into his house and put on his father's old hat to make himself feel   fast and
more grown-up. He looked into the mirror to practice whistling. Still no whistle!   sketchy

46

sum up his understandings about Carla's progress in the summary section of the Primary Language Record (Part B) completed in the early spring:

> Carla is in love with books. She enjoys reading them and is aware of purposes for reading and writing. She understands book protocol—knows what a title is, knows to write "by Carla" when writing her own books, and uses "book language" to discuss a familiar text. Carla correlates pictures and words, using pictures to find meaning in the text. Her attention to meaning may cause her to disregard one-to-one correspondence at times in order to keep going on with the reading. She has developed her own strategies to identify letters and words and knows the difference between letters that make words and those that don't. Carla reads back her own writing—focusing on initial consonants. She is writing more words on her own as time goes by. She is on the road to connecting it all.

Mark reviewed this detailed evidence, collected over the course of the school year, using the Primary Language Record's reading scale.

Based on child development knowledge as well as psycholinguistic theories of literacy learning, the Primary Language Record's reading scale is designed to describe what a child is able to do, with increasing ease, on the road to developing as a reader. One reading scale for younger children (ages 5–7) charts children's progress as readers on a continuum from *dependence to independence.* Another reading scale for older children (ages 6–8) plots the developing *experience* of readers and looks at the ways in which they broaden and deepen their experience of reading many kinds of texts. (See Figures 2.4 and 2.5.)

The reading scale helped Mark to see Carla's progress in the context of a general literacy learning continuum appropriate for students of her age. He used this evidence to determine her place on the literacy learning continuum and to assign her a scale number that could be used to report her progress to the school. He noted that Carla had progressed from stage 1 (beginning reader) to stage 2 (nonfluent reader).

Once this overall description/evaluation was recorded, Mark used it in a variety of ways: to continue developing instructional approaches tailored to meet Carla's needs; to write his final report to Carla and her family about her progress; and to inform Carla's upcoming year's teacher about her achievements, her strengths, and her strategies for learning.

Through the experience of observing and documenting student work, Mark and other teachers who have used the Primary Language Record have come to see how important it is to use concrete evidence about students and their work to inform their teaching and to evaluate progress. They have also come to appreciate how much they can learn by taking careful and up-close looks at chil-

FIGURE 2.4. Becoming a Reader: Reading Scale 1

	DEPENDENCE
Beginner Reader 1	Does not have enough successful strategies for tackling print. Relies on having another person read the text aloud. May still be unaware that text carries meaning.
Nonfluent Reader 2	Tackling known and predictable texts with growing confidence but still needs support with new, unfamiliar one. Increasing ability to predict meanings and is developing strategies to check predictions against other cues such as the illustrations and the print itself.
Moderately Fluent Reader 3	Well-launched on reading but still needs to return to a familiar range of texts. Simultaneously beginning to explore new kinds of texts independently. Beginning to read silently.
Fluent Reader 4	A capable reader who now approaches familiar texts with confidence but still needs support with unfamiliar materials. Beginning to draw inferences from books and stories that are read independently. Chooses to read silently.
Exceptionally Fluent Reader 5	An avid and independent reader who is making choices from a wide range of materials. Able to appreciate nuances and subtleties in text.
	INDEPENDENCE

From Barrs et al., 1988. *The Primary Language Record Handbook for Teachers.* © CLPE, 1988.

dren. Liz Edelstein, a third-grade teacher at Central Park East elementary school in New York City, summarizes it this way:

> Without the written record over time, I would miss some kids. Only by looking back over this record can you start to see patterns in what the child is doing—reading, writing, and how it is all connected. All these bits of information come together into a picture that is particularly useful for kids who are struggling in one way or another. Using the PLR has taught me that whatever conclusions I come to about a child or whatever I am going to try to do next has to be grounded in an observation or a

FIGURE 2.5. Experience as a Reader Across the Curriculum: Reading Scale 2

INEXPERIENCED

Inexperienced Reader 1	Experience as a reader has been limited. Generally chooses to read very easy and familiar texts where illustrations play an important part. Has difficulty with unfamiliar material yet may be able to read own dictated texts confidently. Needs a great deal of support with the reading demands of the classroom. Overdependent on one strategy when reading aloud, often reads word-by-word. Rarely chooses to read for pleasure.
Less Experienced Reader 2	Developing fluency as a reader and is reading certain kinds of material with confidence. Usually chooses short books with simple narrative shapes and with illustrations and may read these silently; often re-reads favorite books. Reading for pleasure often includes comics and magazines. Needs help with the reading demands of the classroom and especially with reference and information books.
Moderately Experienced Reader 3	A confident reader who feels at home with books. Generally reads silently and is developing stamina as a reader. Is able to read for longer periods and cope with more demanding texts, including children's novels. Willing to reflect on reading and often uses reading in own learning. Selects books independently and can use information books and materials for straightforward reference purposes, but still needs help with unfamiliar material, particularly non-narrative prose.
Experienced Reader 4	A self-motivated, confident, experienced reader who may be pursuing particular interests through reading. Capable of tackling some demanding texts and can cope well with the reading of the curriculum. Reads thoughtfully and appreciates shades of meaning. Capable of locating and drawing on a variety of sources in order to research a topic independently.
Exceptionally Experienced Reader 5	An enthusiastic and reflective reader who has strong, established tastes in fiction and/or non-fiction. Enjoys pursuing own reading interests independently. Can handle a wide range of texts, including some adult material. Recognizes that different kinds of texts require different styles of reading. Able to evaluate evidence drawn from a variety of information sources. Is developing critical awareness as a reader.

EXPERIENCED

From Barrs et al., 1988. *The Primary Language Record Handbook for Teachers.* © CLPE, 1988.

piece of work. Observing children closely generally gives me a lot more than a specific recommendation or a particular method or thing to do for a kid. I walk away with some learning that I can apply to all kids.

ENHANCING UNDERSTANDINGS OF DIVERSE LEARNERS

When teachers get into the habit of collecting and reflecting on concrete evidence about their students, they become more able to recognize and appreciate the different ways that different students learn. These understandings enhance the teachers' abilities to provide effective instruction. Iliana Ordonez, who teaches 8- and 9-year-olds in a dual-language classroom, explains:

> Keeping the observational records of the PLR has helped me to become aware that each child is learning at her own pace and that each child knows something and is good at something. I now gear my work to each child, individualizing and giving children the support they need. The children know that I see that, and it makes them feel secure.

Teachers' appreciation for the strengths of different learners resulting from use of the PLR also helps to safeguard against any bias that teachers may have about students' capabilities. As teachers recognize the varying strengths of diverse learners, they become less likely to attach labels to children (e.g., José is a "troublemaker") or to make all-inclusive judgments about them (e.g., Shanta can't read). These labels and judgments often have the unintended effect of becoming self-fulfilling prophecies—the child for whom adults have low expectations dutifully produces what is expected; the child who is labeled with a particular problem conforms to the image held by others. As a result, teachers and schools often inadvertently set limits on the learning opportunities for these students. Although the intent may be to provide appropriate settings for students with special problems, the actual effect is to deny students access to challenging curriculum. This, in turn, constrains their abilities to develop intellectual rigor and to achieve high standards.

The story of Louisa Cruz and her student André illustrates how the Primary Language Record helps teachers to avoid turning their concerns for students into perpetuating cycles of labels and limits. Luisa, a prekindergarten/kindergarten teacher at River East School in Manhattan's East Harlem, worried that 4-year-old André was going to have problems with language development because he had a noticeable stutter. However, her actual observations of André talking and listening in her class demonstrated that André could communicate with his classmates and make himself understood. This evidence kept her from making unfounded judgments about his capabilities and helped to channel her concerns for André into support for his progress. She explains:

> I knew he had difficulty with oral language and that emotionally he was tied up in knots. I worried he was going to have a hard time with language, but I was wrong. Watching and documenting what he was doing with the PLR showed me that he didn't have a hard time. The fact that I was really listening to him and writing down the things he was saying kept me from being biased about what he was capable of doing, from misjudging what he was actually doing, and from limiting learning opportunities for him based on my misjudgments.

In addition to safeguarding against bias, the documentation that teachers collect for the PLR helps them to identify and appreciate student strengths that might otherwise go unnoticed. This recognition consequently leads them to provide better supports for their students' learning. Special education teacher Lucy Lopez's experience collecting evidence about 7-year-old, bilingual Miguel's learning is an example of how this happens.

Miguel was referred to Lucy's classroom after being diagnosed as "learning-disabled" with "attention-deficit disorder." Her early impressions of him were:

> He used to jump all over and never focus in. He could never remember what he had learned. He didn't listen, and it used to make me mad.

Official school records for Miguel provided Lucy with little information that helped her cope with his behavior or that gave her understandings she could use in her teaching. They focused almost exclusively on the details of academic skills Miguel could not demonstrate, with no mention of the strategies, approaches, or learning modalities he employed as a learner. This can be seen in this excerpt from Miguel's Individual Education Plan (IEP), required for all special education students (see Figure 2.6).

When Lucy first received Miguel's records she noted that the phrase "Miguel does not" was used in almost every sentence. Therefore she was not surprised that after presenting Miguel in the light of such deficits, the description of him concluded with the following:

Social/emotional description
    Miguel has a negative self-concept.

This deficit-model portrait of Miguel was shared by all the adults who came in contact with him until Lucy used the PLR to observe Miguel and to keep track of his progress. As she began to identify his learning strategies, the

FIGURE 2.6. Excerpts from Miguel's Individual Education Plan

Academic

Miguel does not demonstrate strong word-attack skills.

Miguel does not read multisyllabic words.

Miguel does not recognize content-related vocabulary.

Miguel does not identify and use signal (key) words to increase understanding of a reading selection.

Miguel does not read for a definite purpose: to obtain answers, to obtain general ideas of content, and for enjoyment.

Miguel does not identify the main idea of a passage.

Miguel does not use context clues to define unfamiliar words.

Miguel does not spell words at grade level.

Miguel does not write complete simple sentences.

Speech/language and hearing

Miguel is not able to use copular and auxiliary verb forms.

specific competencies he was mastering in reading and writing, as well as areas in which he demonstrated strength, she began to see him differently. She began to focus on what Miguel could do, rather than dwelling only on his problems and what he was not able to do. The following entries from Miguel's PLR demonstrate how Lucy's documented observations provided her with information about his learning strategies and behaviors that were useful guides to teaching:

> Miguel enjoys looking at books and can retell stories. He memorized most of his favorite nursery rhymes with intonation and sang some of them. When reading, he points to each word as he reads. He runs his fingers across the page when reading unfamiliar texts and uses picture clues to read unknown words. His sight vocabulary is developing through the use of "key words" [a personal word bank developed from the child's own interests].

This description of Miguel's reading reveals that despite his lack of fluency in English and his inability to decode precisely, he was able to gain meaning when reading from texts. Among Miguel's reading strategies, the observation notes that he relied on pictures to help him figure out the words, suggesting to Lucy that she provide him with books containing lots of pictures to assist him. The observation also revealed information about Miguel's interests, guiding Lucy in her selection of books for him to read and prompting her to encourage the development of Miguel's sight vocabulary by enlarging his personal word bank.

In this way the PLR helped Lucy to see beyond the problems presented by Miguel's behavior, to see that he was indeed making progress as a learner. As Lucy noted Miguel's strengths across the curriculum, she became more able to plan instruction that met his specific learning needs.

INFORMING STUDENT EVALUATIONS WITH EVIDENCE FROM THE PLR

The rich evidence provided in the Primary Language Record can be helpful when making school decisions that affect students and their futures, especially when the students have special needs or learning differences.

This was the case for 9-year-old Kendall, a recent emigrant from Jamaica, who had low scores on standardized reading tests and was receiving extra supports through Title I assistance. Described by his classroom teacher as "nonfunctioning in literacy" and "unable to read, speak, or write," Kendall was referred for a special education evaluation.

However, the broad array of information that Kendall's resource room teacher collected in his Primary Language Record, along with the information obtained from his PLR parent interview, offered a very different portrait of Kendall and his oral language expression. Through the vehicle of the parent interview, Kendall's family was able to present information that revealed cultural differences between their home and the school, differences that were responsible for what Kendall's teachers saw as his "lack of spontaneity" in oral language. Kendall's family explained that their culture expected children to be quiet, polite, and obedient in school, to speak only when spoken to, and to do exactly what the teacher asked. This description of their native country's expectations for appropriate school conduct caused the teachers to question whether Kendall's apparently lagging language development was the result of innate deficits in his abilities or of cultural differences.

The resource room teacher's own observations of Kendall gave strength to the cultural explanation of Kendall's behavior. Her documentation provided descriptions of him in diverse school contexts that revealed him expressing himself well in many situations and demonstrating considerable interest and ability:

Kendall continues to be well-behaved and very quiet in group situations. Yet he appears to be attentive and interested in all curriculum areas. When called upon, he will respond and read confidently. Otherwise, he will remain quiet and not contribute. He is beginning to initiate comments and questions in the classroom and small-group situations. In the playground, however, he is verbal and socializes well. He is noticeably happier in one-to-one situations and when observing and listening.

This data filled in many of the gaps that were distorting the total picture of Kendall as a learner. It enabled those responsible for decisions about Kendall's future to see the strengths in him that had been missed by other conventional assessments, to see that he was making significant progress in his current class, and to avert an unnecessary referral to special education.

Other teachers have also found the PLR to provide information for evaluations and decision making that is richer than that provided through more conventional forms of assessment. By presenting a fuller picture of student progress that includes context and process as well as product, PLR use heightens the possibility that evaluations will be more accurate and fair. Roz Freidus, a resource room teacher at P.S. 84 in Manhattan, explains:

> I learn much more about a child's reading level by keeping track of the books the child has read than by the score received on the standardized test. With standardized tests there's no conferencing, no talking. It's an isolated instance, a one-shot deal. You are basically looking at the product, no process. You don't get the picture of that whole child. You just get a score. But the PLR is an ongoing thing. It's throughout the year. The PLR sees the process as as important as the product. The PLR gives the kid a chance to demonstrate what he knows and can do.

MEETING THE CHALLENGE OF RESPONSIVE TEACHING: TEACHING TO THE CHILD

Teachers use the Primary Language Record in a variety of ways. Some use the form in its entirety; some use it simply as a guide for observations. Some use it for keeping track of all students; some use it only with those students who are puzzling, who are troublesome, or who require special documentation. Some work on the PLR alone; some use it along with other colleagues, sharing insights about the evidence they collect to enhance the assessment of different children.

A variety of structures have been invented by teachers to foster professional collaboration and conversation around use of the Primary Language Record. Some have dialogue sessions within their schools at lunchtime, preparation periods, or after-school hours. Others participate in out-of-school activities—such as courses, study groups, and summer institutes—that feature group opportunities for exchanging ideas about teaching and assessment strategies.

However the PLR is used, most teachers who have had experience with it say that it has deepened and broadened their instructional strategies as well as their thinking about teaching and learning (Falk et al., 1995). Many credit the PLR for teaching them how to be better teachers of reading. Janet Chan, a teacher of 8- and 9-year-olds in Brooklyn, New York, explains:

> Before I started using the Primary Language Record, reading for me was two-dimensional—you either could read an unfamiliar text or you couldn't. I had previously relied mainly on phonics to teach reading and had used books whose only purpose was to teach children to read. The Primary Language Record is the first real reading course I've ever taken. Through the PLR I learned about all the strategies—semantic, syntactic, and phonetic cues—that go into reading. As I learned about all these components of the reading process, I began to realize all the things that my kids could actually do. Even if kids couldn't independently read an unfamiliar text, they could still do a lot of the behaviors that constitute reading. The way that the PLR asked me to observe and record gave opportunities for kids to show their strengths so that I could build on them for future instruction.

Other teachers consider their experience with the PLR as having a powerful influence on their overall teaching. Carla's teacher, Mark, explains it this way:

> The Primary Language Record has helped me learn how to teach. No one ever said to me, "Look at kids." Courses I took just said, "Do this to them, or do that to them." But with the PLR I can really watch kids and see how they develop. It helps me know what to look for. By watching them I can learn. I'm working *with* them, not doing things *to* them. The PLR lays it right out. It is a framework for the kind of teacher I want to be.

The Primary Language Record's emphasis on observing students in diverse contexts across the curriculum calls on teachers to take a closer look at students and their learning. In doing so, the details of the learning process are revealed, clarifying the kinds of environments and practices that support different kinds of learners. Rather than "teaching to the test," teachers are supported to "teach to the child."

The Primary Language Record provides a way for teachers to come to know their students well. It helps teachers to respond to the need of all learners to be seen and responded to as someone special; to answer the universal learner's plea expressed by teacher Lucy Lopez (1995) in this poem about her students:

I Am Special
Teacher, I may not follow
directions as clearly
as you want me to.
I may not speak as clearly as you.
I may not read as fluently as you.
I may not express my ideas in writing as clearly as you.
But I am learning at my own pace.
Can you see that?!!

APPENDIX: PRIMARY LANGUAGE RECORD

Primary Language Record

School	School Year

Name	DoB	Summer born child ☐
	☐ Boy ☐ Girl	

Languages understood	Languages read
Languages spoken	Languages written

Details of any aspects of hearing, vision or coordination affecting the child's language/literacy. Give the source and date of this information.	Names of staff involved with child's language and literacy development.

Part A To be completed during the Autumn Term

A1 Record of discussion between child's parent(s) and class teacher *(Handbook pages 12-13)*

Signed Parent(s) _____   Teacher _____

Date _____

A2 Record of language/literacy conference with child *(Handbook pages 14-15)*

Date _____

The Primary Language Record is reprinted with permission from the Centre for Language in Primary Education, Webber Street, London, SE1 8QW, U.K.

Part B   To be completed during the Spring Term and to include information from all teachers currently teaching the child.

Child as a language user (one or more languages)   *(Handbook pages 17-18)*

Teachers should bear in mind the Authority's Equal Opportunities Policies (race, gender and class) in completing each section of the record and should refer to *Educational Opportunities for All?*, the ILEA report on special educational needs.

B1 Talking and listening   *(Handbook pages 19-22)*

Please comment on the child's development and use of spoken language in different social and curriculum contexts, in English and/or other community languages: evidence of talk for learning and thinking; range and variety of talk for particular purposes; experience and confidence in talking and listening with different people in different settings.

What experiences and teaching have helped/would help development in this area? Record outcomes of any discussion with head teacher, other staff, or parent(s).

B2 Reading   *(Handbook pages 23-28)*

Please comment on the child's progress and development as a reader in English and/or other community languages: the stage at which the child is operating (refer to the reading scales on pages 26-27); the range, quantity and variety of reading in all areas of the curriculum; the child's pleasure and involvement in story and reading, alone or with others; the range of strategies used when reading and the child's ability to reflect critically on what is read.

© CLPE 1998

B2 (continued)

What experiences and teaching have helped/would help development in this area? Record outcomes of any discussion with head teacher, other staff, or parent(s).

B3 Writing *(Handbook pages 29-34)*

Please comment on the child's progress and development as a writer in English and/or other community languages: the degree of confidence and independence as a writer; the range, quantity and variety of writing in all areas of the curriculum; the child's pleasure and involvement in writing both narrative and non-narrative, alone and in collaboration with others; the influence of reading on the child's writing; growing understanding of written language, its conventions and spelling.

What experiences and teaching have helped/would help development in this area? Record outcomes of any discussion with head teacher, other staff, or parent(s).

Signature of head teacher and all teachers contributing to this section of the record:

Part C To be completed during the Summer Term*   *(Handbook page 35)*

C1 Comments on the record by child's parent(s)

C2 Record of language/literacy conference with child

C3 Information for receiving teacher
This section is to ensure that information for the receiving teacher is as up to date as possible. Please comment on changes and development in any aspect of the child's language since Part B was completed.

What experiences and teaching have helped/would help development? Record outcomes of any discussion with head teacher, other staff, or parent(s).

Signed: Parent(s) _____   Class Teacher _____

Date _____   Head Teacher _____

To be completed by the Summer half-term for 4th year juniors.

Observations and Samples (Primary Language Record)

attach extra pages where needed

Name: **Year Group:**

1 Talking & listening: diary of observations

The diary below is for recording examples of the child's developing use of talk for learning and for interacting with others in English and/or other community languages.

Include different kinds of talk (e.g. planning an event, solving a problem, expressing a point of view or feelings, reporting on the results of an investigation, telling a story ...)

Note the child's experience and confidence in handling social dimensions of talk (e.g. initiating a discussion, listening to another contribution, qualifying former ideas, encouraging others ...)

The matrix sets out some possible contexts for observing talk and listening. Observations made in the diary can be plotted on the matrix to record the range of social and curriculum contexts sampled.

(Handbook pages 37-39)

LEARNING CONTEXTS	SOCIAL CONTEXTS				
	pair	small group	child with adult	small/large group with adult	
collaborative reading and writing activities					
play, dramatic play, drama & storying					
environmental studies & historical research					
maths & science investigations					
design, construction, craft & art projects					

Dates	Observations and their contexts

The PLR Observations and Samples form is reprinted with permission from the Centre for Language in Primary Education, Webber Street, London, SE1 8QW, U.K.

2 Reading and Writing: diary of observations
(reading and writing in English and/or other community languages)

(Handbook pages 40-44)

Date	Reading
	Record observations of the child's development as a reader (including wider experiences of story) across a range of contexts.

	Writing
	Record observations of the child's development as a writer (including stories dictated by the child) across a range of contexts.

4 Writing Samples (writing in English and/or other community languages)
Writing to include children's earliest attempts at writing *(Handbook pages 50-54)*

Dates			
Context and background information about the writing: • how the writing arose • how the child went about the writing • whether the child was writing alone or with others • whether the writing was discussed with anyone while the child was working on it • kind of writing (e.g. list, letter, story, poem, personal writing, information writing) • complete piece of work/extract			
Child's own response to the writing.			
Teacher's response: • to the content of the writing • to the child's ability to handle this particular kind of writing • overall impression			
Development of spelling and conventions of writing.			
What this writing shows about the child's development as a writer: • how it fits into the range of the child's previous writing • experience/support needed to further development			

Please keep the writing with the sample sheet

Further information to support teachers in using the Primary Language Record can be found in *The Primary Language Record Handbook for Teachers* by Barrs, M., Ellis, S., Hester, H., & Thomas, A. Published in the United States by Heinemann, a division of Reed Publishing (USA) Inc., ISBN 0-435-08508-5

NOTES

1. The names of the children referred to have been changed. The teachers, however, are identified by their real names.

2. When a teacher keeps a running record, she documents a child's oral reading of a text by noting on the text what and how the child reads and what strategies he uses for decoding.

REFERENCES

Barr, M., & Cheong, J. (1993, March). *Achieving equity: Counting on the classroom.* Paper presented at Ford Foundation symposium on "Equity and Educational Testing and Assessment," Washington, DC.

Barr, M., & Syverson, M. (1994). *Overview of the California Learning Record: Report on regional moderation readings.* La Jolla, CA: Center for Language in Learning.

Barrs, M., Ellis, S., Hester, H., & Thomas, A. (1988). *The Primary Language Record.* London: Inner London Education Authority/Centre for Language in Primary Education.

Center for Language in Learning. (1995). *Connecting classroom and large scale assessment: The CLR moderation process.* El Cajon, CA: Author.

Centre for Language in Primary Education. (1990). *The reading book.* London: Inner London Education Authority.

Centre for Language in Primary Education. (1995). *Language Matters, No. 2/3.* London: Author.

Cohen, D., Stern, V., & Balaban, N. (1997). *Observing and recording the behavior of young children, 4th ed.* New York: Teachers College Press.

Darling-Hammond, L. (1989). Curiouser and curiouser: Alice in testingland. *Rethinking Schools, 3*(2), 1, 17.

Darling-Hammond, L. (1991). The implications of testing policy for educational quality and equality. *Phi Delta Kappan, 73*(3), 220–225.

Darling-Hammond, L., Ancess, J., & Falk, B. (1995). *Authentic assessment in action.* New York: Teachers College Press.

Edelsky, C., & Harman, S. (1988). One more critique of reading tests—With two differences. *English Education, 20,* 157–171.

Falk, B., & Darling-Hammond, L. (1993). *The Primary Language Record at P.S. 261: How assessment transforms teaching and learning.* New York: National Center for Restructuring Education, Schools, and Teaching.

Falk, B., MacMurdy, S., & Darling-Hammond, L. (1995). *Taking a different look: How the Primary Language Record supports teaching for diverse learners.* New York: National Center for Restructuring Education, Schools, and Teaching.

Falk, B., & New York Assessment Network (1995, April). *Authentic assessment as a catalyst for learning: An inquiry model of professional development.* Paper presented at the annual meeting of the American Educational Research Association, San Francisco.

Feeney, K., & Hann, P. (1991). *Survey of reading performance in year 2: Summer 1991.* Lewisham, UK: Lewisham Education.

Garcia, G., & Pearson, D. (1994). Assessment and diversity. In L. Darling-Hammond (Ed.), *Review of Research in Education* (Vol. 20; pp. 337–391). Washington, DC: American Educational Research Association.

Goodman, K. (Ed.). (1979). *Miscue analysis: Applications to reading instruction.* Urbana, IL: National Council of Teachers of English.

Keats, E. J. (1964). *Whistle for Willie.* New York: Viking Children's Books.

Lopez, L. (1995). "I am special." Unpublished manuscript.

Medina, N. J., & Neill, D. M. (1988). *Fallout from the testing explosion.* Cambridge, MA: FairTest.

Miserlis, S. (1993). *The classroom as an anthropological dig: Using the California Learning Record (CLR) as a framework for assessment and instruction.* Unpublished manuscript.

National Association for the Education of Young Children. (1988). NAEYC position statement on developmentally appropriate practice in the primary grades, serving 5 through 8 year olds. *Young Children, 43*(2), 64–84.

National Association for the Education of Young Children. (1991). Guidelines for appropriate curriculum content and assessment in programs serving children ages 3 through 8. *Young Children, 46*(3), 21–38.

O'Sullivan, O. (1995). *The Primary Language Record in use.* London: Centre for Language in Primary Education.

Wiggins, G. (1989). A true test: Toward more authentic and equitable assessment. *Phi Delta Kappan, 70,* 703–713.

Wilson, M., & Adams, R. (1992). *Evaluating progress with alternative assessments: A model for Chapter 1.* Unpublished manuscript.

3

Studying Children

The Philadelphia Teachers' Learning Cooperative

HELEN FEATHERSTONE

From spending decades in schools—as students, as teachers, and as parents—we know about the dangers that a career in teaching poses to the practitioner's mental health and development: Teaching can be isolating—we work alone. Teaching can be stultifying—schools tend to be conservative institutions in which one teacher's efforts to change his or her practice can evoke a hostile or defensive response from colleagues. Teaching is uncertain—since we co-construct our lessons with students, we can rarely predict exactly how they will go. Teaching can be unsuccessful—in order to teach well, we must connect with children who are very different from us and from one another, building relationships and developing insight into their ways of learning. Teaching can be demoralizing—teachers are often answerable to administrators and to a public that neither understand nor respect their work.

Imagine a teachers' group—a grassroots organization of working teachers, without institutional support or accountability—that met regularly and addressed some of these difficulties. What might such a group do in its regular meetings—how would it support teachers' work and development? What difficulties might it run into?

The Philadelphia Teachers' Learning Cooperative (TLC), most of whose members work in the city's public elementary schools, has been meeting after school every Thursday since 1978. A member of a teacher group myself, I know quite a lot about the difficulty, for teachers, of finding time for regular meetings and about the centrifugal forces that can pull groups apart. I had never heard of another teacher group that had met weekly for even 4 years, let alone 19. I had been curious about the TLC for as long as I had known about it—for more than a decade. I had wondered what kept members coming back, week after week, as the shape of their lives changed, as their children grew up and left home, as friends died and retired, as they themselves made changes in their schools and in their teaching. And I had wondered about the group's meetings: How do these support and stretch members? What role do they play in the teachers' professional development?

In the late 1980s, at the annual meeting of the North Dakota Study Group on Evaluation, I met Lynne Strieb and Rhoda Kanevsky for the first time. From them I learned a bit about the history of the group and about the role that the Descriptive Review processes developed by Patricia Carini and others at the Prospect Archives and Center in Bennington, Vermont, have played in the work of the group. Many of the TLC's founding members, including Lynne and Rhoda, had met in the early 1970s in a Teachers' Center that was funded through the public schools as a part of the federally funded Follow-Through Program. In this Center, and also at summer workshops at Prospect, they met Patricia Carini and began to use the processes that she and her colleagues had created for looking at children and their work.

Working with these processes, the Philadelphia teachers found that they were able to make powerful discoveries about children and about teaching. In the late 1970s funding for the Teachers' Center grew tight, and in 1978 it disappeared altogether. The teachers, however, saw no need to give up the conversations that had become important to them. Six years later, in an article about the group, they wrote:

> We couldn't let go of the experiences we had at the Center at those Thursday night gatherings at dinner. We found we didn't have to have a Teachers' Center to do it. Teachers' Learning Cooperative was ours, and we didn't have to answer to anyone. And we didn't have to worry about funding any more. (Philadelphia Teachers' Learning Cooperative, 1984)

Since 1978, the Cooperative has met in the homes of its members—a different one every week.

The more I have learned about the group and about its use of descriptive processes, the more intrigued I have become. In February 1995 I asked Lynne and Rhoda if I could come see the TLC for myself. We agreed that I would visit their classes, attend a regular TLC meeting, and then, after the meeting, talk over pizza with whoever could stay around. I hoped to learn more about the ways in which the teachers in the group saw the role of the TLC in their professional lives.

IN THE FIRST GRADE

I got to Rhoda's first-grade classroom at the Powel School in downtown Philadelphia shortly after lunch. The first-graders were busy at a variety of occupations around the room. Rhoda greeted me warmly; as she began to explain what the children were doing, a small boy tapped her arm.

"Teacher Rhoda?" Rhoda leaned toward him. "Teacher Rhoda, how do you spell 'three'?"

"You know how to spell it, Marcus: You know from *In the City*. What first two letters do you hear?"

"*T*," Marcus paused thoughtfully, "and *H*."

"Good," Rhoda looked pleased. "Now, go and find it in *In the City*."

Marcus carried a copy of the pre-primer to his desk, where he placed it between his science journal and the cardboard shoebox that houses his silkworm.

For the past few weeks, the children in Rhoda's first grade had been studying silkworms. Every April, when leaves begin to appear on mulberry trees, Rhoda brings silkworm eggs to school so her students can watch them grow into caterpillars, spin their cocoons, pupate, emerge as moths, mate, and lay eggs. At the end of June she puts the eggs in the back of her refrigerator, where they stay until she is ready to hatch them with next year's first grade. Until they begin work on their cocoons, the silkworms eat voraciously. Their dietary requirements are even less flexible than those of the average 6-year-old: They eat *only* the leaves of mulberry trees.

Having solved the problem of spelling "three," Marcus wrote in his science journal: "My silk is trng to eat three at a time." He surveyed his words with pride, then located a ruler, measured the silkworm, and recorded his results: "my silk worm is 4 1/2 inch."

Next to Marcus, Lamar had drawn an elaborately detailed picture of a baseball diamond with a game in progress. On the page opposite he had written: "its 1 to 1. Keri picH. Marcus hit a home run." Lamar looked up from his drawing, and together they watched the silkworm devour mulberry leaves. "When silkworm eat they look like a car," Marcus concluded.

A few feet away, Lisa and Keritha struggled with the intricacies of the classroom computer. "Teacher Rhoda," called Lisa, but before Rhoda arrived Dominique had shown them how to open a new document. Having hit the wrong command, the three girls found that they were typing in Greek letters, which they recognized from their study of Greek myths and greeted enthusiastically. After this detour, they chose an Olde English font and begin their story: "Once . . ."

At her desk, Adrienne watched through a magnifying glass as one of her silkworms began its cocoon. Rhoda, pausing to see what Adrienne had noticed, summoned several other children from nearby to share her discovery.

The story on the computer screen now reads:

Once upon a time there lived a widow named *erin*. she had three daughters name Ilnea, Maya, Natalie, Magdad.

"Hey," objected Keritha, "that's not three. We gotta do it all over!"

Noticing the time, Rhoda directed those who were taking silkworms home overnight to get bags of mulberry leaves and bring their boxes to her to be checked. As the buzzer sounded the end of the day, children collected boxes and bags and headed out the door.

Fifteen minutes later, we followed the first-graders down the stairs, carrying the few unclaimed silkworms.

AFTER SCHOOL ON THURSDAYS

After depositing the silkworms and their mountain of greenery on Rhoda's kitchen table, we drove to Judy Becker's house in the East Oak Lane section of Philadelphia, where the TLC was to meet on this particular Thursday. The meeting wasn't scheduled to start until 4:30, but many teachers arrived early to see friends and catch up. At 4:35, the 15 teachers who had assembled moved chairs into a circle. Karen Bushnell, who teaches fourth grade at the Frederick Douglass Elementary School and was serving as tonight's chairperson, laid out the agenda: The group would do a Descriptive Review focusing on Lynne Strieb's student Matthew.

"At the core of our meetings," explains the one-page handout that TLC members give to interested outsiders, "is a particular kind of conversation, guided by the descriptive formats developed by Patricia Carini and colleagues at the Prospect Center in North Bennington, Vermont." These descriptive processes, developed in the 1970s to help teachers to look closely at children and their work, include guidelines for describing and thinking about one child or one piece of work (a child's drawing, perhaps, or explanation of a mathematical idea). They create the context for an inquiry that encourages careful observation, concentrates attention on children's strengths, and capitalizes on the different viewpoints of different participants.

The Descriptive Review of a child has six parts. First, the chairperson gives the child's name (a pseudonym) and age and the teacher's guiding question. Then the presenting teacher describes the child, using five broad headings: physical presence and gesture; disposition; connections with others, both children and adults; strong preferences and abiding interests; and modes of thinking and learning. Third, the chairperson restates the presenting teacher's themes as she hears them. Then the participants ask questions that they hope will clarify the descriptions and the context. Fifth, the chairperson summarizes new information. Finally, returning to the teacher's original question, group members make recommendations (Kanevsky, 1993).[1]

A teacher requests a Descriptive Review because of questions about a particular child: Perhaps the teacher wonders how to help the child work more productively with classmates or wants help in figuring out how to build academic success on a child's fascination with pattern and color. Sometimes the teacher simply wants to see a quiet child more clearly. The group member who is chairing the Review meets with the presenting teacher ahead of time to help clarify the focusing question. Whatever the question, the goal of the review, as a 1986 Prospect Center publication explains, is "to describe a child's experience within the school setting" (quoted in Kanevsky, 1992, p. 43). The teachers focus on the child's *school* experience, aiming to understand and describe this more fully rather than to "fix" the child or to probe the child's family life for explanations of problematic behavior. The design of the Review assumes that a group of thoughtful teachers working together can see more about the child's interests, accomplishments, and experience than any one teacher could see alone. It further assumes that all children work actively to make sense of their world and that a respectful investigation of a teacher's observations can help teachers to gain access to the child's ways of thinking. In the words of the Prospect publication:

> By describing the child as fully and in as balanced a way as possible, we begin to gain access to the child's modes of thinking and learning and to see their world from their point of view: what catches their attention; what arouses their wonder and curiosity; what sustains their interest and purpose. (Kanevsky, 1992, p. 43)

Finding the Descriptive Review a particularly powerful tool for structuring inquiry, the TLC and people from other communities have developed variations on the original descriptive processes for investigating aspects of teaching practice. "A question comes up and we have tried to figure out a way to address it," Rhoda explains. Whatever the focus, certain features remain central: inquiry, observation and description, respect for children and teachers, creating space for all voices, looking for themes and patterns, taking notes. Since 1979, the group has kept notes from every meeting in an ever-expanding collection of three-ring binders. The notes provide a tool for reflecting on past work and planning for the future. They also furnished material for this chapter.

Describing Matthew

Karen and Lynne had met ahead of time to look at Matthew's work, discuss Lynne's concerns, and establish the focusing question. After we formed our circle and introduced ourselves briefly, Karen gave the focusing question: Lynne wanted insights into helping Matthew become a reader. Matthew was a 7-year-old in Lynne's first-grade class.[2]

Karen gave the floor to Lynne. Following the Descriptive Review guidelines, Lynne began by describing Matthew's physical appearance and the way he used his body, then moved on to disposition, connections with others, preferences and interests, and modes of thinking and learning.[3] Karen (as chair) and Betsy Wice (as note-taker for the evening) scribbled notes:

Physical Presence
Matthew is small, an only child, and often considered "cute." His head is big; his body appears squat (short neck, arms stick out). He is fast. He's unafraid to be physical with bigger, older kids. He often looks pale and tired. He can be tired and energetic at the same time. He can sit still when he writes, when he works at project time. He dashes back from the bathroom, knocking over other kids' projects. He's physical with his classmates. He jumped on a child's back and punched a girl in the eye when she tried to get him off. A week ago he kicked a bigger kid in the bathroom. That afternoon he called a kid a name and the kid tripped him. He's not afraid of retaliation. Swinging his heavy bookbag, he hit another kid. Within the class, this physical behavior has improved, but he still sometimes loses control in unsupervised places like the bathroom.

Connections with Other Children and Adults
At project time he can work with others. He taught children origami and how to make paper houses. It's hard for him to sit with a group and read. His group is four or five boys, with one able reader. They tend to take too many books, and they keep getting up for different books. He listens to Lynne, but he used to lie when caught. He can be quite convincing, as when he almost got the substitute to let him out early for the school bus. When caught touching a girl inappropriately, he denied it. He has a volunteer tutor on Tuesdays and Thursdays who works with him on some aspects of reading. They were meeting in the library, but he was so loud and uncooperative he was asked to leave. He used to ask to go home, refuse to work, try to distract the tutor, anything to keep the focus off work. Lynne has helped direct the tutor's sessions, and now the tutor reads to him or plays some game at first.

Matthew is not afraid of adults or other kids. The after-school older kids think he's cute. Other adults think he is not happy. One reported him telling a fantasy story about his family life.

Strong Preferences and Abiding Interests

Matthew loves drawing. He loves the good Magic Markers and takes very good care of them. From Day 1 he was drawn to construction, creating a Lego structure with internal space and walls. He's drawn to the marble track and did an accurate drawing of his structure. He likes to work in clay, making strong people. He's quick at strategy games like checkers and 3-Man Morris. He finds pieces of cardboard and draws on one side. When the second-graders in the adjoining classroom were working on making bunches of paper flowers, he picked up on that and taught the other first-graders. He makes structures out of separate pieces of paper. He wanted to make a whole city, with streets, a mom, a dad, "me." He can actually follow the directions in origami books. His dad is a carpenter, and he probably does work with his dad sometimes. He can measure with a ruler. His interests are: drawing and constructing, cutting paper pictures. The books he likes are wordless books, sports books, books with cartoon animals and speech balloons.

Modes of Thinking and Learning

Lynne explained her schedule and how Matthew works within it. He loves writing time. Lynne tries to fit math into the morning. During "quiet" reading time students are expected to read alone or in groups. Matthew is up and down all the time. Lynne types up transcripts of class discussions as plays. This is good for Matthew. He must be alert so he can say his part when the "play" gets to him.

In the afternoon Lynne reads a story (Matthew loves the ones from the Houghton Mifflin anthology). Then the children work in their drawing–writing books. Matthew's afraid of his writing book. He said it was "too hard"; he erased and tore a page. Lynne sat with him while he wrote what he could and Lynne filled in (wrote) what he couldn't.

Using the notes she had been taking since the beginning of the year, Lynne gave a history of Matthew's reading. In September he knew the alphabet, but if Lynne asked, "Which letter is *M*?" Matthew had to say the whole alphabet, pointing as he said it, until he got to *M*. He had a hard time tracking the print as his group read with Lynne. He was quick to memorize a story. He loved to copy from the Big Book into his own little book. In October he still had trouble remembering letters. Sometimes he paid attention. A breakthrough came in October when he wrote the words *Dad*, *kid*, and *nail*. In mid-November he only knew five letters. The tutor was working with him, reading to him, practicing his flashcards with him, listening to him recite the story he had memorized. He had a strong idea of his own preferences: poetry books, copying words from books.

By December Lynne was getting nervous: The memorizing of books wasn't helping Matthew; it wasn't bringing him to the symbol. But he got an alphabet game and several Step Into Reading books for Christmas and started learning the alphabet. Now he knows lots of letter sounds (he still has trouble with the letter *V* and some other letters). If an adult doesn't direct him to point to the text as he "reads" it, he won't point to each word of a book he has memorized. There seems to be a chasm between his ability to work with his hands and his ability to work with symbols. He can read just as well with the book closed! He seems young in that. With friends, sometimes he points to the words, sometimes he just recites. Sometimes he gets the right word when it's another child's turn and that kid is trying to figure it out. Reading *Toby in the Country, Toby in the City* (Bozzo, 1982) 3 weeks ago, he raised his hand and pointed to words, figured out some words, and asked to read it again. He is working with the tutor with the flashcards. His mother reads stories with him and plays alphabet games. His awareness of print is growing. Lynne wanted to do this Descriptive Review because of the great disparity between his reading and what he can do with his hands. She wanted to know how to use his interests.

At this point Lynne played a tape of Matthew reading. He read *all* as *every*, but Lynne reported that he had corrected his own mistake when he listened to the tape later.

"His modes of thinking," Lynne concluded, "show strength in memorizing, in putting things together, in strategy. His greatest strength is his work with his hands. His greatest vulnerability is his impulsiveness."

Reframing

It was now Karen's turn to reframe what she had heard in Lynne's description:

> Lynne's presentation was full of contrasts: Matthew tired, Matthew energetic. Matthew using his hands, Matthew thinking about symbols. He is small, low to the ground, gets a lot of attention. Though small, he is not afraid of older kids and adults. He can get physical, talk back. He is fast. He will sit and read without abrupt motion, but he will dash back from the bathroom. In September he was often out of control when not supervised, yet he could work with other kids, teach them how to make things. Still, it's hard for him to sit with a group around a book. Matthew listens to Lynne, yet he stretches the truth and denies wrongdoing. When he first started working with his tutor it was difficult, but Lynne has provided

some structures and he's more cooperative now. Other adults see him as unhappy. He loves construction: Lego, clay, paper construction. He's careful that the markers are in the right place. He has been quick to pick up what the older (grade-2) children are doing at project time, and he brings back the activities to the grade-1 kids. He's good at measuring. He makes books but prefers not to put words in them. He likes sports. He liked copying the Big Books. He seems afraid of his writing book—he prefers the drawing–writing book. He has excellent memory but has had difficulty recognizing letters. It is hard for him to focus on print. When he listens to a tape of himself reading, he can recognize his own errors.

Lynne added family information: Both of his parents came to the report card conference at the end of first report period. Matthew's father looks a lot like Matthew in build. If Lynne retains Matthew, he would be in her colleague Eve's class next year, not in Lynne's: Lynne moves on with her class to grade 2.

Following the format of the Descriptive Review, Karen called for questions.

Digging Deeper

"What does he do in math?" asked Betsy: "The picture that showed the letter *A* seems to show an interest in symbols."

"His math is fine," Lynne agreed. "He noticed the vertical pattern of numbers in the hundred chart. He's learning to tell time. He is interested in the 100th day project. He can tell that a dime is enough to get an eraser at the school store. He is not facile with numbers over 100 yet. He does fine with adding and subtracting."

Tamar Magdowitz asked about Matthew's favorite time of day.

"Probably project time," Lynne concluded after a bit of thought. "Also, the time for drawing during drawing–writing time."

"How does he react to the older kids' attention?" asked Susan Shapiro.

"He loves it! He fosters it in the after-school program. They think he's naughty—'cute but bad.'"

"Is he considered 'cute' because he's small?" inquired second-grade teacher Pat Boyle.

"Yes," Lynne nodded.

"When his mother's in class, what's he like?" asked the next teacher.

"When she came in to show us pictures of Native Americans, he didn't seem to like the attention she was getting and he started to interfere," Lynne recalled. "His mom comes at 1:00 on Fridays. He gets anxious if she's late. She gives him a lot of attention when she comes. He loves to show her what he's been working on."

The next questions took the group inside of Matthew's head. "Does he mind being small?" inquired Rita Sorrentino.

Lynne shook her head, "I don't know."

When Rhoda asked whether Matthew was embarrassed about not reading, Lynne said that he was not, perhaps partly because he was not alone: "There are several others who aren't reading yet."

"Are you still as concerned about him as you were before you did this Descriptive Review?" Rhoda wondered.

"Deep down I feel he'll read, yet I'm also unsure."

"I think of my own son," commented Peggy Stone. "It's possible for people to learn how to read and not read. They find other ways to make a contribution."

"On the tape of him reading, was he reading or reciting?" asked Lisa Hantman.

"He'd been working on it, before I started taping him," Lynne responded.

Lisa pressed this distinction a bit: "What do you mean when you say a child has 'learned to read'?"

"When I can hand him a book like *Little Bear* (Minarik, 1957) or *Go Dog Go* (Eastman, 1987) and know he'll be able to read it. For example, today a girl suddenly could read *In the City* (Black, 1973). She'll go home with it and just keep reading it." Lynne's eyes and voice conveyed her delight in these break-throughs. "It's a challenge: Suddenly you're drawn into it and you can't stop doing it because it's so compelling. That magical leap—I *love* teaching beginning readers!"

"On the tape, he *was* reading," Pat asserted. "He kept self-correcting. And at the end, he didn't know a word and he hesitated, so he had to be reading."

"How is it when he reads his journal back to you?" asked Karen.

"Pretty accurate."

"What if it's something he wrote a long time ago?"

Lynne considered the question for a moment. "I don't know."

"It's arbitrary to expect a child to learn in grade 1," Peggy observed. "I think that if a kid learns to read by grade 3, he's OK."

Lynne nodded. "I tell kids—and I believe it, too— that some people learn to read at 3, some at 10; all learn to read." She paused, before continuing. "There's pressure in my school. It affects my question, whether to retain him in first grade. I will talk about it with his mother. I need a cushion, and I also need some way to deal with a class where some children are already reading chapter books and some aren't reading yet."

"Is there pressure from the school to have Matthew retained if he's not reading?" asked Rhoda.

"The school feels they should go to the resource room if they're not reading at the end of grade 1."

Sensing that the group was ready to move on to making recommendations, Karen signaled an end to questions and summarized the new information we had gotten from Lynne's answers to these questions:

Matthew didn't know all the symbols in September but learned fast and seems to have gotten the idea. He does not feel bad about not reading. He is excited when his mom comes, anxious if she's late. We talked about Matthew's reading on the tape. We talked about what reading is to Lynne. There aren't many words Matthew could read in isolation. We talked about becoming. We talked about retaining.

Recommendations: "Keep Him for Second Grade"

Around the circle, raised hands signaled that many of the teachers have suggestions for Lynne. Sharing her notes with me later, Betsy explained this part of the process: "The presenter is not expected to answer recommendations, either to say 'Oh, I could never do that!' or 'That's a great idea! I'll try it tomorrow,' or 'But I already do that.' We make no attempt to reconcile conflicting recommendations. All recommendations are recorded, and we let them stand as is. The presenter feels free to try any of the ideas that make sense and are comfortable for her."

Tamar went first. "Keep him for second grade, so he can stay with you another year. Maybe you need to use letter flashcards and word flashcards, cards with capital and lower-case letters. He doesn't seem to use initial consonants as a way of figuring out words, so you can write down words that start with each consonant sound—words that are things found in the room, or words that are shown in a picture collage. He is good at spatial things. Get computer games. Shareware is only $5. 'Reader Rabbit' and 'Word Rescuer' are good ones. Encourage him to play them at home. Take the books he memorizes and have him rewrite them as pattern books, adapting them—in place of 'Brown Bear, Brown Bear, What Do You See?' you can do 'Matthew, Matthew, What Do You See?' He should have his own markers, in school, to write in colors. If he decorates his writing book, he'll feel better about using it."

Betsy supplied the name of some books that she thought Lynne could use with Matthew as well as some strategies for helping him to focus on words. "Make him point his finger at each word while he reads and rereads them aloud. Once he knows a book well, have him use a window card to mask all the words on the page but one, to try to read it in isolation. This will get him to attend more to the isolated word on the known page. If he can't get the word in isolation, he can take the card off and work his way up to it by pointing to the text and saying the story."

"The step-by-step progression in origami books—that could be his road to reading," proposed Susan. "And use his relationship to the tutor to build his skills. Also, have his mom play alphabet games with him and read to him. Poetry would help.

"For homework, send home a transcript of the class discussion and have him memorize it. He values memorizing. Certain kinds of homework you give can value memorizing." She returned to her first point: "His reading instruction is less step by step than origami, so you need to make it step by step. Make learning to read as coherent as origami. Origami he figures out by himself, but learning to read, that has required answering to a lot of different people and that might be confusing."

"His work with markers is unbelievable!" Helen Lamont exclaimed. "Also, use his interest in sports. He can study baseball cards, learn to read the names. Somebody could sit with him and write the story that goes with the picture, then put it into a book, so he'll have a book that is his own words and is about something he can draw so well."

Pat described a game utilizing cardboard letters that she had made for one of her second-graders—"Kids would play the game with her"—and recommended Dr. Seuss's ABC books. "What computer do you have in the room?"

"The Apple IIe."

"I can bring you a bunch of easy programs to use in it."

"Matthew reminds me of my John C.—he can make anything," said Rhoda. "Over the years, I've had so many boys who are visually magnificent: They are drawers, thinkers, see-ers. They seem distressed by the discrepancy between their ability to grasp reading and their ability in other areas. They feel, 'I can't figure it out, and I should be able to.' Keep him in your room for 2 years. Tell the school he's on the track. When I kept students, if repeating grade 1 or grade 2, I'd say, 'There's not a problem here—they just need time.' A visual kid expects things to be easy. Also, I think there's something about those symbols: They can't make them stop and be what they are. I try lots of things—rhyming, initial consonants. Do these things make a difference? I do it, but I'm not sure it makes a difference. Try tapes and books—total immersion."

"Books on tape are not what he prefers," Lynne demurred.

"Say there's no choice," Rhoda urged, "that that's what he does: He *must* point to every word. The family will support you. It's not an emotional issue; it's that kids who are good in art often have trouble learning to read if they are spirited, excited boys. Also, he *was* reading a lot on that tape. Give him harder books with tapes."

"Don't make it a chore," Helen cautioned. "It's best he shouldn't worry about it yet."

The recommendations came quickly now, as teachers connected what they had learned about Matthew with their own experiences helping children learn to read: Make sentence strips from books he knows and have Matthew put them in order. Write out the words for songs on chartpaper and point to each word with a yardstick as the class sings—"hearing the sound of the word and saying it and seeing it all at the same time helps to lock the configuration in memory." Make step-by-step instruction books for things he knows how to make so he can read them. Use Big Books—or texts made large on the computer—and have him match words on cards. One teacher explained how Matthew could make accordion-like books from 3-by-5 file cards, copying words and illustrating them with markers. Another suggested a collaboration in which Matthew would illustrate a book and another child would take his dictation. Each recommendation built on what we had learned about Matthew's strengths and interests.

"He's made enormous growth this year," Rhoda asserted emphatically. "You can see it in the drawing–writing books: He's moving into reading. On the tape, when he got to the word *said* he tried *who*, but he knew it couldn't be *who*, so he was using initial consonants. Also, see how much work he does!"

"That's what having kids for 2 years is all about!" observed Lisa.

Pat pushed Lisa's point to its logical conclusion: "You can have the mother insist he be promoted, so he ends up in your second-grade class next year."

Suddenly it was 6:30 and time to adjourn. Ordinarily the chair invites the TLC members to move into "critique" at the end of a Review, to evaluate and reflect on the work they have just done. Today, however, a critique was impossible: The recommendations were so full that we were out of time.

AFTER THE MEETING

About half an hour later, when the pizza had been delivered and distributed and we had satisfied our most pressing hunger pangs, I asked the nine teachers who had stayed to talk about two unusual features of the group: that it has continued to meet for 18 years and that it for meets for 2 hours every week rather than once or twice a month, as many other teachers' groups do. What keeps members coming year after year? How do they find the time to meet so often?

"One answer is that most of us are in different schools and we feel isolated," replied Betsy. "This is the place we come to find lifelines day to day. And it does play an important enough role in our lives that we need it more than once a month. A core of six to eight people come every week, but most people come a couple of times a month. There's an easy in and out."

Another teacher elaborated: "If you miss one, and the group only meets once a month, then you have to go 2 months between meetings. This way, you get another chance a week later."

Lynne observed that creating a written schedule—something the group started doing in 1979—has made the "in and out" easier. "You could know what you were missing. And you could know that it wasn't the last time the group would meet."

The teachers began to talk about the range of ways that the TLC had supported their teaching. I had participated in several Descriptive Reviews in other settings and seen how much a group's painstaking, respectful efforts to describe a student can help a teacher to support that child's growth. But several group members emphasized the less obvious ways that this work helps *all* of those present. One noted that spending 2 hours discussing a child's strengths and interests refreshed her spirit and helped to counteract the depressing effect of school faculty meetings. Another talked about the way in which the energy of children's drawing and writing, examined in this context, fed her practice.

All the teachers seemed to agree that the descriptions of one child, one drawing, one classroom yield insights into other children, and into teaching's endemic dilemmas. Betsy spoke of the power of Descriptive Reviews of "children who reappear over the years, in many different classrooms—the child who teases, the child who gets teased, the child who is hard to see because she is so quiet, the child who doesn't learn to read but does powerful drawing, the child who lies, the child whose spirit makes a place for other children to get along."

Some conversations open up difficult ideas and help teachers to deal with recurring stresses—around report cards, for example, or the decision to retain a child in grade. Two mid-winter meetings celebrated teachers' accomplishments and growth: To the first meeting each participant brought a success, a recollection of a time when she felt she had made a difference; to the second, teachers brought examples of professional growth, times when they had made lasting changes in their practices. The TLC examined these stories with the same care that they had, on other occasions, taken with a child's painting or story.

Because the members set the agenda every 6 to 8 weeks, it responds to their current concerns. "When we readdress topics over time," Betsy pointed out, "it is because teachers are continuing to puzzle about them, not because some university professor or school administrator has decided that they are important."

The TLC also serves its members in practical ways. For example, the group collectively owns a number of classroom sets of children's books—bought with a small bequest from a former member of the group—and they pass them around. "It's a little hard to administer," added the teacher who described this arrangement.

"How does it work?" I asked innocently. Peals of laughter answered my question.

"It's hard to keep track of," Lynne explained.

Rhoda elaborated: "When we started, it was really important to us not to have anyone in charge, not to have an administrator, not to be dependent on others for money, not to have people organizing us. There's a price for that: We do things on our own, but these sorts of things are hard to coordinate."

The group rotates the task of chairing meetings, encouraging every member to take his or her turn.

"And that wasn't always easy," noted Rhoda. "People were reluctant. Maybe they saw other people running them who knew how to do it better and they hesitated . . .

"We encourage new people to chair meetings because you *hear* a lot more when you chair—you listen with a different ear. And now, with new people, we do it in pairs. The new person does the restatement first, and then her partner has a chance to add to it. If you do it a few times with an experienced person, it becomes less daunting."

Setting the Agenda

The TLC devotes one meeting every other month to setting up a schedule for the next 7 weeks. They launch this session by going around the circle, putting ideas on the table, figuring out what people want help with. Two or three teachers may ask for Descriptive Reviews of particular children. Another might suggest devoting a meeting to the teaching of writing. Sometimes public events, local or national, demand attention. In 1995, for example, the superintendent of the Philadelphia schools introduced the slogan "Children Achieving"; TLC members raised questions about what the phrase meant and scheduled a meeting in which to explore it.

Once all the ideas are out, the chairperson tries to group them in some way and launches work on the schedule. Sometimes the group decides to combine two issues—taking several Descriptive Reviews of children who like to write as an occasion to look more broadly at the role of writing in the learning of primary-grade children. In addition to addressing the concerns of several teachers, such a combination allows the group to discuss an important issue in its particularity—something educators often fail to do. These planning meetings can be difficult, though, partly because the number of potential topics often exceeds the number of Thursdays and partly because group members differ about how much time to spend exploring issues and concerns before constructing the schedule.

The teachers returned to the earlier question: What draws them to the TLC on Thursday afternoons? "It feels like a place where we look at our work as an intellectual activity," asserted Rhoda.

"It makes everything else bearable," added a colleague succinctly.

"It is very hard to find a place to have a serious conversation about teaching that lasts more than a few minutes," Betsy pointed out. "And here we can get one that lasts a few hours."

"And that continues over time," added Lynne.

"It's really about looking at a whole lot of things differently," Rhoda said. "Looking at something, and having so many perspectives, means we can turn it and see it from different angles. And that is *so* unusual. Everything we experience in the school system is just the opposite. It is so cut and dried. People get nervous if you can't attach a number to something you are describing."

THE DISCIPLINE OF PROCESS

The format of the TLC meetings—the custom of going around the circle during certain parts of the process, getting everyone's comments in turn, and discouraging cross-talk and interruptions—strikes some newcomers as confining and artificial: Why discipline the spontaneous back-and-forth of good conversation?

"I really liked the format from the very first," recalled Betsy. "I am a person who gets a lot of airtime. I talk a lot. But *here* there are strict rules: You don't talk when it is someone else's turn. I liked the discipline: I listened more, and I learned a lot. I always got surprised. I tend to make snap judgments about people—about what they are like or how they teach—and then I'd hear something I didn't expect: 'Oh, you do *that* in your room?' And I'd learn something."

Describing what the TLC has learned from nearly two decades of experience with Descriptive Reviews, teachers ticked off what they see as fundamental to the process: observing and describing; taking turns so as to get as many perspectives as possible; connecting the particular to larger issues; "continually asking ourselves, 'How did we do?'." The Descriptive Review process, Rhoda argued, can create an entirely new kind of conversation in a school faculty. "We did Descriptive Reviews in my school during a period when we were having difficulty talking about some hard issues. We did them two different times and everyone loved it. It was a moment when teachers spoke to each other in a different way and there was common ground in a different sense. The structure made it comfortable for everyone and put the focus back on concerns we all share."

Several teachers mentioned that the TLC had taught them about leadership as well as about teaching. "For one thing," explained one long-time member, "I've learned how to run a meeting so that people can be heard, so people understand what is being talked about. A meeting where there's—not a conclusion necessarily—I'm not sure how to say this—"

"A meeting where people feel they've been heard," offered another teacher.

As an instructional support teacher, Susan Shapiro works with other school district staff in a variety of ways. She described the way in which strategies she had learned in the TLC enabled her to reshape the discourse in a principal's group in which she participates. "The first meeting I went to, two people dominated the whole meeting. I took *copious* notes, and I went home and typed them up and sent them to all the principals.

"Then, in the second meeting, one of the two people who had dominated said, 'Today we're all going to take turns.' And those two people tried not to dominate and," Susan paused and made a face, "it was better, but there was still a lot of crosstalk and venting. So I took notes again and I got them out on Tuesday."

"So, as a member of this group, I take these structures to other groups."

Rhoda noted that Susan's documentation gave the group the power to understand not only the content of the meeting but also its process.

"You see, it isn't just about classrooms and schools," concluded Lynne. "It's also about leadership: We speak with a voice that gets listened to when we speak elsewhere. We speak with authority. And people will ask us, 'Where did you learn to do this? How did you learn to run meetings like this?' It has to do with a different arena than the classroom. It has to do with working with other adults. And people get to practice it here."

A FEW WEEKS LATER

In early June I was able to join the TLC again, this time for a meeting that focused on the classroom of Linda Bean and the work her students were doing during project time. After the meeting, our talk turned to assessment, and Lynne recalled an ordeal of the previous morning: She had had to give Matthew a standardized test that had reduced him to tears "because he was confronted with all the things he *couldn't* do." She contrasted the experience of the test with the Descriptive Review she had done 2 months earlier, recalling how heartening and helpful it had been to concentrate for 2 hours on this little boy's strengths. Listening to Lynne describe the progress Matthew had made since the Review,[4] I was reminded of two sentences from Rhoda's analysis of the values built into the Descriptive Review process (Kanevsky, 1992): "No one is trying to change the child. Rather, the Descriptive Review helps the teacher use the child's interests and values to create harmony in the child's school life."

By focusing on Matthew's gifts and achievements, the TLC had helped both teacher and student.

NOTES

1. Because the Descriptive Review continues to evolve, the language that Carini and the TLC use to describe both the descriptive categories and the process itself has changed. Kanevsky's 1993 chapter, for example, gave the five headings for the descrip-

tion of the child as physical presence and gesture (which remains unchanged), relationships, temperament, interests, and formal learning. The changes in vocabulary reflect experience with the Descriptive Review process.

2. The extraordinarily detailed notes of Betsy Wice, a long-term member of the TLC, provided the basis for the account of the Descriptive Review of Matthew.

3. This Descriptive Review took place several years ago. Several of the teachers who participated in the Review noted that in the years since they have deepened their understanding of reading and that they would make somewhat different suggestions today.

4. Matthew continued to make progress. Lynne did keep him with her the next year, as several TLC teachers had recommended in the Review, as she moved from teaching first grade to second. Matthew then spent a second year in second grade (this time with another teacher, as Lynne was now teaching first grade again). Through both second grade years he displayed pride in his developing skills as a reader; during the second year in second grade, he often visited Lynne with a book in order to show her how well he was reading.

REFERENCES

Black, I. S. (1973). *In the city*. New York: Macmillan.

Bozzo, M. Z. (1982). *Toby in the country, Toby in the city*. New York: Greenwillow Books.

Eastman, P. D. (1987). *Go dog go*. New York: Random Library.

Kanevsky, R. D. (1992). The descriptive review of a child: Teachers learn about values. In J. Andrias, R. Kanevsky, L. Strieb, & C. Traugh (Eds.), *Exploring values and standards: Implications for assessment* (pp. 41–61). New York: National Center for Restructuring Education, Schools and Teaching.

Kanevsky, R. D. (1993). Descriptive Review of a child: A way of knowing about teaching and learning. In M. Cochran-Smith and S. Lytle (Eds.), *Inside outside: Teacher research and knowledge* (pp. 150–162). New York: Teachers College Press.

Minarik, E. H. (1957). *Little bear*. New York: Harper.

Philadelphia Teachers' Learning Cooperative. (1984). On becoming teacher experts: Buying time. *Language Arts, 61*(7), 731–736.

PART II

Protocols for Examining Students' Work

At a national conference of school reformers, teachers, administrators, and other educators engage in a "Tuning Protocol," providing feedback to Greg, a middle school teacher, on an alternative assessment task he has used with his students. Greg listens as participants raise questions and offer comments on the design for the assessment and on samples of student work from it.

In a high school media center in California, a small group of teachers meets for a weekly "protocol" focusing on samples of student work. The discussion, informal but not unstructured, focuses on an Internet writing assignment and helps teachers grapple with teaching and assessing student writing in new media.

In a classroom in the Bronx, a high school senior presents one of her graduation portfolios at a "Roundtable" that includes teachers, classmates, family, and visitors. She relates her work to the school's goals for its graduates and to her own life and goals, then listens as others provide feedback and pose questions.

As methods for student assessment have shifted from tests to more authentic and complex tasks, including portfolios and exhibitions, teachers at all levels of schooling have recognized the need to examine more closely the product of those tasks: students' work.

In the scenarios above, each from a chapter in this section, teachers take part in established, agreed-upon protocols in order to gain a deeper understanding of their students' learning and their own practice. The protocols share important features:

- They are facilitated. The facilitator may be from inside or outside the school.
- They are structured. Time is allotted for different activities and for different participants to speak—and listen.

- All those taking part share *norms* for participation, for example, respect for the student whose work is being discussed.

The protocol structure supports discussions that allow all participants—teachers, educators, and "critical friends"—to share their perspective on the work. The protocols help create opportunities for teachers to get valuable feedback and critique on their work. They allow teachers to examine and reflect on their assignments and standards for students' work in the light of the actual student work that results.

Teachers involved in protocol meetings like these confront many obstacles, including tight school schedules and old notions of student assessment and professional development. One of the toughest challenges for teachers is to break the typical school culture of isolation and expose their students' work—and their own—to a wider audience, one that is both supportive and critical. In doing so, teachers begin to build new and powerful models for professional exchange and professional development.

4

The Tuning Protocol

Opening Up Reflection

DAVID ALLEN

The second "Tuning Protocol" of the day was scheduled to begin at 1:15 PM. The group of 14, including teachers, administrators, coordinators of regional school reform efforts, staff members from the Coalition of Essential Schools, and other educators, took their places around the tables set up by the hotel staff in a hollow square. At one end of the table, Kara, a young researcher from the Coalition staff facilitating the group, and Greg, a middle school teacher, were talking quietly. Behind them a VCR and monitor were set up.

Kara turned to the whole group and asked for its attention:

OK. Just like this morning, we'll hear a presentation about an exhibition or project and examine some of the student work that comes out of it. This morning we "tuned" a high school graduation portfolio project presented by a team of three teachers. This time we'll hear about a middle school exhibition presented by Greg. Take another look at the schedule you have in your packet. [See Figure 4.1.]

During Greg's presentation, there'll be no interruptions for questions or comments. After he's done, we'll take a few strictly clarifying questions, things you need to be clear about in order to offer your feedback. Then, I'll ask you to identify one or two comments or questions you'd like to address to Greg. It may help to think in terms of "warm" feedback, that is, supportive comments—what you found strongest, or most promising, about the student work or the exhibition structure—and "cool" feedback, more critical comments or questions—what's missing or not

FIGURE 4.1. Schedule for Tuning Protocols (Chicago)

I. Introduction *10 min.*
- Facilitator briefly introduces protocol goals, norms, and agenda.
- Participants briefly introduce themselves (name, school).

II. Teacher(s) Presentation *20 min.*
- Context for student work (describing exhibition vision, coaching, scoring rubric, etc.).
- Samples of student work (these might be photocopied pieces of written work and/or video clips).

III. Clarifying Questions *5 min. max.*
- Facilitator will judge which questions more properly belong in warm/cool feedback.

IV. Pause to Reflect on Warm and Cool Feedback *2–3 min.*
- Participants may choose to write down feedback items they'd like to share (generally no more than one example of each).

V. Warm and Cool Feedback *15 min.*
- Participants offer feedback while teacher-presenter is silent.
- Facilitator may try to give some focus by reminding participants of an area of emphasis supplied by teacher-presenter.

VI. Response *15 min.*
- Teacher-presenter responds to those comments/questions he or she chooses to.
- Participants are silent.
- Facilitator may intervene to give response focus, clarify, etc.

VII. Debrief *10 min.*
- Begin with teacher-presenter ("How did the experience compare with what you expected?").
- More general discussion of the Tuning Protocol may develop.
- Frustrations, misunderstandings, etc., as well as positive reactions participants may have experienced.

Note: This schedule represents an early version of the Tuning Protocol. See Figure 4.4 for a more recent version.

strong enough? During that time Greg is silent. In the next part of the protocol, he'll respond to any feedback he chooses, while the rest of us are silent again. We'll save time at the end for a debriefing of the process. Any questions?

A junior high school teacher asked, "What about suggestions to the presenter? Where do they fit in?" Kara thought for a moment, then asked for the group's opinion. One of the presenters from the morning protocol said she thought some suggestions offered during the feedback were really helpful. Another participant said, "I think suggestions are OK, but we have to be careful about getting into a quick-fix mentality here. These issues are too complex." The group nodded in agreement.

Kara began the protocol by introducing the presenter: "Greg is a sixth-grade middle school teacher from Ramparts Middle School in Ohio. He's going to present an exhibition about designing a community center for the town. He's identified one area he'd especially like some feedback on: Are students demonstrating an ability to apply math concepts and explain how they used them when they make their presentations? He'll say more in his presentation."

Greg began to speak, nervously at first. He apologized for having such a "rough" project, especially after the "great work" the group had seen in the morning. "This is the first year we're trying this," he said. "I'd like to do more, but I have to get my kids ready for state tests in reading and math, so I only have 3 or 4 weeks out of the year to do this kind of thing."

Greg became more comfortable as he continued. The group was very attentive as he described the assignment. Teams of students had been given the task of designing a recreational center for the town. He talked about how the class had worked on calculating area and how he had given them town maps with the site outlined in red. One of his goals, he said, was for students to apply the formulas for area they were learning to "a real problem, as well as to use their addition and multiplication skills"; they had to come up with a budget for the center with each item accounted for by its unit price. He described how students worked in groups; how he started each 45-minute class with a mini-lesson, then "roved" from group to group to provide help and answer questions; how the students kept individual "project logs"; how the final product, including a blueprint for the center, a budget, and a written proposal of the center, was to be presented to a panel of "experts"; and how he evaluated their work on the basis of "teamwork, creativity, presentation skills, and math accuracy."

"I have a scoring rubric, but I didn't bring copies because I'm not really happy with it." Greg passed around one of the blueprints and copies of one group's report. "I made a videotape of the presentations, and I'm going to show you the group whose work you've seen." The participants watched as three boys stood in front of a chalkboard on which they'd hung their blueprint. The tape was poorly made: The boys looked distant; the blueprint was much too small to read in any detail; and the sound was grating—replete with coughs and chairs scraping the floor. Nevertheless, participants strained to catch every word of the 5½-minute presentation and the few questions from classmates and the panel that followed.

When the lights came on, Greg seemed a little unsure of whether to add anything, settling for a quick, "Well, that's about it."

Kara checked her watch, then leaned forward. "Thanks, Greg. Let's take a few clarifying questions."

A high school principal asked, "Who were those adults we saw in the video?"

"Oh yeah," Greg said. "Sorry, I should have told you. One is a parent who agreed to come in and the other one, the woman, is a substitute teacher I was able to get to sit in on her free period. I wanted more outside judges, but it was just too complicated to get them in."

After a few more questions, Kara asked participants to identify one or two comments or questions for Greg, reminding them of the warm/cool distinction. Participants reviewed their notes. Some jotted down a few words, others looked at the ceiling.

"OK, let's get started," Kara said. "Greg, we're putting you in a kind of isolation booth here: You can see, hear the comments, take notes if you like, but you *can't* speak. You'll get your chance to do that later." Turning to the group, she said: "We're a pretty small group, so I won't ask for hands, and I won't ask that we do only warm then cool, but I'd suggest you start off warmer and then move to cooler feedback. I'll try to keep quiet, but I may step in from time to time to keep us on track. Who'll start?" (See Figure 4.2.)

FIGURE 4.2. Norms for Tuning Protocol

---

1. *Be respectful of teacher-presenters.* By making their work more public, teachers are exposing themselves to kinds of critiques they may not be used to. Inappropriate comments or questions should be recast or withdrawn.

2. *Contribute to substantive discourse.* Many teachers may be used to blanket praise. Without thoughtful, probing "cool" questions and comments, they won't benefit from the Tuning Protocol.

3. *Be appreciative of the facilitator's role,* particularly in regard to following the norms and keeping time. A Tuning Protocol that doesn't allow for all components (presentation, feedback, response, debrief) to be enacted properly will do a disservice to the teacher-presenters and to the participants.

A moment went by before anyone spoke. A middle school teacher from Florida started to raise her hand, saw Kara nod to her, and said: "Well, I just want to say, I think it's great to see kids with a challenge like this. I mean something more complex than just 'answer this word problem' or maybe 'make a drawing.'"

Another teacher said she'd enjoyed seeing students working together on math problems, "that's too rare."

The next few comments were equally warm. Greg jotted down a few notes and seemed to relax.

A regional coordinator of Coalition schools said she liked the question-and-answer period. She hesitated, then said, "This might be a cool comment, too. I mean, maybe it could be even longer, with more people asking questions. It seemed like a good opportunity that wasn't really taken advantage of."

Without any explicit acknowledgment or direction from Kara, the feedback became cooler, more probing, often coming in the form of questions:

"Could the kids have spent time outside of school, measuring the site or taking photos of it?"

A staff member from a school reform organization offered, "I'd like to see some more preparation for public speaking, maybe using videos of other presentations as models."

"It seemed like one of the boys in the presentation didn't really speak. How could you evaluate what he learned? Even with the kids who spoke a lot, I mean, if I were a judge I'm not sure I could have evaluated their math ability, or their accuracy—and those were the goals, right?" Greg nodded emphatically; he seemed eager to respond but kept quiet.

A senior high school math teacher added, "I'm not sure I do see a lot of real math going on." He proceeded to list a few kinds of problems that might have been emphasized.

An elementary teacher asked, "Does estimation come into this at all? I spend a lot of time with my children on estimating, and I'd like to think they use it later on."

The feedback continued for 10 minutes more before Kara spoke up. "OK, I think we've had a good mix of warm and cool, a lot for Greg to think about. But for the next part of the protocol, I'm going to ask that all the participants except Greg be silent. We'll give him a couple minutes to look over his notes, then he's free to respond to whichever of the comments and questions he chooses to. Greg, it's all yours."

Greg flipped through the two or three pages of notes he'd made, then looked up. "Well, I guess I'll begin with something a couple of people noticed about the preparation for the presentation. I think it would be a good idea to give them more practice before they actually present, especially for those kids who don't really like getting up in front of the class." He talked about the one practice presentation he had built into the class: "I know now it's not enough, and some kids didn't really take it seriously. . . . We could probably spend one more day working on that, maybe looking at some videos from the year before, now that there's going to be a year before." A ripple of laughter went around the table.

In an increasingly relaxed fashion, Greg went on to talk about his dissatisfaction with the unequal distribution of work in the groups. "Jason, the kid who didn't speak at all, actually did contribute to his group's project. I wish I'd brought some of his log entries to show you. But I've still got the problem of how to grade him on presentation." Greg came back a few times to the shortage of time. "I'd definitely like to have them spend a whole day at the site, and I think taking photos would be a great idea. I don't think it would be that difficult to do, and it would make it more real to them."

"The comments about not enough real math, that's tougher. I need to find ways to require them to show how they used the formulas. I'd like to talk more with some of the math teachers here who made some good suggestions."

Greg turned to his notes again, when Kara interjected, "Sounds like you've got a lot more to say, but we're going to have to end there." Greg and the participants seemed surprised at how quickly time had passed. "We've only got a few minutes for a debrief of the process. Let's start with Greg. How'd it feel to be in the hot seat?"

"Well, I was pretty nervous at first, especially since the morning presenters seemed so well prepared. But a lot of the comments were kind of a relief. I thought I was on the right track with this thing, but I feel more confident about that now—I just wish my principal was here to hear this. [Some participants laughed with Greg.] Some of the cool comments I'd definitely thought about, but a couple, like the idea of using video to coach the presentations, were new, and I think they'll really help."

Kara opened up the discussion to the whole group. Most participants shared a general sense of appreciation for the process.

"It really lets you get into the important classroom issues."

"It's just so interesting to see the real stuff, I mean the kids' work."

One participant agreed but added, "I have to admit I really felt stifled by the rules, when you can talk and when you can't. I feel like our chance to really get into it with the presenter was always being cut off."

Another participant agreed, "It just feels so artificial. I think it works against real discussion."

A third spoke up, "I disagree. I thought at first this was going to be way too 'soft,' but I like the structure. I think it kept us focused and gave everybody a chance to say something. That doesn't happen a lot, at least not in my school."

More discussion followed, with most participants agreeing on the value of the "norms" for the protocol. "I'm going to bring it back to my district for our professional development planning meetings," one middle school principal said.

"It's 3:00 now—one final comment?" Kara offered.

"I'm exhausted," said a high school principal, and the entire group laughed.

A NEW TOOL FOR NEW ASSESSMENTS

Each Tuning Protocol is a unique event, shaped by its goals, who takes part, the nature of the student work, and many other factors. In the section above I've tried to portray a "typical" Tuning Protocol. To do so, I've created a composite from the more than 30 Tuning Protocols that took place at a national meeting of the Coalition of Essential Schools in Chicago with the theme of "Standards and Student Work." While the characters and dialogue are fictional—based on interviews with facilitators and presenters, and survey data from participants from the meeting—I believe they provide some idea of what it's like to take part in a Tuning Protocol.[1]

The Tuning Protocol was originally developed by Joseph McDonald and colleagues from the Coalition of Essential Schools' Exhibitions Project[2] as a resource for the five high schools participating in the project. Each school was engaged in developing an authentic assessment, or "exhibition," to determine students' readiness to graduate according to the school's own criteria or standards; these included a series of Socratic seminars, a "position paper," and a year-long research project culminating in a public presentation (McDonald, Smith, Turner, Finney, & Barton, 1993).

Changing the ways in which students were assessed from familiar test-based evaluations to the new and largely untested exhibitions called for different ways of planning, teaching, and judging student work. Along with the faculty from the schools, the project staff wanted the meetings of the schools to provide more than just a chance to commiserate or show off; instead, the meetings became opportunities for the schools to provide each other with critical feedback on their exhibitions as *works-in-progress*.

The Tuning Protocol that emerged from the Exhibitions Project is a structured, facilitated process that brings teachers and others together to examine student work and the exhibition design for it. This close examination leads to critical feedback and reflection on the work presented. The feedback and the reflection it triggered, we believed, would help teachers "fine-tune" their exhibitions to better support student performance and learning.

From its first tryout in 1992, the Tuning Protocol has been used in and adapted for many contexts: in individual schools, professional development institutes, and school network meetings (McDonald, 1996). The most sustained, programmatic use of the Tuning Protocol has occurred in California, where it has been adapted by the state's Center for School Restructuring as a key element in the Center's statewide school restructuring initiative (see Chapter 5).

In this chapter, I introduce the Tuning Protocol to educators who may find its approach and structure useful in their work. To do so, I consider the national Tuning Protocols in Chicago, referring often to Greg, Kara, and their group's experience. I also draw on other sessions from which we have collected data, including interviews, field notes and videotapes, and my experience as a facilitator of Tuning Protocols and trainer of facilitators.

My second goal for this chapter is to critique the Tuning Protocol and how it has been used so that it may become a more effective tool for supporting teachers' practice. To do so, I borrow from the format of the protocol and provide warm and cool feedback on the Tuning Protocol itself.

As Kara explained, warm feedback points out what's strong or promising in the student work or the exhibition structure. Cool feedback asks participants to take a more critical stance, offering comments or questions about what's weak or missing in the work. The line between warm and cool feedback is often difficult to discern. Warm comments often contain questions and suggestions that suggest changes in practice or an extension of practice ("You could go further with . . . "). Cool comments may well start from an acknowledgment of a strength but point to some aspect of the work that may not have been considered. Perhaps for this reason, Kara did not try to maintain a strict division of warm and cool, although she encouraged participants to begin with warmer comments.

The warm and cool feedback that follows really comes from many voices, primarily from the Chicago protocols from which we collected data, and I act as a kind of reporter. The coolest feedback with which I conclude the chapter represents some of my own reflections on the Tuning Protocol and its potential to be a more effective resource for teachers.

WARM FEEDBACK

It's difficult to generalize across the 16 different groups and 32 Tuning Protocols from the Chicago meeting. Beginning with very warm feedback, it is possible to say that all the Tuning Protocol sessions were marked by a high level of engagement. All the presenters I spoke to afterward described their protocol session as valuable and enjoyable, and some described the experience as "exhilarating"; many participants concurred.

In the sections that follow, I summarize a few of the factors that contributed to the participants' appreciation of the Tuning Protocols. I don't intend these as a set of "dos and don'ts" for Tuning Protocols. Instead, I hope these points are useful for understanding the Tuning Protocol and, for some, for preparing for Tuning Protocols in their own work.

Everybody Participates

The Tuning Protocol does not divide participants into categories, beyond those of presenter, participant, and facilitator. The Tuning Protocols in Chicago—and as it is usually practiced—made no distinction between classroom teachers, education researchers, and state education department officials. In other words, no one sits outside the circle.

This broad and equitable inclusion serves several purposes. It allows teachers to hear, and respond to, direct feedback from people whose perspectives they do not normally have much access to: superintendents, education researchers, teacher educators, and other teachers. For Greg, some of the most valuable feedback came from math teachers at different levels of schooling.

Educators often talk about the importance of bringing the business and higher education communities into closer contact with schools. The Tuning Protocol may offer one vehicle for doing that in a way that is useful to teachers, as well as informative to those outside the classroom. The focus on student work keeps the discussion grounded in the realities of schooling—as opposed to the generalities, abstractions, and polemics that often arise ("If we only had national standards . . . "). The protocol structure and facilitation help to make sure that every voice is heard and none dominates.

When everybody participates, everybody learns. Teachers benefit from the observations and questions of those from outside the classroom and school. The "outsiders" learn about what is really happening within the classrooms: What do the students actually do? What does their work look like? How do teachers assess the work? One participant described the protocol as "a great way to further substantive dialogue between professionals."

Depending on the purpose for the "tuning" and practical considerations, the participant list will not always be as diverse as in Chicago. For example, within some districts, the Tuning Protocol has been used to bring together teachers from different subject areas and levels of schooling to look at student work and discuss cross-district standards for student performance. Still, the Tuning Protocol seems to thrive when it integrates multiple perspectives.

Video Animates and Informs Discussion

As the Tuning Protocol has developed, video has become a regular part of the teachers' presentations. Together with samples of student work in other formats—for example, essays, journals, posters, and models—video provides an important "angle" on student work and learning (Collins, Hawkins, & Fredericksen, 1991).

Video is particularly useful in allowing participants to visualize the students at work and the classroom reality. Even a poor-quality tape of a few minutes—for example, Greg's boys' presentation—is viewed with great interest and appreciation by protocol participants and informs the feedback and questions participants offer. A comment about one boy's silence during the presentation, for example, led to Greg's reflection on how his assessment can be fair and individualized.

While student presentations are often "featured" in teachers' presentations, participants also benefit from video that captures some of the process of developing exhibitions. In some cases, the teacher even appears in the frame, working with groups of students or leading a discussion about criteria for performance.

The positive response to video argues for more taping and more occasions for viewing, analysis, and discussion of student work. However, it is not enough simply to turn on the camera or, at the other end, to select the best moment of the best presentation to show during your Tuning Protocol. As Erickson and Wilson (1982) advise, video case studies can "help us get closer to the action of life in schools. But being close, in and of itself, may not help us develop new insights" (p. 2). When presenters bring slickly edited tapes or only "best works," they may cut off the most useful feedback (of course, this is also true with written work and other visual student products). Adding to a video case study the questioning, feedback, and reflection of a Tuning Protocol may help in acquiring the insights to which Erickson and Wilson refer.

A Process for "Doing It"

As one facilitator in Chicago put it, "Everybody knows we need to do this, we say we should do this, and we don't do it." For many participants, the Tuning Protocols seemed to be a very "practical" way in which teachers in one school or from a number of schools in a district or network could work together. While several participants in Greg's Tuning Protocol reacted negatively to the confining "rules" of the protocol, most appreciated the value of the structure.

It's not surprising that teachers feel the need for a structure for talking about student work and their own work, if only for the "safety" it offers, an issue I discuss later. Few professionals, in any field, engage in frequent, impromptu analytical discussions of their work; it is for this reason that other professions have developed forms for such discussions (for example, doctors' rounds). The Tuning Protocol, as well as other processes described in this book, may begin to provide some of the "process and discourse tools" (Szabo, 1996, p. 87) teaching will need to become itself more professional.

FIGURE 4.3. Guidelines for Facilitators

1. *Be assertive about keeping time.* A protocol that doesn't allow for all the components will do a disservice to the presenter, the work presented, and the participants' understanding of the process. Don't let one participant monopolize!

2. *Be protective of teacher-presenters.* By making their work more public, teachers are exposing themselves to kinds of critiques they may not be used to. Inappropriate comments or questions should be recast or withdrawn. Try to determine just how "tough" your presenter wants the feedback to be.

3. *Be provocative of substantive discourse.* Many presenters may be used to blanket praise. Without thoughtful but probing cool questions and comments, they won't benefit from the Tuning Protocol experience. Presenters often say they'd have liked more cool feedback.

Qualities of Facilitation

Tuning Protocol facilitators always juggle a number of responsibilities. Facilitators are concerned with the focus and coherence of the Tuning Protocol and the inclusion of all participants; sometimes these goals may compete. For example, in Greg's Tuning Protocol, a math teacher chose to offer feedback in the form of a list of suggestions. "Why not try this, I've done this in the past . . . " In this case, Kara saw the relevance of the recommendations to the presenter's focus question and did not intervene. (As it turned out, Greg expressed gratitude for the suggestions.) In another case, such a list, or the way it was offered, might have set a tone of problem solving rather than of reflection on issues that don't lend themselves to quick fixes; in such a case, the facilitator might have intervened.

Other issues related to facilitation emerged in Chicago—and will continue to emerge as the protocol develops. Should the facilitator be involved in giving feedback like other participants? Should the facilitator set a tone of informal collegiality or efficiency and adherence to the schedule? In the "guidelines for facilitators" (see Figure 4.3), organizers tried to bring to the surface some of the competing responsibilities and tensions. After Chicago, we recognized that individual facilitators will employ varied styles with equally effective results.

Advance Organization and Preparation

Facilitators, presenters, and participants in Chicago had a pretty clear idea of the goals and norms for the protocols. Advance communication with presenters, including "phone-coaching" from experienced facilitators 3 weeks before the meeting, ensured that no one came unprepared to present or surprised by the process they would take part in. Presenters met their facilitators over breakfast to briefly discuss how they'd start off the protocol.

Facilitators were prepared for both the logistical aspects of the event—how the room would be arranged, how much time they would have, and so on—and the potentially dangerous, or at least disruptive, exchanges that might call for intervention. In fact, facilitators who had experienced and debriefed a particularly thorny "mock Tuning Protocol," complete with planted "difficult participants," a month before the conference found the real protocols in Chicago "took care of themselves." Several facilitators described their group as not just respectful of the norms of the protocol but virtually "self-regulating."

Some of the participants in Chicago had taken part in Tuning Protocols previously, and, in general, all shared a knowledge of exhibitions and support for this kind of teaching and learning. Greg did not encounter any resistance to the form of assessment he presented. This will not always be the case, and participants raised important questions about using the protocol in less like-minded groups.

One participant pointed out that in this "unnatural" setting, the trusting environment necessary to do the protocol was not a problem, but in many schools it will be. Because schools are often fraught with internal divisions (Muncey & McQuillan, 1993, 1996), careful preparation, informing presenters and participants of the goals and structure for the Tuning Protocol, and openness to questions and comments about the process will be even more important. A facilitator from outside the school may also be beneficial, especially for a first protocol.

COOL FEEDBACK

From the cooler feedback we received from participants, I now consider two areas of concern for the continued use of the Tuning Protocol: (1) how to focus on student work, not just (or primarily) on teacher work; and (2) how to emphasize reflection rather than response. Finally, I conclude the chapter by considering how "tuning" may become part of a larger school and professional culture that provides multiple resources for teachers.

Student Work Versus Teacher Work, or Product Versus Design

The Tuning Protocols in Chicago turned out to be a very effective way to focus on teachers' work. As one teacher noted, "we got into many issues about our work. How can we improve pedagogy, coaching." Several participants commented that their groups really got at "design" issues—and that that was important.

The sessions were less effective in focusing on the actual student work and the learning demonstrated there. Several participants and presenters remarked on the lack of connection between the morning panel on "Standards and Student Work" and the Tuning Protocols that followed, although they may have appreciated both. "Standards were not truly explored, but the effectiveness of opening up issues was high," commented one participant. Another participant concurred: "Standards were brought up; however, most of the feedback offered to presenters did not address standards or student work in particular."

Facilitators tended to agree. The protocol was most successful in exploring *teachers'* work. Participants gained a clearer idea of what was happening in Essential School classrooms, and teacher-presenters got many ideas about how to revise or extend their exhibition designs and their instructional practice. Greg's experience is illustrative; he left the meeting confirmed in the soundness of his assessment and with some concrete ideas for his support for student exhibitions, for example, adding photography to the assignment.

In general, the groups did not address the more difficult questions about the quality of student work and the standards teachers apply to it. One facilitator remarked that no one in her group ever asked: "Are we asking students to do enough?" In another group, the facilitator noted that the cooler, more critical comments about the student work itself led to a much better discussion about design of the exhibition but that the presenter said later that he had felt "stung" by some of these.

Unlike some of the other processes described in this book, the Tuning Protocol has always considered within its scope the context for student work, including teachers' practice, as well as the student work itself. However, as we have learned, it's very easy to lose sight of the student work almost entirely and become caught up in issues of context and design, for example, how Greg could integrate photography into his exhibition plan.

A balance between context and content (student work) was the goal of one modification to the protocol structure we made after Chicago. Reacting to participants' comments, we added a new component to the protocol: *examination of student work.* This adds approximately 15 minutes to the entire process and follows the teacher's presentation of the context for the student work and the clarifying questions (themselves an earlier modification of the protocol). During this period, participants have time, for example, to carefully read several contrasting samples of written work or watch a videotaped presentation twice. (See Figure 4.4.)

Even with modifications such as the one suggested above, teachers may not be ready for a full-scale exploration and critique of their students' work,

FIGURE 4.4. Schedule for Tuning Protocols (1998)

I. Introduction   *5 min.*
  • Facilitator briefly introduces protocol goals, guidelines, and schedule.
  • Participants briefly introduce themselves.

II. Teacher(s) Presentation   *15 min.*
  • Context for student work (assignment, scoring rubric, etc.).
  • Focusing question for feedback.
  • Participants are silent.

III. Clarifying Questions   *5 min. max.*
  • Facilitator judges which questions more properly belong in warm/cool
    feedback.

IV. Examination of Student Work Samples   *15 min.*
  • Samples of student work might be original or photocopied pieces of
    written work and/or video clips.

V. Pause to Reflect on Warm and Cool Feedback   *2–3 min. max.*
  • Participants may take a couple of minutes to reflect on what they would
    like to contribute to the feedback session.

VI. Warm and Cool Feedback   *15 min.*
  • Participants share feedback while teacher-presenter is silent.
  • Facilitator may remind participants of teacher-presenter's focusing
    question.

VII. Reflection   *15 min.*
  • Teacher-presenter speaks to those comments/questions he or she chooses
    to while participants are silent.
  • Facilitator may intervene to focus, clarify, etc.

VIII. Debrief
  • Open discussion of the tuning experience the group has shared.

especially the first time they meet to engage in the Tuning Protocol—I consider some of the possible explanations for this below. The enthusiasm with which teachers and others greeted the opportunity to discuss *teachers'* work signals a real need for more such opportunities to focus on instructional practice. A closer focus on the student work may be seen as a goal for the Tuning Protocol but not its sole purpose.

Reflection Versus Response, or Openness Versus Defensiveness

The facilitator of one group noted the tendency for the teacher-presenters to reply to cooler feedback with more information, "defending" their work rather than "thinking hard about the feedback." A common response to feedback often began like this: "Oh, I forgot to tell you that . . . " Greg did not react defensively to feedback, but he began his presentation somewhat defensively by apologizing for the quality of his students' work and he explained several times that he was constrained by time and the pressure of state tests.

In putting together collections of exhibitions and other authentic assessments from schools, we have learned that the hardest dimension of an assessment to document is the actual student work (Allen & McDonald, 1993). Many of the same teachers who are very willing to frankly share their own work—providing the assignment and scoring criteria for the student performances—are hesitant to bring the student work itself out for public consideration. This may reflect a natural protectiveness toward the students themselves. It may also stem from a recognition that by exposing the actual product of schools' and teachers' work, educators become most vulnerable to the critiques that will stifle or strangle the fragile process of developing new methods of teaching—methods they may not yet feel very confident about. It is one thing to show a neat, organized plan for an exhibition and another to show what an individual student made of it.

There is no ready answer to this problem. The Tuning Protocol, in asking teachers to present samples of student work along with accounts of their own work, may be useful in simply framing the questions for teachers to discuss: Why are we hesitant to show our students' work? What will be gained by doing so?

To defuse some of the defensiveness and create a safer and more productive environment, it has been suggested that we adopt the term *reflection* rather than *response* in describing the time reserved for the presenting teacher to speak to the feedback (see Figure 4.4). When a teacher "responds," it suggests a defensive pose, as if answering charges at a hearing. When a teacher is asked to "reflect," it suggests a more thoughtful activity—of course, the reflection has an outward expression. The facilitator may encourage this rhetorical change to become a real one by using follow-up questions or asking the presenter to delve deeper into a question or comment raised as feedback—something Kara did not do.

The California Protocol emphasizes reflection by providing presenters—always a group—time to discuss the student work among themselves while other participants "listen in"; then the situation is reversed and the "reflectors" discuss while the presenters listen in (Larmer, 1994). Other changes and adaptations will certainly emerge to support more reflective and more purposeful Tuning Protocols.

GOOD PROTOCOL, NOT NEARLY ENOUGH

As we saw in Chicago, participants, presenters, and facilitators often emerge from a Tuning Protocol enthusiastic about the experience. At the same time, they may find it difficult to define the purpose of the protocol in which they've just taken part.

This lack of clarity is not surprising. The protocol structure helps create a forum for exploring questions that lead in different directions, for example, from discussing strengths and weaknesses demonstrated in a student's work to debating whether the criteria for scoring work help or constrain students' performance. The focusing question asked by the presenter may be the last one to receive attention, sometimes to the chagrin of the facilitator.

Even if the focusing question is addressed, as Greg's was, it doesn't always answer larger questions. Is the Tuning Protocol really intended to focus on Greg, his exhibition, and his students, presumably so that his practice will improve? Or is it a chance for discussion of topics of interest to the whole group, using Greg's presentation as a starting point? Or is it intended to provide a better picture of what's going on in progressive schools (or at least, in progressive teachers' classrooms) for educators and other "critical friends" from outside the school?

In practice, the Tuning Protocol often serves multiple purposes at once—dependent on the context and participants. In the Chicago conference, for example, the organizers planned an exploration of "Standards and Student Work." We imagined that teachers would bring neat lists of criteria and not-so-neat samples of student work and that the protocol would provide a structure to analyze, discuss, and reflect on the relationship of the two. Instead, participants took the opportunity to learn about other teachers' authentic assessments and to discuss how teachers can best design exhibitions and prepare their students for them.

Given the overall good reviews of the day, should the organizers—and participants—be concerned that the original purposes weren't met? I think so, although not because the stated purpose was necessarily the right one for the meeting; rather because our concern may help us to learn from what did happen—and consider what may happen in future protocols.

As we reflect on the Tuning Protocol in Chicago, we might conclude that the form is better for some purposes than others, for example, looking at exhibition design rather than actual student performance. Or we might tinker with the structure to make it more effective at doing one thing well: "Next time we'll try . . . " Both responses are natural and appropriate. At the same time, they might overload and undersell the Tuning Protocol.

Rather than focusing only on how the Tuning Protocol can get better, we should also consider how the Tuning Protocol, through its weaknesses and strengths, reveals teachers' important questions, concerns, and needs. What other activities, resources, and opportunities can complement the Tuning Protocol in addressing these needs?

Greg commented that he found very useful the suggestions made by other teachers, especially math teachers, on how to better emphasize math skills in his student exhibitions. Will he now have the discussions with math teachers from different levels he asked for in his response time? What about other resources that might be hinted at during a protocol, but by no means supplied: examining samples of other teachers' exhibitions, including samples of their students' work; a stint as panelist at another school's exhibitions; or summer workshops to collaboratively develop exhibitions?

Teachers often value the "collegiality and camaraderie" they feel in the Tuning Protocol (Chicago Learning Collaborative, 1996). This is, in itself, a valuable goal for Tuning Protocols, but an occasional Tuning Protocol shouldn't provide the only chance—or form—for collegiality. The more opportunities teachers have to work together, the more purposeful those meetings may become, including—but not limited to—meetings that use the protocol structure. When the protocol is used within faculty groups or networks of teachers that meet regularly, the structure is often adapted to better address specific questions or issues, as it has been, for example, by the California Center for School Restructuring (Chapter 5).

Structuring or facilitating the protocol too narrowly, however, may destroy some of its benefits. Facilitators and participants will rightly reject a protocol that programs them to offer only certain kinds of feedback or ask certain kinds of questions. The freedom to offer the feedback and ask the questions that come to mind is an essential aspect of the protocol's success.

The Tuning Protocol is perhaps best thought of a medium for opening up and identifying questions for reflection and further inquiry and discussion. These questions are among the most important ones to ask about teaching and learning, because they come from contact with its essence: the real work of teachers and students.

NOTES

1. An earlier, significantly different version of this chapter appeared in the *Studies on Exhibitions* series of the Coalition of Essential Schools, Brown University.

2. The Exhibitions Project was generously supported by IBM. For more information about the project, see McDonald (1996).

REFERENCES

Allen, D., & McDonald, J. (1993). *Keeping student performance central: The New York assessment collection* (Studies on Exhibitions, No. 14). Providence, RI: Coalition of Essential Schools, Brown University.

Chicago Learning Collaborative. (1996). *Report on the Chicago Learning Collaborative, 1995–1996.* Chicago: Author.

Collins, A., Hawkins, J., & Frederiksen, J. R. (1991). *Three different views of students: The role of technology in assessing student performance.* New York: Bank Street College.

Erickson, F., & Wilson, J. (1982). *Sights and sounds of life in schools: A resource guide to film and videotape for research and education.* East Lansing: Institute for Research on Teaching at Michigan State University.

Larmer, J. (1994, December 20). The Tuning Protocol. *The Educator's Guild*, p. 2.

McDonald, J. (1996). *Redesigning school: Lessons for the 21st century.* San Francisco: Jossey-Bass.

McDonald, J., Smith, S., Turner, D., Finney, M., & Barton, E. (1993). *Graduation by exhibition: Assessing genuine achievement.* Alexandria, VA: Association for Supervision and Curriculum Development.

Muncey, D., & McQuillan, P. (1993). Preliminary findings from a five-year study of the Coalition of Essential Schools. *Phi Delta Kappan, 74*(6), 486–489.

Muncey, D., & McQuillan, P. (1996). *Reform & resistance in schools and classrooms.* New Haven, CT: Yale University Press.

Szabo, M. (1996). Rethinking restructuring: Building habits of effective inquiry. In M. McLaughlin & I. Oberman (Eds.), *Teacher learning: New policies, new practices* (pp. 73–91). New York: Teachers College Press.

5

Three Takes on Accountability

The California Protocol

JOEL KAMMER

Faculty in reforming schools spend more time planning change strat-
egies than going through the crucial process of assessing existing
practices to uncover basic beliefs, attitudes and assumptions that
drive their work in schools. Their reticence to engage in serious
analysis seems to suggest that planning for tomorrow is much more
attractive than examining what happened today, yesterday, or histori-
cally. In many cases, because that analysis does not take place, the
faculty merely tinker with change instead of building significantly dif-
ferent possibilities for students.

—Wasley, King, & Louth, 1993, p. 1

In 1994, on the last day of the California Center for School Restructuring's first
Spring Symposium of Restructuring Schools, in a small room at the Disneyland
Hotel in Anaheim, Piner High School (PHS) was paired for a reciprocal Protocol
with Central Valley High School (CVHS).[1] On paper the schools seemed an
ideal match: Both were about the same size and had vaguely similar demographics; both had been leaders for change in their regions and had been part of the
Research and Development Project that had developed the original format for
the Protocol process. But nearly a year after the R&D phase had been completed, the ground rules and focus of the Protocol had shifted somewhat, and
the two schools had used it differently.

The room was small and only 10 people were present, including the moderator, the two school teams, and two observers. While I am a teacher at Piner,

on this occasion I was an observer, not a member of the team. Central Valley presented first. Their analysis of student work began with a slickly produced student video overview of a program that included several innovative aspects: integrated subjects, block classes, and extensive use of technology. At the end of the 15-minute videotape, the three-person team took turns presenting carefully scripted explanations of the program, accompanied by computer-generated overhead transparencies; in fact, the CVHS team used all its presentation time expanding on various elements of that same program.

During the "clarifying questions" that followed, the team acknowledged, rather reluctantly, that the program they had described enrolled only a small percentage of the school's students and made up only a portion of their school day. It had also received the bulk of the resources the school had received from SB 1274 (California state restructuring legislation) for that year, and that had engendered serious resentment from the rest of the school.

As the facilitator moved the session into the feedback phase, the Piner team offered questions, qualms, ideas, and commentary on what they had heard. The CVHS team sat quietly, only occasionally making brief notes. Finally, in the time allotted for their own reflection on the feedback and planning for future changes, the CVHS team chose to respond to several specific points raised by the reflectors by assuring them they had misunderstood important aspects of the presentation. They seemed in no mood to have their work questioned or criticized.

Piner's team began its presentation by shuffling papers and discussing who should start. Eventually, one of the four teachers began outlining a structural overview of the school; a minute or two into his explanation, he was interrupted by another team member who disagreed with his analysis, a pattern that recurred throughout the presentation. At times, animosity surfaced between the two presenters, defused through the intervention of an administrator on the team; the disagreements seemed well-worn, as though the two had frequently visited the same issues without resolving much. The presentation proceeded, accompanied by hand-lettered posterboard signs and sheaves of paper and folders, presumably containing student work, although these functioned mainly as props.

When the moderator called time, the teacher presenting complained that she wasn't finished and chastised her teammates for taking too long. As feedback, the Central Valley team, which hadn't always seemed particularly attentive during the presentation, mostly preached, often citing the way things were done at CVHS as a possible solution to problems or issues Piner had raised. The most tangible suggestion they offered involved simplifying Piner's vision and mission statement of expected outcomes for students. To be effective and attainable, one reflector suggested, the text had to fit on a business card or small poster. After the session was over, he illustrated his suggestion by distributing

CVHS business cards and posters. The Piner team accepted the offerings with little enthusiasm.

CCSR AND THE PROTOCOL

About a month after this event, members of the California Center for School Restructuring (CCSR) leadership team met to review the reflection sheets and their own observations of the Protocols. It's safe to say that the Protocol experiences of most of the 140 schools that took part in the Symposium were more satisfying than the one I've just described. The team considered both "warm" and "cool" feedback—building on strengths and learning from weaknesses—as it redesigned the Symposium for the next year and, especially, how the Protocol would be used.

By the time of the Symposium I've just described, the schools had been working for about half a year on the restructuring plans to transform teaching and learning for which they had been selected and funded. The California Center for School Restructuring had come into existence in 1992 as a result of California Senate Bill 1274, innovative school reform legislation whose overarching purpose was "to dramatically increase the ability of schools and districts to engage all students in rigorous, powerful learning" (CCSR, 1993c, p. 1).

The CCSR staff, led by Maggie Szabo, Joel Shawn, and Steve Jubb, defined their task this way: helping to develop "effective learning communities producing powerful learning outcomes for every student" and inventing and developing "an ongoing system of accountability, learning and support" (CCSR, 1994, p. 1). The CCSR staff shared a conviction that a new conception of school accountability was inextricably linked to developing communities—within and across schools—in which all members were engaged in teaching and learning from one another.

Pursuing these goals, the staff recognized, would mean meeting difficult challenges. One was supporting a large number of schools, each working on its own restructuring plan. Another was to confront the tendency—evident in the history of school reforms—for comprehensive initiatives to shrink to mere program implementation within schools (CCSR, 1993a, p. 1). Perhaps the most difficult challenge would be to keep the focus on children, not on adults, by developing systems for accountability strongly grounded in actual student work rather than numeric distillations of simulated performances—scores and grades.

To begin to take on these challenges, CCSR sponsored a 5-month Research and Development Project involving representatives of 24 restructuring schools from around the state, as well as the newly chosen "regional leads" and some "regional fellows" from the 10 regions of California. The leads were mostly county-level administrators who coordinated SB 1274 efforts throughout each region, while the fellows, including myself, were mostly teachers and site administrators assigned to work directly with the funded schools, coaching and acting as critical friends. The R&D Project would design the tools that would eventually be used to support all participating schools. This early learning community would share its experiences and lessons with the statewide community.

The R&D Project produced a design for an "Accountability/Learning System" of three interconnected "central vehicles": the School Change Portfolio; the Spring Restructuring Symposium; and the Protocol. All have changed over time, and new ones have emerged. Work on the Portfolio continues, with a number of models being developed in different schools. The Spring Symposium has grown and changed in focus somewhat; as of this writing, three annual Symposia have been held. Of the three original elements of the system, however, the Protocol is the one that has been used most extensively, has focused most closely on classroom teaching and learning, and has proven to be most adaptable to different contexts and situations.

In developing the Protocol, the R&D team was strongly influenced by the "Tuning Protocol" developed by Joe McDonald and his colleagues (McDonald, Smith, Turner, & Barton, 1993) at the Coalition of Essential Schools (see Chapter 4). One of McDonald's questions, based on the Tuning Protocol's initial use, spurred the R&D Project's work: "What if such tuning conferences were held semi-annually among schools within a single geographical region, perhaps crossing district lines to ensure differences in perspective?" (McDonald et al., 1993, p. 54).

CCSR developed its Protocol to accomplish two main goals. It would be "an interactive process designed to provide a safe, constructive setting for critical dialogue about the work and progress of restructuring schools." At the same time, the Protocol would become "an inquiry tool to use regularly *within* the school community to keep change efforts focused on the real, specific learning needs of all students" (CCSR, 1993b, p. 1).

Consistent with those goals, the CCSR Protocol has been used in two main contexts, at the yearly Symposium and within schools. While certain features are common to both, the differences are marked. McDonald (1996)—coming to see the legacy of the Tuning Protocol in California—compared the Protocol at the Symposium to "a high mass sung in a cathedral . . . an elegant manifestation of a ritual designed to be pervasive and generally much simpler. Like the high mass also, it is meant to inspire lower efforts—that is, to be picked up and modified for local and even internal use" (pp. 221–222).

For the Protocol to be effective, it must serve as an impetus for change as well as a method for assessing the effects of change. The very public, culminating Symposium versions of the Protocol serve as a combination of celebration, demonstration, and accounting. The ongoing, presumably frequent, even habitual versions practiced within individual schools and within the regions are the "lower efforts" McDonald wrote about.

The Symposium format has changed each year based on reflection on and analysis of the feedback from the previous year. The Protocol, however, has remained a central part of the Symposium. In the remainder of this chapter, I describe two additional instances of the Protocol that involved Piner High School—one "high mass" version from the 1996 Symposium and one "lower effort." Before I do, I return to the 1993 Symposium and the Piner–Central Valley Protocol with which the chapter began.

PERFORMANCE OR PUBLIC INQUIRY?

Coming as they did at the end of the first half-year of SB 1274 funding and implementation, no one knew quite what to expect from the 1993 Symposium Protocols. This was, after all, the first public "high mass" after a limited number of "lower efforts" for many schools.

One difference between the two versions emerged early on. While the emphasis of schools' restructuring efforts was to be on examining student work, it was impractical for schools to try to replicate that work at the Symposium. Instead, schools were asked to step up to a more "meta" level, presenting their work in examining student work. That is a slipperier and less tangible prospect as well as a more difficult presentation to structure and plan.

While some schools felt their Protocol was remarkably successful, that they had indeed established critical friendships with partner schools that would continue and would improve their future work, not all were so fortunate, and experiences such as the Piner–CVHS session described earlier led to several changes in subsequent years.

A fundamental misunderstanding, perhaps disagreement, marked the first year's Protocols. Was the purpose of this public display to document and, for public relations reasons, put the best face on each school's restructuring efforts? Or was it to use critical but knowledgeable and supportive colleagues to dig deeper into a school's work, exposing discrepancies, questions, weaknesses, and other areas for improvement? In other words, were Tuning Protocols intended to be performance or public inquiry?

CCSR was clear on that point. "Keep in mind that this is developmental—a work in progress—and not a finished work," they cautioned schools in 1993. "Remember that the purpose is to provide an honest and authentic account of the work you are doing now, especially focusing on those areas where you may be puzzled, stumped or facing obstacles. Only in this way will you be able to capture useful feedback, information, or suggestions, which may help you break through some of the barriers you are facing" (CCSR, 1993b, p. 12). But not all schools had the confidence to expose their flaws to the world.

Central Valley came into the Symposium self-confident and ready for its hard work to be acknowledged and admired. There was no indication at the Symposium of the type of pressure the school may have been facing at home from parents or school board members—even other teachers—critical of their change efforts; perhaps they knew all too well the costs of airing their self-doubts in public. For them, the Protocol was a performance, and the only appropriate response may have seemed to them to be applause, appreciation. When the Piner team pointed out flaws and asked probing questions about future approaches to problems, the CVHS staff members reacted by closing ranks, becoming defensive, and formulating excuses and explanations rather than listening carefully to the cool feedback as a prompt to rethinking their assumptions about their work.

Piner's team, too, got much less out of the process than they might have. In part this was because the Central Valley team was not inclined to listen and reflect thoughtfully, but rather tossed out canned solutions—some of which may have resulted from their defensive reaction to the feedback they had received from Piner earlier.

But the Piner team was poorly prepared in a different way. Working through disagreements and clarifying issues is healthy and useful, a sign of a group engaged in collaborative inquiry, but all that should have been done long before the Protocol. A half-hour of presentation time is little enough to touch on more than a few aspects of the complexities of school change. They would have gained much more had they arrived with a few clearly defined areas of concern and a few focusing questions to elicit the sort of feedback they needed from reflectors with some distance and detachment from their ongoing problems.

Using Tuning Protocols effectively requires everyone to understand his or her role; presenters as well as reflectors must come into the room ready to be honest and straightforward, and to listen carefully and be reflective rather than reactive and judgmental. The public nature of this discourse means that there is some risk. Exposing a school's weaknesses and doubts to audiences that might contain parents and district or state officials—perhaps even those who might have a stake in making the presenting team look bad—could produce setbacks in a school's progress that will affect its efforts for years. And yet, unless and until schools are willing to take that risk and lay their work out for public scrutiny, only limited growth is possible. Schools need critical friends; they need outside perspectives to balance and augment their own necessarily limited views of their work.

The trick is in careful preparation and clear understanding by all parties of the purpose of Tuning Protocols: making schools better by making the work of those within those schools better. Within that context, it is possible for the session to be a powerful learning experience for all participants: presenters, reflectors, moderators, and observers. By last spring's Symposium, the process had evolved into something quite different, and Piner's experience was far more useful and worthwhile.

Symposium Protocol: Three Years Later

The San Diego hotel conference room was filled to capacity; at least 40 people, including the Piner school analysis team, were present. Chairs from adjoining rooms had been dragged in, and the doors were closed and an appropriate warning sign posted in the hall: "Do Not Disturb, Protocol in Process." The nine members of Piner's team, including the new principal, a counselor, and a student, sat in a semicircle in the right front corner; the facilitator, a school principal from Mendocino County who had been asked by Piner to preside, was front center.

In this year's iteration of the Protocol, all of the audience were to be reflectors. Among those arranged around tables of six or seven were leaders of CCSR; representatives from school reform organizations active in California; and teachers, administrators, and school board members from different districts.

The Piner team members were mostly young; only two or three of the staff members had been at Piner longer than 3 years and a student was included. After each member identified him- or herself, one of the more experienced teachers, who had introduced herself as an "elder of the tribe," sketched in some background and context; when her introduction threatened to run beyond the budgeted 5 minutes, the facilitator intervened (see Figure 5.1). Time was allowed for the reflectors to review Piner's entry in the CCSR "School Previews," including demographic and statistical information as well as a description of what the school considered its central issues.

After a few minutes of reading time, the presentation began. Team members briefly described some aspects of the school's work and posed questions for consideration. The team was most interested in looking closely at relationships and the culture within the school, a large school subdivided into five "learning communities" (in structure, similar to "houses"). After answering some clarification questions, they moved from presentation to conversation.

The conversation that ensued was clearly practiced, not spontaneous, but it was no less heartfelt for that, especially as some underlying disagreements among team members surfaced. The student raised the issue of gender diversity and the lack of clearly articulated schoolwide standards. A Latino teacher spoke feelingly of other kinds of diversity and raised concerns about tracking and stereotyping in the school's learning communities. A counselor stated flatly,

FIGURE 5.1. Format for 1996 CCSR Symposium Protocols

5 minutes: Moderator welcomes participants and reviews the purpose, roles, and guidelines for the Protocol.

20 minutes: Reflectors review the school's preview and self-assessment on the Rubric for Progress on the Four Goals of SB 1274 Restructuring. The "Four Goals" are: 1) Deepening Inquiry by Examining Student Work for What Matters Most; 2) Shaping Strategies and Actions to Address Issues of Diversity and That Meet the Needs of Every Student; 3) Shaping Strategies and Actions to Impact the Whole School; and 4) Supporting Districts to Rethink and Restructure to Support School Progress on the First Three Goals.

5 minutes: Analysis Team provides an introduction, perhaps referring to one or two highlights of the written materials provided to reflectors.

5 minutes: Reflectors ask brief questions for clarification. The Analysis Team responds succinctly with clarifying information about the preview and introduction.

25 minutes: Analysis Team gives its analysis of what it learned from examining student work—what it means and what the school should do about it.

20 minutes: Reflectors form groups of four to six to provide feedback. Each reflector group chooses one of its members to chart questions and statements. The reflector groups summarize their comments as concise, essential questions and supportive statements. Each group will post chart pages as they are completed so Analysis Team members can see them. The Analysis Team observes and listens in on the reflectors' discussion. They may also wish to "caucus" informally as the comments emerge and discuss which points seem most interesting to pursue in the reflection time to follow.

15 minutes: The Analysis Team engages in reflection, planning, and discussion with one another (rather than in direct response to the Reflectors). This is a time for everyone else in the room to hear the Analysis Team's discussion in which they reveal how they reflect, think, plan, and adjust.

20 minutes: The Analysis Team and the reflectors engage in an open conversation about the school's work.

Source: Steve Jubb and Joel Shawn. (1996, February/March). Protocol for Restructuring. *Thrust for Educational Leadership*, p. 20. Used by permission.

"There is a belief that some communities are 'flushing out' undesirable students." Her voice broke as she added, "This is kind of emotional for me." A science teacher posed a question of student and parent choice versus equitable distribution of students. The conversation was becoming more heated when the facilitator gave a time warning. The team finished with each member posing a single question for reflection.

Reflectors then gathered around tables to discuss and reflect on what they had heard. One person at each table was designated to write the group's conclusions on chartpaper. The Piner team members each joined a table, not to participate but to listen and observe. I sat with a group from a Los Angeles school, who were at first very thoughtful, then increasingly animated as their discussion progressed.

Insights and perspectives I had never before considered emerged. About the choice and tracking issue, which had been referred to as a choice between apples and oranges, a teacher asked whether the choices were viable ones for students or were between "a shiny red apple and an old withered orange." Another added, "If I'm a 15-year-old girl, I want to be in Miss Lee's government class with all my 'homies.' That's how I'd make a choice." Several observers remarked on how much data the school had been able to collect and how little any of the information therein seemed to figure into its decision making; a CCSR staffer wondered aloud whether the school needed help with that.

Commenting on the changing student demographics, someone suggested that the school seek out some training in strategies to deal with increasing diversity. Someone else posed a provocative question: "How many schools is Piner? Is it one or five? Why are they trying to have it both ways?" In a flurry of conversation, one teacher offered comfort: "I don't see it as something that can't be worked out." Another responded, "It's easy to say that. But they're out there. They're drowning. They're asking for help." As the facilitator called time, someone added the last word: "They're going to have to figure this out themselves."

After the analysis team's public reflection and brainstorming, the last segment of the Protocol called for a facilitated conversation between the reflectors and Piner's analysis team. Lasting about 15 minutes, the discussion was animated and free-flowing. It included some advice-giving from the reflectors and some defensive positioning from the team, but it also ventured into some new territory. At one point a team member admitted that at least some of the school's changes as well as structural elements that hadn't changed were prompted more by teacher preferences and agendas than by what would be good for students.

The session ended with thanks from the facilitator to the analysis team for their honesty and to the reflectors for their hard work and engagement, and, then, sustained applause from everyone.

Reflections on Two Protocols

Comparing the two Symposium Protocols, a few design principles seem apparent. More reflectors usually mean better feedback. The most effective reflectors are those who are experienced and knowledgeable, with some insight to offer and sufficient concern to offer it. They should have a stake in the outcome and care about the presenters and their school but be distant enough to stay objective; the point, after all, is to generate both warm and cool feedback.

Preparation by the presenters is vital, but not the sort of preparation that leads to a slick or glib presentation. Instead, grappling with issues to decide what's most important and how to convey essential information clearly enough to reflectors is what pays off. Honesty is a Protocol virtue. In the long run, there's little to be gained by glossing over painful areas and questions. Lastly, a willingness of presenters to listen to and take seriously reflectors' feedback is essential. Thoreau (1854/1971) concludes *Walden* by reminding us, "Only that day dawns to which we are awake" (p. 333). I would paraphrase that as, "Only that feedback which we are willing to hear can be effective."

The Piner team left the 1996 Symposium having learned quite a lot. The school defined a question to drive inquiry during the next school year: How does staff culture affect student learning? A number of other initiatives can be traced to the Symposium Protocol, including budgeting for a data gatherer from the staff to collect and organize information on the school's change process. The most significant "lower effort" to result from the Symposium, however, has been the Thursday Protocols.

A THURSDAY PROTOCOL

It's a Thursday afternoon in April. A small group of Piner teachers from three of the school's five learning communities gather in the career center adjacent to the school's library. A few months ago, this year's Symposium-bound school analysis team, made up of representatives from each of the five communities, began organizing and sponsoring regular "Thursday Protocols," beginning during common planning time following early dismissal of students and continuing on into the late afternoon. Everyone on the staff is invited to present or reflect on work, but, although different people show up each week, there are only half a dozen regulars. The afternoon is warm and the career center is stuffy; several students are scattered around the room working on computers or chatting in English or Spanish. There are snacks and sodas, however, along with a colorful array of folders and binders on the table around which the teachers have gathered.

After small talk and snacks, the teachers halfheartedly discuss the operating

Protocol. All those present are quite experienced with sharing and critiquing student work in such exercises; a high degree of familiarity, trust, and comfort with one another and the process is apparent in their conversation. The questions they consider have to do with the amount of time to spend on individual portions of the process, who has brought work to examine, who will facilitate, and, given the small number of participants, whether the facilitator will also serve as a reflector. Before any real decisions are made, the presentation begins, and no one seems especially concerned about the informality of the arrangements.

The work being examined today comes from Fulton Valley Prep, one of the small learning communities. It is being presented by two of the three members of a "lower-division" (freshman and sophomore) collaborative planning and teaching team. They have brought several examples of "autobiographical anthologies" written and compiled by students as part of a "Growing Up" unit and an assortment of the associated teacher work—calls for exhibitions, assignment sheets, grading rubrics, and so on. The assignment required students to put together "writer's journals"; write and revise five or six stories about critical incidents in their lives; put them together in anthology form; and send off at least one story for feedback via the Internet to distant "critical friends."

The presentation of the work begins with the two presenters discussing with each other which framing questions they want reflectors to focus on. Although this presumably should have been decided earlier, and the discussion takes away from the time available for the rest of the process, the reflectors seem patient, even interested in the conversation. In the daily rush of school, the desirable level of advance preparation was probably impossible. The atmosphere is informal and collegial; they are here to share ideas and learn from one another as much as to "tune" a given piece of work.

The framing questions are asked and written on a sheet of paper in the middle of the table. One has to do with the Internet sharing of work: Was that ultimately something that caused students to take their writing and revising more seriously and thereby really improve their writing skills, or was it merely an add-on, an attractive distraction from the real work of writing? The second is a standards question: How good was the writing represented in the samples? How could it, and the teacher work that prompted it, be improved?

As the two presenters finish defining the framing questions and, in the process, sketching in the relevant context, an English teacher from another of the school's communities makes the first move toward facilitation, suggesting they move to clarifying questions. As the participants look over the assignment sheets, several questions emerge: Was there a requirement that students do something with the on-line responses? Were there categories or required elements to the anthologies? Where did the interviews fit in? Each is answered by one or the other presenter, often building on each other's response. The questions are accompanied by commentary and expressions of appreciation: "Gosh is this great!" "So there are people just hanging around out there on the Net waiting to do this?" The presenters are effusive in their praise of the e-mail responders to the students' work. I am conscious that the time for clarifying questions seems more like a conversation, which doesn't really follow the norms for a Protocol, but no one seems to mind.

Finally, in lieu of any active formal facilitation, a presenter responds to the abstract nature of the conversation by suggesting they spend some time just looking at the samples of work. They do, and this phase lasts for nearly 20 minutes. Across the table, presenters and reflectors share striking or interesting passages. One anthology that garners a lot of attention is collected in a cover embellished with a collage of photographs that cover the front and back. Amidst the snapshots of healthy and smiling teenage girls with big hair dressed in cropped-top T-shirts and shirtless boys beside cars or next to stereos is a small picture of a gaunt man in his mid-30s sitting hunched over staring into the camera with a hollow but ethereal look in his deep-set eyes. "My Toughest Experience" and an e-mail exchange about it (see Figure 5.2) are included in the collection.

This anthology is passed among the readers along with four or five others; whispered side conversations between the presenters as well as the reflectors accompany the exchange of materials. Finally, someone calls for a return to the Protocol process: It's time for the reflectors to offer feedback. The presenters take out notepads and pens, and listen quietly as the reflectors talk among themselves.

The discussion begins with analysis of the anthology that includes "My Toughest Experience." Although the reflectors include teachers from a variety of disciplines, each has opinions on the quality of writing. They consider the question of where and how the story should begin; they talk about the piece as a story but also as a real account of an extremely painful event in a student's life. They disagree about whether the feedback from the electronic "critical friend" is enough by itself and about how prescriptive the teacher should be about ongoing revision of the story. Someone reminds the others that the piece was written by a freshman. Specific discussion of the piece leads to a broader consideration of the anthology and the importance of the pictures and layout, and, in turn, to the assignment itself.

"I'm just blown away. It's fascinating. I'm not all that interested in the Internet stuff, but getting work out that way makes it seem like a really authentic writing experience."

"I like the idea of sharing the work. The problems with consistency and delays come with the (electronic) territory."

"In science we'd love to do something like this, but instead coordinate it with another class, pair kids up with partners somewhere else. The sharing could become really important to the student."

FIGURE 5.2. Excerpts from Jody's Anthology

A: Request for Internet feedback

Date: Fri, 15 Mar 03:11:40 -0800

Hi, my name is Jody, and I am 15 years old. I wrote this piece on AIDS. It is talking about my toughest experience in life. I would really appreciate it if you would read it and write back.

Thanks,
Jody

B: Excerpt from story

My Toughest Experience

The toughest experience that I have gone through would definitely have to be when I found out that my uncle was infected with AIDS. I never even suspected anything until one day I heard my mom say to him that he was getting awfully skinny. She would ask him if there was anything the matter, but he would always say, "I'm fine." I never thought that anything was the matter because I thought it wouldn't happen to my family. At that time, we were living with him and his friend in Windsor. I'll never forget the day that I found out the truth.

It all started one day when I was sitting on the floor in the bedroom. We were staying in doing my homework, when all of the sudden I heard a knock on the door. As soon as I heard it, a really weird feeling came over me. I yelled for who was knocking to come in. When I looked up and saw that it was him, an even stranger feeling came over me. I could just tell by the look in his eyes that something was seriously wrong. My uncle asked me if I could please leave the room, because he wanted to talk to my mom alone, I gathered my things, and went to the part of the bathroom where there was just a mirror and two sinks, and through the next door was the shower and the toilet. As I sat there it began to get cold and dark. I had a feeling that I can't explain. It was like a cold and damp feeling. All I could hear was a dead silence, the sound of murmuring voices, which sounded so distant, and the sound of the water coming from the shower. I tried to make out the words, but I couldn't . Then as if someone was shouting at me I heard the words so clearly.

My uncle said, "I lied to you." Then I heard my mom say, "About what?"

Out of nowhere, my uncle said, "I'm not OK like I said I was; I have full-blown AIDS".

I couldn't believe what I just heard. At first I thought that I misunderstood him, but deep down, I knew that I didn't; I just didn't want to believe it. I heard my mom begin to cry. As I sat there listening to my uncle comforting her, I was listening to his voice, not his words, just his voice. I began to wonder how much longer I would get to do that. I was confused and scared, I started shaking, and began to cry hysterically. I felt like my whole world came to an end. Then out of nowhere, I heard my name being called . . .

C: Internet response from "critical friend"

Date: 15 Mar 05:47:27 EST

This message is for Jody—Core 2

Jody, I've been thinking about your splendid writing piece. This, from me, is being written at about 5:30 in the morning on Friday, March 15th, in the eastern time zone: you must still be asleep (it's 2:30 in the morning with you, as far I can figure) so maybe you'll find this when you get to school.

Your writing really communicates to me even though I don't know you. You make me feel as if I *did* know you, your mother, your uncle, your pain, your sadness. I feel part of it all.

The part about your uncle's illness bringing your family closer intrigues me, and I wish you'd said more about it. It reminds me of a conversation I had a couple of years ago, when I heard from a woman colleague about how she had taken someone with AIDS into her home for his last months. His own family had rejected him. She said that the love that developed then was the strongest, most tangible, she had ever known.

About your writing style, my only suggestion is that you use fewer words. (Your first sentence might be, for instance: My toughest experience was when I found out my uncle had AIDS.) Some people say "less is more" (but I don't think those people remember what it's like to be in school and have to write to a specific word length!).

Anyway, congratulations on your piece. It is strong, it is real, it rings true, it is universal. I ache for all of you. Let me know how it goes for you.

Alice

"The great thing about the prompt that went out to responders is that it was cross-generational. I noticed that lots of them cited their own experiences. Kids could see what was universal about their stories and their experiences. But I still think you should have 'forced' them to do something with the responses. Some great ones weren't used for anything. I'd make it a required part of the assignment."

"Was there any room to vary the genre? I like the essential question: How can words tell the truth about our lives? But is prose narrative the only way to do that? You had them read poetry about growing up. What about writing it, or writing songs? Could they have explored some other areas?"

"How about more of a social studies tie-in? What if kids identified the world events that they felt most shaped their thinking, and then talked to people from another generation. . . . "

This conversation continues for about 10 minutes, with the reflectors taking turns talking to each other and the presenters listening silently but intently, scribbling notes as they try to keep up with the flow of ideas. After the conversation slows a bit, the facilitator asks if there are any more comments, then turns it back over to the presenters for their reflections on and responses to what they've heard. They talk to each other rather than to the reflectors, taking turns speaking and responding to each other's as well as the reflectors' comments. One begins:

> Geez, I need these reminders. We torture ourselves writing the essential
> questions, agonizing over every word. Then we just put them out there
> and hang them on the wall and lose sight of them in the daily classes and
> assignments. . . . Brigette really tied things together for me, brought me
> back to the essential question. . . . Steve reminded me that the responders
> addressed the truth-telling we were after and we just let that sit. . . . I
> loved Steve's comment about songwriting! Kids really think of songs as
> telling the truth. And what about the interviews?

As she pauses, her partner picks up the thread:

> My sense of this is all the lost opportunities. . . . But that's good!. . . . I re-
> ally like the idea of their having to do something with the e-mail feed-
> back. And the social studies tie-in. . . . As we planned this, the whole no-
> tion of the logistics of kids just getting something out on-line seemed so
> overwhelming, but now. . . . Should there have been more emphasis on
> getting kids to send out their best work? . . . I noticed how many respond-
> ers wrote back, "Send me the next version," and how many kids never
> did. . . . Next time. . . .

As their brainstorming tapers out, the decision to end the session is collectively made. People begin packing up papers and cleaning up. Then, as has happened each time the group has gathered, the discussion breaks out again. The facilitator hands out an assignment she had brought but hadn't had time to share, which prompts another round of "Next time . . . " conversation. There is talk about the nature of kids' lives growing up in the 1990s, as revealed through the autobiographical writings: "Kathy's class is 'The Wonder Years'; the rest of us have 'ER.'"

SO?

In a non-linear world, the slightest twitch can amplify anywhere in the system; and . . . small-scale efforts can have large-scale effects.
—Wheatley, 1995, p. 5

The "elegant manifestation" of the California Protocol at the yearly symposium is not in and of itself an adequate means of assessment or accountability for a program, school, or system. And in the absence of other formal and informal examination of student work, the "lower efforts" of school-level Tuning Protocols are hardly sufficient to provide any real insight into the overall quality of work students are doing. Really, in the overheated, deadline-driven daily atmosphere of most schools, it's probably impossible to keep both the macro and micro views of school change in focus at the same time.

Why bother, then? What about either of these similar but distinct processes is worth the time, energy, and effort they require? I would suggest that the answer is the same as the answer to many questions about learning itself: The process is at least as important as any result, and the preparation for undergoing the process is even more important. In the chicken-and-egg world of school restructuring and "reculturing," the habits of work and behavior that are formed and reinforced by engaging in the Protocol processes are exactly what must exist for schools to change to better serve students' needs.

Six or seven years ago, as the Piner staff envisioned the school we wanted to have in the far-off future world of 1997, we imagined lots of aspects of structure, curriculum, governance, and assessment. We gave little of our time and attention to thinking about culture and relationships, especially to the relationships between and among the adults in the school. Of course, in the school-change literature that has emerged since then, such relationships have taken on paramount importance. Wheatley (1992) goes so far as to say that "relationships are not just interesting; to many physicists, they are all there is to reality" (p. 32). Other observers, including Milbrey McLaughlin and Joan Talbert (1993) and Fred Newmann (1994), suggest a direct connection between the quality of professional community in a school and the level of achievement of that school's students.

The sharing of student work in local Tuning Protocols and the collaborative inquiry and preparation that goes into getting ready for a Symposium Protocol involve building and nurturing exactly those sorts of professional relationships. It hardly matters whether the process of Protocols has led to our developing a more collaborative culture at Piner, or whether the building of a more collaborative and inquiry-based culture has led to our being better able to use Protocols more regularly and effectively.

In the preface to *Redesigning Schools*, McDonald (1996) confides, "Indeed, I do not believe that even the best designs of today's school reformers will last beyond the first few years of the twenty-first century" (p. xii). Given the pace and complexity of change these days, it's easy to imagine that any structures we can invent today will be obsolete not long after they are implemented. In anticipating this world of the next millennium, however, it is also easy to imagine that asking important questions and taking seriously their answers, adapting and adjusting for continuous improvement, and making use of varied perspectives will always be useful. So Protocols that allow us to regularly examine samples of student and teacher work for evidence that changes are having the desired effects, as well as more formal and public meta-protocols for sharing efforts made, hoped-for results, and future plans with some set of exterior critical friends, seem a wise use of time and resources.

Though the SB 1274 funding has expired and the 1997 Symposium may have been the last such statewide event to be held, I believe the California Protocol will continue to be of use and will continue to change to suit changing conditions. Five years ago, it was a daunting prospect; it was hard for me to imagine that schools could have the honesty and nerve to make public their work, with all its uncertainties and blemishes, and could invite cool and critical feedback from outsiders. Now it's hard for me to imagine working in a school that doesn't assume that such public and open-ended inquiry is essential to doing business.

NOTE

1. Piner High School, where I've taught since 1983, is located in Santa Rosa, California. "Central Valley High School," however, is a pseudonym used to protect the privacy of the Protocol presenters.

REFERENCES

California Center for School Restructuring (CCSR). (1993a). *A first draft of an accountability/learning system.* Redwood Shores, CA: Author.

California Center for School Restructuring (CCSR). (1993b). *Guidelines for the protocol: Examining student work for what matters most.* Redwood Shores, CA: Author.

California Center for School Restructuring (CCSR). (1993c). *Summary of the SB 1274 RFP.* Redwood Shores, CA: Author.

California Center for School Restructuring (CCSR). (1994). *Cycles of inquiry: Whole school impact.* Redwood Shores, CA: Author.

Jubb, S., & Shawn, J. (1996, February/March). Protocol for restructuring. *Thrust for Educational Leadership*, pp. 18–21.

McDonald, J. (1996). *Redesigning schools: Lessons for the 21st century.* San Francisco: Jossey-Bass.

McDonald, J., Smith, S., Turner, D., & Barton, E. (1993). *Graduation by exhibition: Assessing genuine achievement.* Alexandria, VA: Association for Supervision and Curriculum Development.

McLaughlin, M., & Talbert, J. E. (1993). How the world of students and teachers challenges policy coherence. In S. H. Fuhrman (Ed.), *Designing coherent education policy: Improving the system* (pp. 220–249). San Francisco: Jossey-Bass.

Newmann, F. (1994). School-wide professional community. *Issues in Restructuring Schools* (Issure Report No. 6). Madison, WI: Center on Organization and Restructuring Schools.

Thoreau, H. D. (1971). *Walden.* Princeton: Princeton University Press. (Original work published 1854)

Wasley, P., King, S., & Louth, C. (1993). *Collaborative inquiry to create better school* (Studies on School Change, No. C1). Providence, RI: Coalition of Essential Schools, Brown University.

Wheatley, M. J. (1992). *Leadership and the new science.* San Francisco: Berrett-Koehler.

Wheatley, M. J. (1995). *Leadership and the new science.* (Professional Development Brief No. 3). California Staff Development Council, Santa Rosa.

6

Taking Responsibility for Our Work

Roundtables at University Heights High School

PAUL ALLISON

It's just before 9:00 on a Thursday morning. Students, members of their families, and invited guests will soon join me in Room 403 of University Heights High School for a portfolio Roundtable. I had been here earlier to arrange the tables in a tight circle, leaving a space where a student aide is now setting up a tripod with a video camera.

Around the tables, I had distributed about a dozen copies of Anna's and Mario's cover letters, and I had placed each of their portfolios on a table at the front of the room, ready to be studied by the Roundtable participants. At each place around the tables, I had put a copy of our "Roundtable Assessment Rubric." I had also posted a piece of newsprint with our Roundtable Protocol listed for all to see (see Figure 6.1).

Before I greet Anna and Mario, their parents, and the guests, I consider what I've learned over the past several years of teaching at this small, alternative public school in the Bronx. My mind goes to an essay by bell hooks called "Keeping Close to Home." In it she argues that "the most powerful resource any of us can have as we study and teach . . . is full understanding and appreciation of the richness, beauty, and primacy of our familial and community backgrounds" (hooks, 1989, p. 83).

Perhaps today's Roundtable will be one of those experiences that "transform and enrich our intellectual experience," which come when we work to make education a "practice of freedom . . . not a force which fragments or sepa-

FIGURE 6.1. Roundtable Protocol

9:00–9:15	Orientation
9:15–10:15	Reading Hour
10:15–10:30	First Presentation and Clarifying Questions
10:30 –10:45	Warm and Cool Feedback (given without presenter's response)
10:45–11:00	Presenter's Response and Further Dialogue
11:00–11:15	Consensus Decision, Recommendations, and Report to Presenter
11:15–11:30	Second Presentation and Clarifying Questions
11:30–11:45	Warm and Cool Feedback (given without presenter's response)
11:45–12:00	Presenter's Response and Further Dialogue
12:00–12:15	Consensus Decision, Recommendations, and Report to Presenter

rates, but one that brings us closer, expanding our definitions of home and community" (hooks, 1989, p. 83). That, I reflect, is why we do these portfolio Roundtables, if for no other reason: to expand our understandings of how the home, the community, and the school can work together; to bring families and members of other important communities—the university, research, business, social services, government, and so on—to the table to work with us in assessing students and their work.

UNIVERSITY HEIGHTS HIGH SCHOOL AND ITS STUDENTS

Established in 1987 by Nancy Mohr and colleagues, University Heights Middle School and High School depend on many different co-sponsors and collaborators. We are an affiliated school of the City University of New York, located on the campus of Bronx Community College; a member of the Coalition of Essential Schools and the Center for Collaborative Education; and a participating school in the Networks for School Renewal, a project funded by the Annenberg Institute for School Reform.

Although each of these networks is important to us, arguably our most precious collaboration occurs at Roundtables, when parents and invited guests come to the school, sit with us, and participate in the assessment of students' portfolios. Our alternative assessment system has been a vital link among teachers, parents, students, and "critical friends" in the educational and broader community. Teachers, family members, and critical friends assume the role of a:

> trusted person who asks provocative questions, provides data to be examined through another lens, and offers critique of a [student's] work as a friend. A critical friend [as well as the teacher and family member] takes the time to fully understand the context of the work presented and the outcomes that the person or group is working toward. The friend is an advocate for the success of that work. (Costa & Kallick, 1993, p. 50)

Like most young people who come to University Heights High School, Anna came to us after having been failed by large, traditional high schools. Many come with a strong desire to finish high school but with little notion of going on to college after graduation. By finding academic success at University Heights, most students leave with plans to go to college. Yet by the time they graduate, many students still lack such common currency for college admission as a good score on the Scholastic Aptitude Test or smooth, excellent academic records. Most also lack other resources important for college: family tradition, social support, and money. For many, they are the first in their families to graduate from high school and the first to think about going on to college.

It's our students' ability to succeed in spite of obstacles—to consistently bounce back from difficulties with renewed hope for their future—that has pushed us to develop alternative ways to help them become successful students in college and in their lives. In place of state competency tests, content-area requirements (credits or Carnegie units), grades and rankings, we have developed several processes of assessment and accountability, at the heart of which are portfolio Roundtables.

ANNA'S FINAL ROUNDTABLE

9:00–9:15: Orientation

Anna nervously straightens her clothes as we chat. Downstairs guests and family members gather for a brief orientation. Phil Farnham, one of our teachers, tells the guests, "We've found that the best way to get to know our school is to look as deeply as you can over the next couple of hours at the work of two students, and to talk to the students about their experiences here." Then he describes the two most vital documents in the folder they have before them.

Warm and Cool Feedback Sheets. Toward the back of the guest folder are two "Warm and Cool Feedback Sheets." In essence, these are blank grids or rubrics with "warm" and "cool" feedback across the top and three "phases" of assessment—reflection, evidence, and dialogue—down the left side.

Participants are encouraged to keep notes on this page during the reading hour and during the presentations. When responding with warm feedback, participants are asked to take a believing, supportive, appreciative perspective. The goal of this type of feedback is to say what is clearly there. Cool feedback is the time in the process for everybody to take a doubting, constructively critical, discerning perspective (McDonald, 1993). Students, parents, teachers, and invited guests are asked to describe those aspects of the work that seem unclear or missing.

Students are assessed in three different ways at a Roundtable—through a review of cover letters, through a description of the work in their portfolios, and through presentation and conversation during the Roundtable. The form provides sets of questions to provoke warm and cool comments for each phase of the process:

> *Reflection*: What does this student's cover letter reveal about how meaningful this work is for him/her?
>
> *Evidence*: What does the work in this student's portfolio seem to show about his/her habits, knowledge, values, and abilities?
>
> *Dialogue*: What do you notice about this student through the conversation in his/her Roundtable? What do this student's questions and answers show about his/her habits knowledge, values, and abilities?

Domains and Habits of Learning. The second essential document is the school's Domains and Habits of Learning. This is a list of the habits of heart, mind, and work that we require of our graduates. The first version of this list was "finalized" in 1991 after several years of interviewing students, parents, staff, and critical friends about what they believed a graduate should value, know, and be able to do (Farnham, 1989).

Following a list of abilities developed by Alverno College (1988, 1992), our faculty organized these expectations, or outcomes, into seven (later five) categories. These categories became our "domains," a word we used to describe the relatively distinct skills and ways of thinking that we believe exist within all disciplines of study (see Figure 6.2). This is not a conventional list; and it's important to set aside the traditional subject areas when you read it. Our aim is to distill the central organizing concepts—for example, a whole can be investigated through its parts (from biology)—from each of the disciplines, then to select those concepts that seem important to all or most of the subject areas, and finally to consider what is appropriate for secondary school learners.

The domains describe the areas of learning or the kinds of thinking and doing that a student needs to develop in every class and represent the content of our curriculum. It is around these five domains that portfolios and Roundtables are organized.

FIGURE 6.2. Domains and Habits of Learning

Communicating, Crafting, and Reflecting

GENERAL HABITS OF LEARNING

Level 1   Identify own strengths and weaknesses in using writing, speaking, numbers, the arts, media, and second language to formulate, clarify, and reflect on ideas.

Level 2   Appreciate and examine models, and use peer feedback to revise and polish work.

Level 3   Use extended writing and speaking to show understanding of important concepts and processes in academic disciplines.

Level 4   Exhibit, publish, perform, or speak publicly for an authentic audience in the school building using both English and a second language.

ADVANCED HABITS OF LEARNING

Level 5   Show an understanding of the creative processes and standards used by artists, writers, mathematicians, scientists, or other creative thinkers.

Level 6   Exhibit, publish, perform, or speak publicly for an authentic audience outside of the school building using both English and a second language.

Recognizing Patterns and Making Connections

GENERAL HABITS OF LEARNING

Level 1   Identify, assess, and articulate own strategies for recognizing patterns and connections.

Level 2   Analyze and experiment with different strategies for understanding patterns and connections.

Level 3   Analyze patterns and make connections using the content and processes of math, science, history, psychology, literature, language, and the arts.

Level 4   Connect learning from disciplined inquiries and exhibitions to each other and to personal life.

ADVANCED HABITS OF LEARNING

Level 5   Show an understanding of how patterns and connections are used in similar and contrasting ways in math, science, history, psychology, literature, language, and the arts.

Level 6   Connect personal, local, and global issues through interdisciplinary research.

Critical Thinking and Ethical Decision Making

GENERAL HABITS OF LEARNING

Level 1   Articulate and evaluate own problem-solving processes and values.

Level 2   Analyze and use different strategies for solving problems and making moral choices.

Level 3   Employ important concepts and processes from academic disciplines to analyze and solve problems.

Level 4   Identify problems of personal significance and implement solutions using the important concepts and processes that have been learned.

ADVANCED HABITS OF LEARNING

Level 5   Apply strategies, tools, and models from ethics, logic, mathematics, or
other disciplines to support and defend positions.

Level 6   Do independent research and find solutions to important social problems
for people beyond the school building.

Taking Responsibility for Myself and My Community
GENERAL HABITS OF LEARNING

Level 1   Identify and assess own habits of health, respect, and commitment needed
to be successful school and community members.

Level 2   Analyze and consider other perspectives on what deep respect and
decency are.

Level 3   Use disciplined inquiries to evaluate personal and organizational
characteristics, skills, and strategies that facilitate accomplishment of mutual
goals.

Level 4   Give service to the school and outside community.

ADVANCED HABITS OF LEARNING

Level 5   Explore and identify the expectations and support systems necessary to
succeed in college, career, and in other roles one may have after high school.

Level 6   Do independent research and take action to demonstrate an understanding
of interconnected local and global issues.

Working Together and Resolving Conflicts
GENERAL HABITS OF LEARNING

Level 1   Identify own behaviors in group problem-solving situations.

Level 2   Participate in various group problem-solving experiences and identify
successful group behaviors.

Level 3   Design exhibitions that show an understanding of the theories of
mediation, negotiation, consensus, social psychology, and group dynamics.

Level 4   Apply theories and skills learned in inquiries and exhibitions to group
problem-solving situations that show personal connections to the learning.

ADVANCED HABITS OF LEARNING

Level 5   Demonstrate the use of key concepts and processes within the disciplines
of social psychology, sociology, or cultural studies.

Level 6   Facilitate effective interpersonal and intergroup relationships with groups
beyond the school.

Two other resources are available for Roundtable guests in Room 403. The
first is a set of two or three "exemplar portfolios" from last year, which were
determined good enough for graduation, to give an idea of what has been expected for "mastery," or passing, most recently. The second, a document called
the "Roundtable Assessment Rubric," represents our collective standards for
Roundtables at University Heights High School.

Across the top of the rubric are the three levels of achievement that we use: progressing, mastery, and distinction. Down the left side are our "phases" of the Roundtable process: reflection (which includes preparation), evidence (or the work in the portfolio), and dialogue (at the Roundtable itself). Without going into more detail here, the rubric represents a set of criteria for student learning and work that we have adapted from those identified by Fred Newmann and Gary Wehlage (1995):

Construction of Knowledge

Standard 1. Higher Order Thinking: Instruction involves students in manipulating information and ideas by synthesizing, generalizing, explaining, hypothesizing, or arriving at conclusions that produce new meanings and understandings for them.

Disciplined Inquiry

Standard 2. Deep Knowledge: Instruction addresses central ideas of a topic or discipline with enough thoroughness to explore connections and relationships and to produce relatively complex understandings.

Standard 3. Substantive Conversation: Students engage in extended conversational exchanges with the teacher and/or their peers about subject matter in a way that builds an improved and shared understanding of ideas or topics.

Value Beyond School

Standard 4. Connections to the World Beyond the Classroom: Students make connections between substantive knowledge and either public problems or personal experiences (p. 17).

This account of Anna's Roundtable will help readers understand our domains and Habits of Learning and will illustrate how her work demonstrates the criteria listed above.

9:15–10:15: Reading Hour

On the table in front of each participant are copies of Mario's and Anna's cover letters and the other documents I've described. Extra pencils are available, as well as water, because it tends to get hot in Room 403 in May.

Anna's portfolio for "Taking Responsibility for Myself and My Community," like all of her portfolios, includes, as a minimal requirement, work from mathematics, science, and technology; the humanities and the arts; and service and health. The portfolio also includes work from interdisciplinary projects that demonstrate Anna's work in writing, literature, health, civics and citizenship, history, art and music, a second language, global studies, political science, journalism, school leadership, occupational education, and college planning.

Anna ends her cover letter for "Taking Responsibility" with a review of her senior year. It's worth quoting at length, because she says more clearly than I can how our domains and portfolio assessment process helped to structure her learning at University Heights. What follows are excerpts from Anna's cover letter:

> This year is one of the years that will be most remembered in my life. I had many obstacles that I had to hurdle through this year. I found myself dealing with a lot of stress and pressures from school and home. I'm proud to say that I got through it all with a positive attitude. Thinking about what I wanted in life and knowing that there were so many glorious things that will come to me in the future I realized that my life won't always be like it has been recently . . .

Anna reviews her portfolios and Roundtables for the first six domains:

> At this, my last senior Roundtable, I am presenting the domain "Taking Responsibility and Preparing for the Future" which is now called "Taking Responsibility for Myself and My Community." I prefer the old title because that's what I've been doing since I arrived at University Heights High School. As I present this domain, I think it will become obvious that I am preparing myself for the future. In this domain all of the other domains tie together. Because they all were preparing me for my next step in life. In this final cover letter I was able to prove that I am truly ready to move on, because in addition to learning how to care for others in my community, I've also learned how to take care of myself. I have secured a job, I've been accepted to college, and [I plan to move] out of my mother's apartment into one of my own.
>   In conclusion I will always be thankful to the University Heights community. They gave me a chance to express myself freely which helped me to excel academically. To my community I owe my thanks by giving me the strength to move on and make something of myself.

10:15–10:30: Anna's Presentation and Clarifying Questions

The 12 participants plus the 2 presenters introduce themselves. I go first, saying what a pleasure it has been to work with Anna for a year and a half; then a high school principal from Rockland County (just north of New York City) introduces himself, explaining that staff from his school had been visiting to get ideas for an alternative assessment system of their own. Next to introduce themselves are Gene, a counselor and college adviser at the school, followed by a teacher from a recently opened small high school in the Bronx and two students from her school. Anna's mother and her older brother introduce themselves proudly. Anna's boyfriend, who is also a classmate, introduces himself, followed by a recent graduate of the school. Next, a researcher from the Coalition of Essential Schools and Mario's mother introduce themselves, and, finally, Anna and Mario.

It's 10:20. The time has come for a student to present. "I'll not have much more to say until the end," I say. "Anna?"

Anna begins her presentation more or less the way she begins her cover letter for this domain:

Dear Teachers, Students, Parents and Invited Guests:

Good Morning, how's everyone doing? I hope fine. I'm glad that you are able to attend my last senior Roundtable. I will be presenting the domain "Taking Responsibility and Preparing for the Future" which is now called "Taking Responsibility for Myself and My Community." I prefer the old title because that's what I've been doing since I arrived at University Heights. As I present this domain to you it will be obvious that I am preparing myself for the future. In this domain all of the other domains tie together. Because they all were preparing me for my next step in life. Now I'm writing my final cover letter to present and to prove that I am truly ready to move on.

The projects that I will include in this cover letter to show that I am ready to graduate are:

1. Community Service
2. Stress Project
3. College Courses
4. NYNEX and Future Plans
5. The Year in Review

Community Service. Last year in my second semester at University Heights I began doing community service. Every Wednesday students who were not seniors from team Visiones were to attend the job site of their choice for the hours 9 AM to 3 PM. There were several job sites, for example Morris Heights Center, Love Gospel Soup Kitchen, Bronx Museum, Cross Walks Network, day care centers and a few elementary schools.

The job site I chose was Morris Heights Health Center. I chose this site because I have always been interested in the health field and I thought that working there would be a nice experience.

Anna goes on to describe meeting with her supervisor and some of her responsibilities there. She refers often to the journal she kept, which is included in the portfolio as an "exhibit." She concludes:

Working at this place for the short time that I did had me demonstrating a lot of responsibility by being committed to a job and striving to accomplish tasks. The responsibility of going out and working in my community was important. It gave me a chance to work face to face with people in my community and provide them with quality service. Too many times I have entered public clinics and other places where the receptionist and others that work there have an attitude. They are supposed to be helping people, not hassling them and making them feel worse. One thing that I appreciated about the Childbearing Center was that it was a family team who's main interest was to satisfy the patient. [Anna included Exhibit 1c: a letter of recommendation]

Stress Project. Anna then describes a project in which she investigated the health problems surrounding stress and produced a booklet about her findings. As Anna writes in her cover letter, students:

had to tell the etiology of that particular condition and list some support groups people can go to for that condition. [The project] included a statement of any treatment that can be used and prevention methods. I had to do a statistical analysis and graphs to show who is infected with this health issue.

After writing a personal story about stress, Anna did some library research to find articles, books, and pamphlets about stress. As she did, she stopped at key passages to write summaries and personal reactions. These "dialectical notes" are included in her portfolio to show how she came to understand the important concepts and processes of the health and medical research related to stress. In addition, she interviewed a counselor who specializes in stress reduction and collected health statistics regarding stress.

After she had finished the booklet, Anna read it to her seminar and then wrote an eight-page self-assessment of her work during this project. All of these items were available at Anna's Roundtable.

College Classes. Next Anna describes her learning in two different college classes that she had taken—at Bronx Community College—during her senior year at University Heights High School: a chemistry class and a philosophy class. She decides to read excerpts from a paper, a 3,000-word essay, she had written for her philosophy class. Anna describes this class as being "more about thinking about problems, being a witness, and analyzing issues in life." The paper is titled "Violence," and it begins with her account of the Polo Grounds, a housing project in upper Manhattan where she had recently been spending a lot of her time. Anna reads:

> When you look down from the roof of building 2991 which is set in a right angle corner of the Polo Grounds, located at 155th Street and 8th Avenue, you have a clear view of the other three buildings and it's surroundings. In the daylight you see kids playing in the playgrounds surrounded by dirt, glass, crack vials, and negative influence. Cops patrolling, crackheads scheming, trying to sell things including their own bodies to support their habit. You wonder if the people living further downtown live in an environment like this one. When you look downtown, it looks as if their buildings are gray, white, clean, and well kept. . . . As my eyes look back down on the activity, I hear gun shots, but it's nothing new. It becomes like a beat to a tune that you didn't necessarily like, but has grown on you.

Anna goes on in the essay to explain her project, her questions, and some of her reasons for exploring the topic of violence, for which she interviewed three informants from the neighborhood: Mr. W., an elderly "White male [who] remembers when he used to walk to the stadium (which is now a housing project) with his father"; Ali S., "a Black male in his mid-30's who "explained his growing up as an everyday struggle"; and Ali's teenage son, "who lives with his parents in the Polo Grounds."

Skipping to a place toward the end of her essay, Anna talks about her research on the health and science of violence:

> Violence is also a health issue. When we speak of health and living healthy lives, we usually think of eating vitamins, doing exercises, etc. We hardly ever associate violence and health. Violence is one of the biggest health issues in the medical field today. Some of the concerns of the medical professionals when they think about violence as a health issue are: funding for treatment for those that don't have insurance and who might have been victims of violence; funding for correctional facilities; researching and studying the minds of murderers; trying to find a cure for this condition. . . .
>
> Scientists and doctors are beginning to feel that they can monitor the problem of violence. Yes, they may do research, analyze, and conduct tests on its occurrence, but what is that going to do for prevention? This is the beginning of genetic-centered health, I think. Physicians are going to look at genetics for everything as a way to predict the future, the fu-

ture in violence. Doctors want to monitor those who they feel fit the profile of a likely candidate to violent behavior. . . .

Anna ends her reading by going back to the question about violence being choice or chance:

> I think that violence is brought on both by the choices people make and also from the things that people have no control over. But in the other part of the question about what society can do about it: I feel that violence is a part of nature, but now it has become a culturally accepted thing, and that's the thing that bothers me. I don't think medicine alone can be the source of prevention by finding likely violent candidates and doing studies. I believe that this nation needs to observe themselves as a whole, travel back in history, and analyze where these problems come from. Yes, society can do something about the level of violence and crime in this nation, but do they want to do something about? This is my question.

Future Plans. Anna begins to conclude her presentation with a bold account of her future plans, which include a job with the phone company and a scholarship from them to attend Empire State College in the evenings:

> I live with my mother, and I'm not so happy with my living conditions. . . . Me and my mother were evicted from our home. At that time I had a lot of anger towards my mother, because she didn't take care of business the way she was supposed to. She let a man take over control of her finances. From that situation, I learned to always have some kind of security for me and my family, and that's when I started to think about my future and plans for my security. . . . I always wanted to go to college, have an apartment, and work. But my question was how was I going to do all of this: have an apartment, go to college, and have a job that will pay enough to do all of this? That's when the NYNEX Corporate–College Program cam up. It did it for me.

Anna ends with her "Year in Review," a summary of the seven cover letters she had presented in Roundtables like this one.

10:30–10:45: Warm and Cool Feedback

By now it is 10:45, and we are behind schedule. I remind everyone that we will now be giving Anna warm and cool feedback on her cover letter, her work, and her presentation. I also explain that Anna will not be responding immediately to this feedback; instead she'll keep notes and respond in the next step of the Roundtable process. Finally, I ask participants to keep their feedback short, "giving just two or three comments at a time, and allowing others to make their comments before coming back to more. We'll give warm feedback for 5 minutes, then cool for 5 more." I check my watch. "OK, who would like to start?"

Anna's boyfriend begins by reading from notes that he has made:

> Knowing Anna on a personal level, and knowing all the tribulations she went through both here in school and out in the community, I know Anna has the energy that most students need to be successful in life. She has shown a great reason why one should live up to their responsibilities, and she has already had a major impact on our school community. She will always be known as a role model here.

Then the principal from Rockland County speaks:

> Not knowing Anna at all, I see that she's got effort. I see that she shows motivation, basically in being a very focused young lady. She shows perseverance in her work, a very nice portfolio. I also see that she will make something of herself, which I think is very important.

Next, the teacher from a new, small Bronx high school:

> I admire you for sitting here in front of all of these people with this pressure. I was noticing a lot the pressure and whatever was happening during the year that was kind of laying on your shoulders, and just how directed you are. That was what came across to me . . . that you got something you were interested in and you tied it all together in your portfolio, and you talk about the future and being interested in health, and the chemistry class, and the community service project, and the stress project. And how you've got this idea for the future about how you're going to make your dream, your goals happen. And that, to me, was so impressive, just how articulate you are about it. Not just that you can talk about it, but you can show us things that you've done in setting up things for the future to back up your words.

When she finishes, I ask for "anyone younger than 17 to make the next comments," trying to involve students in the process more. After a few giggles from the students who were guests, a recent graduate from University Heights High School speaks up: "I was impressed with your presentation. You were so focused. Your portfolio had a lot of work, and you explained everything."

Mario says:

> I like the way you explained yourself. Your were calm, and very man-
> nerly. You don't even seem nervous, and I'm like, "Oh, my God!" I love
> your work. I like how you put your work in your portfolio, and how you
> showed all of your cover letters at the end. I feel like your work is yours.
> Like this is your work. You have ownership of this work, you know. And
> I admire the way you've taken all your motivation to try.

Next, holding back tears, Anna's mother speaks:

> At some points this year, I never thought I'd be sitting here now, watch-
> ing this. As she has said, things haven't been the easiest recently. I'm just
> glad that Anna was able to make it all into something positive. I can see
> how her school work helped her, and I'm most impressed with her work
> in her college classes.

"What about you, Paul?" Mario wants to know, and I respond:

> One of the things I noticed was the range of the kinds of experiences that
> are in your portfolio, from a very structured science class to service learn-
> ing or philosophy class where there was a lot more independent work. So
> I noticed a real range of learning experiences in your portfolio. And I'm
> impressed with a student who has a clear career goal, like "I want to be a
> health patient advocate." That feels realistic to me. Even though you may
> not end up as that, it feels interesting that you've been able to carve out
> that role for yourself.

The 5 minutes allotted for warm feedback have passed, and I ask, "Anybody else?" The researcher from the Coalition of Essential Schools has a final
warm comment:

> I do have lot of notes repeating lots of things. I was jotting down an
> awful lot. There were some nice things that came out of your presenta-
> tion. I liked that you defined terms as you went. And at one point you
> asked, "What works best for me?" I underlined it, because I think that's
> an important question. And you answered it! With each project you ex-
> plained it. . . .

Thanking everyone for their comments, I move us to cool feedback:

> Again, it's not necessarily critical, but no matter how wonderful we think
> Anna might be, there are still areas where she might grow. So where

might she go next? What might she think about, especially in terms of this domain. And I want to caution us a bit here. I found eight or nine grammatical errors. That's not what we are evaluating here. We're evaluating her ability to take responsibility for herself and her community. So in terms of that domain, let's give her cool feedback. Who would like to start this time?

As often occurs, a guest asks me to start so she'll have an idea of what to say herself, and I agree to model cool feedback:

I had one question. I'm impressed that you've set your goals really high: You want to go to college, get an apartment, and a job. I just wanted to know, does that ever make you angry that you have to do all of this now at this age? You are so focused, that I wonder how you handle it, how you've gotten there.

The guest then adds:

I wasn't sure what to think about the part of your cover letter and presentation where you talk about your mother and allowing a man to take over her finances, and how you got angry at that point. Perhaps you could explain that more? It may just be me. It may be that people take that very differently. And in terms of presentation, some things in the portfolio were hard to read because they weren't typed.

After a long silent minute, Anna's mother speaks about her goals:

Like everyone here, I was impressed with your goal, but I was looking for more of the baby steps. Perhaps a monetary budget for how you are going to do all of these things, you know those kinds of practical things.

Anna's boyfriend has the last cool comments:

Even though you've come a long way, I still think you could be a bit more alive when you present. And I'm not just commenting about being a performer or anything. That thing you wrote after your stress project was all you, you know what I mean? I wish I could see more of that kind of writing in your cover letters, too. No offense.

10:45–11:00: Anna's Response and Further Dialogue

Anna has been silently taking notes, but now she takes back the spotlight. She explains how she is budgeting her money already and looking for an apartment with her boyfriend. She says:

Right now we have bills, and we budget our money. We save money. We know what we can spend, and what we can't spend. We have to make a lot of sacrifices. We can't get that new pair of sneakers, because we have to pay the Macy's bill, something like that. We know our responsibilities, and we'll be able to make the sacrifices to get what we want.

She gives more details of her mother's situation with her former boyfriend. Looking at her mother, she says what she seems to have said before, "I feel you should have taken more control over the situation."

Her mother responds, "Are you going to do that?"

Anna shoots a glance at her boyfriend and says with confidence, "Yes I am! That's something I'll never let happen. I always want to know a bill has been paid or whatever is going on." She answers other questions about the difference between work and school and about the stress she feels having to be patient about getting an apartment and doing well in school and working.

To conclude, I ask one more question: "What have you learned from putting this portfolio and presentation together?"

She answers:

When I was putting together this particular portfolio, I just looked back on my different cover letters and different projects that I used. And in reading over my work, I saw that I learned a lot over here in this school. I think the things that I learned, I will be able to take with me into the future. A lot of things I learned I feel I'll take them with me.

After apologizing for being close to tears at one point during her presentation, Anna agrees to wait in the hall for our decision about her habits in the domain of Taking Responsibility for Myself and My Community.

11:00–11:15: Consensus Decision, Recommendations, and Report to Anna

It's 11:15 already, and I'm aware that we need to reach consensus quickly so that we have enough time for Mario to present. Still, I take the time to explain the consensus process.

"We need to make some judgments now in terms of Anna's habits of heart, mind, and work when it comes to taking responsibility for herself and her community. We need to decide whether she has reached the level of progressing, mastery, or distinction in each of the three phases listed on the left sides of both the Roundtable Assessment Rubric and the Warm and Cool Feedback Sheet where you've been keeping your notes: the reflection in the cover letter, the evidence in the portfolio, and the dialogue at the Roundtable.

"One way to ask the question is this: Is she ready for college in terms of taking responsibility?" I continue, "And I'd like to ask the students here to give us their thoughts about where they think she is on the Roundtable Assessment Rubric within each phase.

"We want to hear all voices as we try to reach consensus. Not that all voices are equal. I know some things having been Anna's teacher that her mother doesn't know, and her mother obviously knows things that I don't know. . . . So we don't think that every voice has the same weight in these decisions, but we value all of your thoughts. It will be my job to craft a consensus with you all, so that we can leave feeling good about our assessments and our recommendations, which we'll end with.

"What seems important about this conversation is that each of us emphasize our reasons for our evaluations, and that all of us listen carefully, confront respectfully, and work together. Does all of this make sense? Then let's get started."

A student guest is the first to speak: "I think she should get distinction, because she worked hard on her work and she's dedicated to what she wants to be, to go to college."

Mario adds:

I think she explored so much, and even though there's so much more to explore about life, she's ready to do that. She's really motivated. She's being stubborn about it. She's going to do whatever it takes to be responsible, and to be on her own.

The teacher from the Bronx mentions three pieces of evidence that haven't been talked about yet: Anna's search for an apartment, her letter of recommendation from McDonald's, and her persistence even when she didn't want to do a project. Her conclusion:

I don't get any sense of her being a quitter, and as was said earlier:
Even when she almost cried during her presentation, she kept going. You need that. You need to push forward and stick to projects once you've started.

Gene, the college counselor, comments on how careful Anna was in getting her college applications and financial papers in on time, and on how much energy she showed in following through with the NYNEX program.

At this point, I say, "OK, she has at least mastery here, and now we need to decide if she has reached distinction. Would anybody disagree with that?"

Anna's boyfriend mentions her commitment to two college classes, chemistry and philosophy, as evidence that she should receive distinction.

The principal from Rockland County agrees, saying:

> With all the work I've seen students do and how they present it, Anna
> has distinction here. I would just be repeating what a lot of people have
> already said. She was so committed. She's such a hard worker. She's so
> competent. If distinction is the highest rating, that's what she deserves.

Anna's mother nods in agreement, "Yes, I'm impressed."

I mark that she has achieved distinction for all three phases: reflection,
evidence, and dialogue. Then I ask if there are any recommendations. "What
recommendations could we give her? Even though she has distinction, what
might she think about as she leaves high school? Anybody?"

The college adviser answers:

> I have one. Dealing with her stress. Anna is someone who works so hard
> that she puts all of her emotions behind her. Then, as we can see, she can
> become overwhelmed. She doesn't think about all the stress in her life un-
> til she reaches that point where she's ready to explode. She needs to real-
> ize how hard she works, and she needs people to confide in. My recom-
> mendation is that she make time for herself more. Stopping more.

It's 11:30, 15 minutes overtime, and her boyfriend goes to the hall to get
Anna. After we tell her that she has reached distinction in this domain, the
college adviser repeats his recommendations, which she takes with a smile.

HOW WE CAME TO ROUNDTABLES AND
WHERE THEY'VE TAKEN US

For her last Roundtable, Anna selected work from an interdisciplinary high
school course, a college chemistry class, and a college philosophy class, as well
as work from her service learning at a health clinic and from concrete plans she
had made for the future—plans which would enable her to go to college. Multi-
plying Anna's final Roundtable times 7 (for her seven presentations done over
at least a year) provides a pretty good idea of what our assessment system seeks
to accomplish.

Roundtables have evolved from the culture of teaching and learning that
we began building from the school's beginning in 1987. Early on, we realized
that the most successful young people were those who experienced little separa-
tion between home and school. We've found that when teachers and parents
work together on common goals, when school life and personal life are brought

together, when academic and cultural goals are the same, students find more success. As Reginald M. Clark (1983) puts it:

> The most pedagogically effective instruction occurs when the role demands and cognitive functioning in the classroom are compatible with, or built upon, those in the home. To the degree that the activities and experiences in these two settings reinforce each other while facilitating mutual trust, mutual goals, and personal autonomy, the child will show a greater proficiency with the basic skills (academic knowledge and social skills) that schools are expected to teach. (p. 5)

Like the Primary Language Record (Barrs, Ellis, Hester, & Thomas, 1989) (see Chapter 2), on which we've drawn, Roundtables give us a vital opportunity to show parents that they and their children will be treated fairly by a school. Central to the purpose of Roundtables is to include parents as partners in student assessment. Our aim is to build trust with parents and to help them feel empowered, to make clear that we value and need their voices in describing their adolescent's strengths and areas of weakness.

Long before we began experimenting with portfolios and alternative assessment, we were committed to collaborating with families and with community and university partners. Roundtables came from our commitment to build standards by consensus with parents and critical friends of the school.

It may sound strange after the extended description of Anna's Roundtable, but we are less committed to any particular protocol or process of assessment, for example, the Roundtables, than to the principles these processes exemplify: ongoing inquiry into what students need to know, be able to do, and value; making assessments as public as possible; involving authentic audiences in assessment decisions; including family members in the process; and keeping the focus on both the work itself and on students' self-assessment of that work.

We don't promote Roundtables as a model for others to follow. Rather, we would ask others who are interested in alternative assessment to look to the questions we've been asking. From the beginning, three areas of inquiry have been the focus of our work: standards, assessments, and systems. Even though the portfolio Roundtable process has become a cornerstone of our school culture, we are always looking to find new answers to these questions:

Standards. What do we want graduates to be able to do, know, and value? What habits of learning—of heart, mind, and work—do staff members, students, parents, and critical friends want high school students to have before they go on to college and work?

Assessments. How can we assure ourselves, as well as parents, students, and critical friends, that our graduates are ready for college and work? How can we fairly and reliably assess the broad range of social and academic qualities and habits that we have all agreed (in our answers to the standards questions) we were looking for in a graduate?

Curriculum. How well do our systems of assessment inform our curricular designs and instruction? What structures, requirements, evaluation systems, or tests inhibit or constrain our ability to teach in the ways that we know are best? What needs to be cleared away, and what systems need to be developed, to allow effective, innovative approaches to curriculum and instruction to take root and to blossom?

It's important to be clear about what we have found necessary to change or eliminate in order to make a new assessment system work at University Heights High School. For example, when we began working with alternative assessment we were convinced that the same students who would be putting together impressive portfolios would also be scoring high on state- and university-sponsored or standardized tests. We thought we could do both, but, after a few years of trying, we decided that we couldn't. Students were telling us that we seemed "schizophrenic." The world of alternative assessment and the world of testing are incompatible.

As Nancy Mohr (1994) describes it:

> The change from a reliance on state testing . . . came about because we experienced, as a group, a year of alternative assessment and saw what many staff described as a deep inner sense that if a student demonstrated mastery, through Round-tables, in each of our seven domains of learning that we, ourselves, could truly believe that they were well prepared to leave high school. And having that deep inner sense (that valuing) we have less of a problem with either taking on the responsibility or feeling justified in making a change. We also, as a group, saw that we were shirking our own responsibility if we were teaching one way and assessing another.

We sought, and received, a waiver from the New York State Regents Competency Tests. This is just one example of what we are not doing. There are no content-area departments (e.g., Social Studies Department); all subjects are taught in interdisciplinary ways. No letter grades or numbers are used to evaluate students, and Carnegie units or credits are not used to determine when students are ready for promotion or graduation. The portfolios and Roundtables, then, are not an add-on to our regular work—they are our work.

The results of our work have justified our decision: Over 90% of our students apply for and are accepted to college, even without a high score on the SAT, grade point averages (of any kind), class ranks, traditional transcripts, or a score on a state-sponsored competency test.

There's much more to say about University Heights, its students, and its ways of working with them, but the best way to get to know us is to come and visit, and take part in a Roundtable. All are welcome.

Curriculum: The Highest Phase of Assessment Integration

After 5 years of building an alternative assessment, where have we come? One of our partners during the development of Roundtables has been a group of researchers from the Center for Children and Technology (CCT). In a report on their work with us, they describe our history with alternative assessment and suggest next steps.

The researchers at CCT write that the "highest phase of assessment integration" is when a school revisits the curriculum "to see if it provides enough opportunities for students to do quality work" (1997, p. 5). This is indeed where we find ourselves now.

Roundtables have put our students' work at the center of our assessments; each Roundtable is grounded in a student's portfolio. At a Roundtable the work is evaluated in the context in which it was produced, by the people to whom it matters most: teachers, parents, critical friends of the school, and the students themselves.

Roundtables have also made public the strengths and areas of weakness of our curriculum and instruction. Our work in assessment has, in fact, led us back to professional development and curricular change. While each Roundtable reminds us of how much work we have left to do, these conversations we have around student work are also a constant reminder of how many critical friends and parents there are ready to join us in this "practice of freedom . . . that brings us closer, expanding our definitions of home and community" (hooks, 1989, p. 83).

REFERENCES

Alverno College Faculty. (1988). *Ability-based learning program.* Milwaukee, WI: Alverno College Institute.

Alverno College Faculty. (1992). *Liberal learning at Alverno College.* Milwaukee, WI: Alverno College Institute.

Barrs, M., Ellis, S., Hester, H., & Thomas, A. (1989). *The Primary Language Record: Handbook for teachers.* Portsmouth, NH: Heinemann.

Center for Children and Technology (CCT). (1997). *Executive summary: New York–based alternative assessment project.* New York: Author.

Clark, R. (1983). *Family life and school achievement: Why poor black children succeed or fail.* Chicago: University of Chicago Press.

Costa, A., & Kallick, B. (1993, October). Through the lens of a critical friend. *Educational Leadership*, pp. 49–51.

Farnham, P. (1989). *What do students need to learn?* Internal publication, University Heights High School, Bronx, NY.

hooks, b. (1989). *Talking back: Thinking feminist, thinking black.* Boston: South End Press.

McDonald, J. P. (1993, February). Three pictures of an exhibition: Warm, cool, and hard. *Phi Delta Kappan.* pp. 480–485.

Mohr, N. (1994). Internal memo. University Heights High School, Bronx, NY.

Newmann, F. M., & Wehlage, G. G. (1995). *Successful school restructuring.* Madison, WI: Center on Organization and Restructuring of Schools.

PART III

Contexts That Work

Fourth-grade teachers in Croton, New York, in the midst of developing a schoolwide portfolio assessment, bring samples of their students' work to monthly meetings. The school principal regularly joins the meetings, helping to keep the group stay clear about its purpose: not to grade the work, but instead to provide a means for students to reflect on their own work and for teachers to reflect on their instructional practice.

An external review team of educators and parents from southern Maine spends a week inside a high school talking with teachers and administrators, "shadowing" students and examining student work. Team members discover that the most illuminating conversations happen when samples of student work are right there to examine and discuss.

A high school class in Kentucky works on assembling their own "digital portfolios." With guidance from teachers, students select pieces from their work—including scanned-in graphics and digitized video clips—that best demonstrate the school's (and the state's) learning goals. The technology allows readers of the portfolios not only to view the work but also to add comments or questions about it.

Teachers learning from student work is a good idea. The protocols for structured conversations around student work described in this book can help to deepen teachers' understandings of their students' learning and their own practice. But like other good ideas in education, this one requires resources, support, and caretaking.

Leadership from principals and superintendents is essential in shifting the focus within a school or district from grading student work to learning from it. Leadership can also identify and provide resources to help maintain the focus on student work and learning, resources as diverse as a regular meeting time for teachers, an off-school-site retreat, or a consultant to work with a group of teachers over time.

Networks of schools or teachers—often partnering with a university—offer possibilities for developing tools for examining student work, such as protocols; honing skills through institutes and workshops;

and sharing expertise and perspectives on the school's work, for example, through "quality-review" teams.

Technology has long been used as a means to provide instruction. Newer applications, such as digital portfolios, suggest how interactive, multimedia technology can facilitate examination of and reflection on student work by teachers and by students themselves.

As teachers come to value the learning possibilities in collaborative examination of—and reflection on—student work, the conditions of their own work must change.

7

Portfolios, Students' Work, and Teachers' Practice

An Elementary School Redefines Assessment

SHERRY P. KING and LAUREN CAMPBELL-ALLAN

In Croton, New York, and all across America, refrigerator doors display samples of student work and teachers' comments on the work. "Excellent," "98% Keep Up the Good Work!," and smiling faces are among the ways teachers give students feedback on their progress. Indeed, because of these evaluations, many teachers might question the need for a book on student work and teacher learning. "After all," they might argue, "haven't we always marked papers and graded tests? And doesn't that tell us where students need additional instruction—when we can make time for it in our crowded curriculum?"

What teachers have done at the Carrie E. Tompkins (CET) Elementary School in Croton has gone beyond *grading* papers to *examining* student work. They have done so to meet three school- and districtwide goals:

1. To break the isolation of classroom practice and create a collaborative, reflective community
2. To establish collective standards that will demonstrate students' proficiency
3. To improve instruction

FIGURE 7.1. Key Activities for School Change

Year 1:
- Community Focus Groups
- K–2 Wing
- Curriculum Mapping
- Development of Alternative Assessments
- Candy House Project
- Monthly Grade-Level Meetings

Year 2:
- District Mission and Vision Statements
- Consultant Bena Kallick
- Analysis of Reading Scores
- Principal and Teacher Participate in New Standards Project

Year 3:
- Elementary, Middle, High School Participation in New Standards Project
- Portfolio Project (All 4th-grade teachers, one 2nd-grade teacher, students in all other classes)
- Teachers' Journals
- Establishment of Assessment Committee

Year 4:
- Districtwide Development of Digital Portfolios
- Elementary Portfolios for All Students in All Classes of 36 Teachers Keep Journals

This chapter tells the story of school change over 4 years from the perspective of the school principal and the district superintendent; it incorporates the voices of teachers, the wisdom of outside experts, and the work of children. While it focuses on the elementary school, it's really the unfinished story of how an entire district has begun to orient its programs around student work and student achievement. (See Figure 7.1.)

DISTRICT GOALS FOR CHANGE

In 1992–1993, the Croton-Harmon Board of Education and new superintendent decided to put systems in place that would allow the district to work toward continuous improvement. Rather than simply embrace temporary goals, for example, multiculturalism one year and technology the next, the central administration decided to create a climate in which the staff, the board of education, and the community would continually assess and refine the educational program. Despite the grades and test scores the teachers regularly collected, no records indicated specifically what students were actually learning.

As a first step to creating a district characterized by self-reflection, the superintendent conducted a series of meetings throughout the community, resulting in the development of vision and mission statements for the district. The Croton-Harmon school district serves a suburban community with 1,200 students in a single elementary school, middle school, and high school. Involving the community ensured that these statements reflected the values of the community. Printing them in the local newspaper and the calendar the district sent to all residents helped make public the goals.

Another priority for all the schools became breaking the traditional isolation by classroom, which created schools where teachers rarely shared teaching practices. The schools developed practices that involved more student-centered learning opportunities as well as more varied assessment methods. For example, at the high school, students in a tenth-grade humanities program would present their work to panels of teachers, students, and community members. In the middle school, eighth-grade students created computerized "digital portfolios" as evidence of their readiness to move to high school (see Chapter 9).

Teachers began working together on a regular basis, technology was integrated into classroom practice, and teachers developed interdisciplinary courses as steps toward creating a system in which students and teachers publicly shared their work. Despite these initiatives, administrators were hard-pressed to answer the question posed by one of the board members: Were all the efforts and initiatives resulting in improved student achievement? While many believed that creating a learning community was essential for school reform, improved student learning, not greater teacher collegiality, was the reason for fundamental change. In order to answer the board member's question about student achievement, the schools had to move beyond anecdotal evidence of greater student engagement to a systematic way of demonstrating student achievement that provided much better information than standardized test scores or subjective, nonspecific teacher comments, such as, "Great work."

In 1994–1995, the district decided to take a more focused look at student achievement. Drawing inspiration and resources from the district's involvement in the Coalition of Essential Schools and the New Compact for Learning, the state's school reform initiative, the superintendent helped the principals of each school scrutinize the work of their schools and develop initiatives that would yield data about student achievement in light of changing instructional practices. In order to maintain sharp focus, the superintendent encouraged principals to examine only one initiative. The high school principal decided to examine a pilot program in which all eleventh-grade students were assigned to the college preparatory–level English course. Students could self-select periods of extra help if they needed it or choose enrichment activities that could result in their receiving honors credit.

The middle school principal, in collaboration with teachers, chose to examine the science curriculum with a view toward creating coherence within the school and cohesion with the elementary and high school curricula.

At the Carrie E. Tompkins Elementary School, the principal focused on development of portfolios with two main purposes: (1) to use student work as a vehicle for creating grade-level and, eventually, whole-school agreement about standards of work; (2) to use the assessment of actual student work—in this case, writing—to inform instructional practice.

SETTING THE STAGE AT CARRIE TOMPKINS

The principal and staff at CET engaged in a number of initiatives that prepared them for the development of portfolios. When Lauren Campbell became principal in November 1992, the elementary school was well poised for change. Early in her tenure, she noted that while students' test and achievement scores were, on average, high, instruction lacked uniformity from classroom to classroom and cohesion from grade to grade. She also realized that teachers were ready to begin to reflect on and change their assessment system. In part, their readiness was a result of working with an outside consultant who had assisted teachers in refining appropriate developmental instructional practices.

Teachers moved their classrooms to create a K–2 wing in order to facilitate—and provoke—collaboration. In addition, teachers engaged in a process of "mapping the curriculum," which required them to examine what they were teaching at a particular grade level, determine its appropriateness, and make appropriate changes. Teachers generated questions such as: Why are fractions being taught in grade 3? Why are Native Americans taught in grades 2 and 4? Where does electricity best fit in the curriculum?

Addressing these curricular questions on a schoolwide basis was new for the teachers at CET. As conversations led to curricular adjustments, teachers also began to develop assessments that would demonstrate what students knew and were able to do at the end of a given unit of study. Performance-based tasks and checklists of mastery replaced multiple-choice, fill-in-the-blank tests. In examining what was being taught, the staff focused on three questions: Do we value what we teach? Are we teaching in ways that ensure that all students can succeed in learning? Does the assessment appropriately and effectively evaluate student learning? This effort to define developmentally appropriate practices allowed the principal to begin to engage teachers in examining their own practices, an important step in building a culture of reflection—but by no means the last step.

Candy Houses and "Kid-Watching"

The principal, during her first year, was urged by the superintendent to create a special opportunity for teachers to work together in grade levels and between grade levels as a way of breaking the isolation of their work and seeing the value of collaboration. The Candy House Project was an early initiative that involved all kindergarten, first-grade, and second-grade teachers in the design of a developmentally appropriate math unit that included new, more performance-based assessments. During the project, teachers also engaged in "kid-watching," during which they observed and recorded students at work, which included the creation of blueprints, estimation, counting, and knowledge of coin values. Teachers took notes on students' math skills as they planned houses, estimated the amount of candy necessary to cover surfaces, decided how much candy needed to be purchased, and determined how much money it would cost. The project culminated in the construction of individual candy houses, which were shown off during the celebration of winter holidays.

While the project had no direct link to portfolios, it resulted in several benefits: Teachers shared actual examples of student work with parents; kid-watching provided teachers invaluable information about the process of student learning; and teachers amassed anecdotal evidence of learning of specific mathematical skills.

Teachers and parents were pleased by how much math students learned in this project-based, hands-on unit. Teachers were particularly surprised at how much they themselves learned about their students through focused kid-watching. The project enabled teachers carefully to record the ways students worked alone, in groups, and in pairs. In addition, teachers collaboratively developed checklists to help them focus on teaching specific math skills and to assess the mathematical achievements of individual students throughout the project.

The Candy House Project prepared the staff to work collaboratively, look more deeply at student work, and more willingly share student work with others. A project that was designed primarily to be developmentally appropriate had opened the door to reflection on instruction through the examination of student work.

Teachers began to engage in conversation about the ways students were being assessed, the ways the teachers shared their information with parents and colleagues, and the helpfulness of kid-watching in assessing the whole child. These conversations began during the monthly grade-level meetings. With the help—and probing questions—of the principal, the teachers began to talk openly about new assessments they were trying. In some cases, teachers across the grade level began to develop grade-level assessments, including one math assessment, intended to replace a section of the Stanford Achievement Test and Reading Records, in which teachers recorded student skills at decoding and miscuing words.

Despite the many benefits of the Candy House Project, collegial conversation about teaching and learning, and more discussion of actual student work, teachers did not seem to make use of these benefits in the ongoing work of their classrooms.

Bringing the Outside In

Realizing teachers required assistance to meet the goal of using the results of student assessments to influence instruction, the administrators met with a consultant to define the next steps in the process. The consultant assisted the principal in analyzing the school's reading scores. Just as the Candy House Project revealed an inconsistency among teachers in approaches to math instruction, reading scores revealed that the school had been ignoring weaknesses in certain aspects of the instructional program. The scores not only revealed gaps in students' basic reading skills but also suggested that the school did not share a common approach to teaching reading and writing.

A way to address these gaps and to bring the faculty together around issues of reading came in the form of a pilot project conducted by New York State and New Standards.[1] During the year of the Candy House Project, the principal participated in the New Standards program, in which she worked with teachers from across the country in collecting samples of student work and developing criteria for a Language Arts Portfolio that focused on developing higher standards. Through activities with New Standards, she discovered the enthusiasm of teachers from across the country for examining students' work. In many cases, participation in New Standards was the first time teachers looked at and assessed students' work in a way that enabled them to rethink their instruction.

At New Standards meetings, teachers shared ideas and strategies about steps for teaching and learning. For example, after looking at fourth-grade writing samples, teachers decided that teaching paragraphing skills was not appropriate until students were writing effective opening and closing sentences for their stories. The principal saw this approach as a way to help her staff in three ways: (1) promoting discussions about student work that would open doors for teachers to reflect on practice and assessment; (2) implementing changes that would make instruction and assessment more student-centered; and (3) involving the faculty in discussions about a schoolwide approach to teaching and learning that would build continuity and consistency in grades K–5.

During the second year of the New Standards project, the principal invited a fourth-grade teacher known to be a risk-taker to become involved in the New Standards project and to pilot portfolios in her class. This teacher immediately saw ways that building portfolios could influence her practice. Her excitement for the project confirmed for the principal the efficacy of teachers' coming together in a supportive environment to share student work and reflect on their practice. The New Standards model of bringing a small group of six to eight teachers together to work over an extended period of time helped build a trusting environment for sharing. Teachers came to trust one another because they developed a culture of respect in which they were able to be critical of one another and to ask hard questions about standards, rigor, and practice. Here was a model the principal wanted to re-create in her school.

Upon completing the second year of participation in New Standards and piloting portfolios, the teacher explained that she had learned more about her students, their learning styles and abilities, as well as her own instruction, than ever before in her career. She and the principal were anxious to pilot a New Standards–type portfolio system, which they believed would help the school pay particular attention to literacy standards, instruction, and student achievement. Developing a schoolwide portfolio, with assessment tasks and a scoring system, could help the school agree on a common approach to reading and language arts instruction and contribute to a more logical and explicit continuum of instruction in grades K–5. They saw the process of developing such a portfolio system as one way to meet the school and district goals of using student work to break the isolation of classroom practice and create a collaborative, reflective community; to demonstrate that students were using their minds well; and to use actual student work to influence instruction.

THE PORTFOLIO PROJECT

The Candy House Project, examination of reading scores, and the teacher's and principal's participation in the New Standards project all came together during the summer of 1994, when the principal asked the fourth-grade teachers to consider piloting a portfolio system. She felt that entire classes needed to be involved in the pilot so the school could gather information about a portfolio's impact on curriculum and instruction. Encouraged by the teacher's enthusiasm for New Standards and the principal's commitment to portfolios, all fourth-grade teachers agreed to participate with all of their students.

With support and funding from the district, the teachers met during the summer to plan for the portfolio pilot. Realizing the interdependence of skills both in the primary and the intermediate grades, the teachers decided that the pilot would benefit from a primary classroom teacher's participation, so a second grade teacher was enlisted in the project.

The portfolios were not developed as grading instruments; rather, they were envisioned as vehicles for a different kind of assessment: student self-reflection, teacher reflection on student work, and teacher self-reflection. An Assessment Committee, made up of the fourth-grade teachers and additional teacher representatives from each grade, developed an outline of the way teachers would pilot portfolios during the school year. Using the New Standards Portfolio as a guide, the committee designed portfolios, the purposes of which were to *collect* student work, *select* the best work, *reflect* on these selections, and *direct* next steps for instruction based on these samples of student work. All teachers were also asked to keep journals of this work throughout the year, reflecting on the pilot—its strengths and weaknesses. The teachers would use this information in assessing the pilot and making necessary changes.

> *Journal Entry—Mrs. D.*
> September—first week
> As I think about collecting student work for portfolios, I hope that the reason I'm doing so is to look at each child's work and see their strengths and needs. For me, the portfolio should be the raw data from which I feed my curriculum back to each child. For instance, if in one portfolio I see a child consistently has trouble organizing her work, I will work with that child on organizational strategies. If, on the other hand, a child has trouble coming up with ideas for writing but is a fluent visual artist, I might try to tie the drawings to the writing. Draw first, write from the drawing.
>   I hope the portfolio project will teach me to respect the work of each child, to use her work as a springboard for individualized coaching, and to give the child a sense of growth and accomplishment.

While the portfolios would not be graded, they would help teachers demonstrate student learning to children and their parents in ways that went beyond the school's report card, with its traditional S for satisfactory work, G for good work, and N for needs improvement.

> *Journal Entry—Ms. F.*
> September 12
> Why are we engaged in exploring portfolios and using them for assessment? I realize we need a better way to measure student growth other than a "formula," which is oftentimes a false assessment of a child's ability. The report card is too confining and does not really measure what can be noted for a kindergartner's growth.

During the summer's planning stages, the Assessment Committee decided that portfolios from grades K–5 would be used to demonstrate evidence of student growth in the areas of reading, writing, and oral communication. The committee specified that all grades 3–5 portfolios should include a table of contents, a letter of introduction, eight to ten pieces of writing with an entry slip on which students explained the purpose of each piece, written "reflection" on at least three pieces, and a reading log. In addition, students made tapes of at least one piece that demonstrated oral language.

Because the teachers valued process writing, they determined that drafts should be included with final copies. Since primary students are not proficient writers, portfolios for K–2 students, in addition to writing samples, would include student illustrations, audio recordings, photographs, and videotapes. The committee also developed year-long portfolio timelines for students and teachers to help them collect, sort, and reflect on their work at regular intervals throughout the year.

The district's consultant helped the principal begin to think about the ways examining student work could form an integral part of the portfolio project and help the school to focus on the place of language arts in the larger context of the elementary curriculum. The consultant also encouraged the principal to expand the pilot. Beyond the involvement of all fourth-grade teachers and one second-grade teacher, the principal decided to ask all teachers, including all special education and special-area teachers, to pilot portfolios with at least two of their students.

This decision helped the principal move ahead on the goal of developing a common approach to the teaching of reading. It also supported the goal of whole-school change; every teacher would use portfolios and consider their value to the school's assessment of students. The principal recognized the danger that the portfolio project would belong only to a small group of "entrepreneurial" teacher volunteers if everyone was not included.

The principal introduced portfolios to the staff at the faculty meeting on the first day of school in September 1994. Over the summer, in preparation for the opening meeting, she sent teachers several articles on assessment. At the meeting, the Assessment Committee joined the principal in explaining the pilot program for the fourth- and second-grade classes. The principal then asked that the rest of the staff be involved in the pilot on a much smaller scale by keeping portfolios on at least two of their students. Teachers, however, were encouraged to keep portfolios on students at all levels of achievement. During that meeting, teachers were given a 3-year portfolio plan, developed by the Assessment Committee. The plan called for the expansion of the pilot in the first year to include all teachers and all students in the next 2 years.

The plan also emphasized the portfolio goals of helping students become more reflective about themselves as learners, demonstrating evidence of student growth and achievement, and influencing instruction. Initially the portfolio would support and help explain the present grading system; later it might be used as an evaluation tool.

After this initial meeting, the entire faculty met monthly to discuss portfolios. In preparation for faculty meetings, the Assessment Committee and the principal distributed relevant articles summarizing current research on portfolios. These articles were discussed during the initial 20 minutes at faculty meetings. The teachers then broke into mixed-grade groups of six, facilitated by one teacher from the Assessment Committee, to share and discuss portfolios. Tasks varied from month to month and included sharing tips on ways to "teach reflection"; ways to look at student work without being judgmental; and ways to help students "weed," that is, select pieces for their portfolios.

Looking at Student Work

The district's consultant helped frame the next steps for the entire staff, including how to reflect on student work rather than actually grading student work, which was crucial to this project. The principal, superintendent, and consultant were concerned that teachers not look at portfolios merely as another batch of work to grade. While agreeing with this decision, the principal was particularly torn about it because she felt that scoring portfolios, as she had experienced with the New Standards Project, was an excellent use of portfolios. However, all three feared that teachers would become so involved in scoring that they would lose sight of the primary goal of the portfolios: the examination and description of student work and use of those observations to influence instruction. The staff, therefore, agreed that at no point during the first year would they grade portfolios.

During the school's first staff meeting in September 1994, the consultant helped teachers to look at the work by asking them simply to describe what they saw in student work. The activity consisted of showing a sample of student work, describing what it told about the child as a person and as a learner, and discussing what this piece indicated as next steps for instruction. Repeating this practice at monthly meetings began to change the school's culture and practices so as to be more consistent with the district goal of teacher collaboration.

Journal Entry—Mrs. L.
October 10th
This week working with the district's consultant was very helpful. It was helpful in that I liked her suggestion of doing lots of writing—first drafts only—for a while. Then take those drafts and only a few will go to revision and finally into the portfolio. This sounds much more manageable.

The idea of taking each piece of writing through the whole process was mind-boggling.

The consultant's suggestion for commenting on only what is there was quite interesting. I enjoyed the activity as a group. Yet when I went to correct pieces of writing this weekend, I found it very hard to be nonjudgmental. I wonder if students need some positive feedback?

Well, I am taking this past week's two writing assignments (Jeremy's story and immigrant picture response). I have made comments and will add to the students' collection. Then some time in November we will pick two pieces to revisit and revise.

Teachers in the school, especially those who were beginning to dabble in more authentic assessments, were used to sharing assignments and scoring rubrics. However, while trying to describe the actual student work, teachers discovered that they were more facile in talking about their own adult work than in describing children's performance. By holding students' work, not their own, up to scrutiny, teachers had no choice but to develop a shared vocabulary to discuss the elements of learning demonstrated in student work. Looking at multiple portfolios led teachers to identify ranges of student achievement and to consider the specific writing needs of their students. For example, teachers and students made specific reference in the portfolios to the use of concrete details and clear topic sentences, two aspects of writing important to fourth-grade teachers.

These observations led to discussions about standards for student work and the development of norms of accountability for teachers, beginning with asking all teachers to bring two samples of student work to share at each meeting.

The principal reminded teachers that the portfolios were an organized way of providing information to parents about the current grading system—not a new grading system. Throughout this first year, the principal kept reminding the staff that this was a pilot, that everyone was learning together, and that the pilot would change based on experiences. In this way, the principal was able to help the teachers feel comfortable about taking risks, trying different strategies, sharing what they tried, and noting what worked and what didn't.

Reflecting Together

The monthly faculty meetings became important occasions for teachers to share samples of student writing with colleagues from across the grades. Teachers were surprised at what students were able to accomplish, particularly in the lower grades. Teacher journals revealed that seeing what students accomplished in other classes caused some teachers to raise their expectations of student achievement. For others, sharing student work forced them to think more about writing instruction simply because they had to provide evidence of student work on a regular basis. Still other teachers shared teaching techniques with their colleagues that they had previously shared only with the students in their classes.

Teachers also remarked on the power of having their colleagues from other grade levels share strategies that they could try in their classes. One teacher wrote: "I can't believe a first-grade teacher told me how to do this with my fourth-graders and it worked." Teachers in grades 3, 4, and 5 were impressed by how much writing primary students were doing; primary teachers were gratified to see how their students had grown and developed as they looked at student work in intermediate grades.

> *Journal Entry—Mrs. D.*   .
> September 20
> At the faculty meeting today we sorted through a portfolio and found it somewhat confusing. Why were these pieces selected? Were they independently done? Is the work supposed to speak for itself? I question just giving a student a 1, 2, 3, or 4 based on a rubric. No one is across the board 1 or 4. I would find it much more useful for instructional purposes and reporting to parents to state exactly what areas are 1's, exactly where are the weaknesses of the 4 writer.
>
> My daughter has been attending PVC [Pierre Van Cortlandt Middle School], and I find the rubrics of the school's expectations for projects somewhat informative. Yet they are almost impersonal. I always want personal comments tailored to her specific strengths and weakness so we can work on it at home or they can focus on it in school. Will parents really be satisfied with a rubric number/a page of details and work samples or do they need specifics? I don't know yet.
>
> After playing with the unorganized portfolio during the teacher meeting, I realize that I must do the following when setting up my portfolio pilot:
>   1. Put date and assignment on each page
>   2. Add child's reflections

During the first year of the portfolio pilot, students were taught how to select their work by going through a weeding process, during which they would sit with folders filled with up to 10 weeks' worth of work and choose two or three pieces that they believed best represented them as learners. Of these two or three pieces, students then chose one piece on which they reflected. In their written reflection, they were asked to articulate the reasons they believed the pieces were evidence of how they were growing and learning (see Figure 7.2).

While reflection, according to the teachers, was the most difficult skill to

FIGURE 7.2. Sample Student Reflections

Student Reflections

Students respond in writing to these questions:

- I selected this piece for my portfolio because . . .
- Which goal does this piece provide evidence of?
- Explain your evidence using specific examples. (For example, I used correct punctuation and spelling.)
- Describe what else you could have done to make this piece even better. (For example, I did well with my goal of spelling, but I should have paid more attention to my punctuation.)

Sample Student Reflections

B.:

For once, my story was well detailed and a variety of sentences.

I used good detail, but I could of had neeter handwriting.

R.:

I thought it was a fun project, and I like sharing a story in a letter.

I wrote in paragraphs but I feel I could have done better on punctuation.

S.:

I enjoyed working this piece because I liked studying immigration.

I did well with my goal on spelling, punctuation, and capatalization, but I
    could have put more detail into the writing.

teach students, it was also the most worthwhile. Because few students or adults spend much time reflecting on their work, the principal modeled reflection with teachers at the end of each faculty meeting on portfolios. In early meetings, she reflected on a portfolio of her own work; in later meetings, she asked teachers to consider how the work she collected related to student achievement. She helped teachers to see how their students' work and anecdotal records on their students could form the basis for similar reflection and questioning.

An unanticipated issue that emerged from the project involved the faculty in rich debates about why students, at times, chose writing that teachers did not deem their best work. The school became involved in discussions about "How can we define best work?" and "What does it mean if students' ideas of best work and teachers' ideas of best work are different?" Were there differences in the characteristics of writing praised by elementary students and teachers? Whose portfolios were they anyway? If the school's premise was that they were student portfolios, did the teacher have the right to say a particular piece was not a sample of best work? If the school maintained focus on its initial purpose, which was to collect, select, reflect, and direct, was it important if students did not select what teachers deemed best work? Those questions became part of the ongoing dialogue among the faculty.

> *Journal Entry—Ms. A.*
> October—Bena Kallick [district consultant] Meeting
> I had a moment of clarity as Bena steered us away from rubrics toward the notion of the portfolio as learner-centered. Words like student "ownership" rang loud and clear. I then began to understand my pilot as a way to help children "self-assess"; I would, in fact, be giving them the power to judge themselves. Once they learn to "self-assess," they then will learn to set their own goals that are within their reasonable limit. The child will learn to describe his/her own work and will learn to reflect on that work; then, hopefully, the child can see the next step or goal to reach for.

Lessons Learned, Changes Made

Some ideas became clear throughout the year, others only when the staff gathered to evaluate the first year of the pilot. All had significant impact on the direction of professional development in the school. For example, as teachers on all grade levels met to analyze the range of skills within a particular grade level, they became aware of the need to identify teaching strategies for students with a wide range of abilities. Writing samples revealed that some students needed more direct instruction in basic skills such as paragraphing. Clear evidence emerged of the need for assignments that would better stretch more talented writers. Teachers, even those who had long been advocates of the process approach to writing, commented in their journals that the practice of sharing student work with colleagues gave them new insights into their own practices. The link between sharing student work and instruction was so great that teachers planned a language literacy summer workshop to help hone their skills in teaching writing.

At the end of the first year, the entire staff agreed that the portfolios were a valuable piece of the school's overall assessment practice. The staff agreed that every teacher would become involved in portfolios in the second year and that certain changes needed to be made to the contents of the portfolio. Among the most valuable assets of portfolios, teachers listed:

- Looking at student work through a different "lens"
- Using student work to plan next steps for instruction
- Gaining a better understanding of the prior experiences of their students and of what their students would encounter in the following year
- Diagnosing student capabilities (also through such strategies as kid-watching)

- Using portfolios as a means for teachers to assess instruction as well as student growth
- Realizing the effect of student reflection on learning

Teachers also experienced the power of having work samples from September to demonstrate to parents in conferences the ways children had grown in the areas of reading, writing, and oral language skills.

Journal Entry—Ms. J.
April
Shared the portfolios with parents during conferences.
   I found that by putting in work samples, I did not need to retest some items prior to conferences. It also made them more authentic. Parents actually saw growth in their children by comparing work from fall to now. Portfolios are very graphic.

As the work for the second year of the pilot began, the staff made changes in the management of portfolios and in the table of contents. The portfolios would no longer be called "best work" portfolios, because students and teachers do not always agree on what "best work" means. A compromise emerged: Teachers would choose at least two pieces they deemed best work; students would choose the rest.
   With the consultant's help, the Assessment Committee examined discrepancies between student and teacher selections of best work. Analyses indicated that students often limit what they write when they are given a specific writing assignment. They tend to pick as their best work free-writing samples in which they are allowed to be more creative. Teachers began to reflect on why students view teacher assignments as more restrictive and less satisfying. Teachers recognized that assigned writings tend to limit creativity. This recognition influenced writing tasks as teachers strove to balance the need for student choice and their need to have writing samples that demonstrate a range of language skills.

Journal Entry—Ms. H.
May
Faculty Meeting
One thing that really troubled me during this meeting was that the child's work we looked at seem so unchildlike. I saw that the teacher shined through more than the student. I could see the teacher's outline, the teacher's suggestion format for the reflection letter, even the teacher's ideas. This child's portfolio did not show a child, but the techniques of one fairly uncreative teacher. Portfolios do tell more about the teacher than we expect. Are there problems inherent in this, too?

Portfolios are not the only way to focus the school on student work and student achievement. The Descriptive Review (see Chapter 3) provides another strategy for examining student work and has helped to deepen classroom practice at the elementary level. At the district level, teachers have practiced the Tuning Protocol (Chapter 4); and the elementary, middle, and high school have all implemented some form of the Digital Portfolios (Chapter 9). All these have helped to make the examination of student work more collaborative and reflective as well as influencing instructional practice.

As the school continues work on portfolios, the focus has turned to deepening the Descriptive Review process, helping students and teachers become better at self-reflection, and beginning conversations about where the portfolio fits into the overall assessment picture of the school and the district. The faculty is also trying to make the portfolio more integrated across the curricular areas. While the portfolio is rich in reading, writing, and oral language, there are now only limited opportunities for math, science, and social studies pieces to be incorporated. Understanding how to bring work from these disciplines into the portfolios in a meaningful way will be a further challenge.

ELEMENTS OF SUCCESS

The culture of the school has been changed from isolated classroom practice to an environment in which teachers willingly share and discuss student work with their colleagues. Careful examination of student work is beginning to have a direct influence on classroom practice; instruction and assessment are becoming more student-centered. Teachers use portfolios in parent–teacher conferences. Sharing student work with other students, teachers, and parents has made the school's work—and standards—more public.

Several elements have contributed to the success of this project:

- The principal was deeply committed to the work and project. Staff development around this project was a non-negotiable priority. Each month a 2-hour meeting was set aside for portfolio work and only portfolio work. Regardless of what else was going on in the school, that meeting time was kept "sacred."
- A long-term consultant was essential to provide a steady sounding board who could help plan for next steps and deepen the work. The outsider's eye forced the school to ask new questions at each step. Her monthly meetings with the Assessment Committee and regular meetings with the principal and superintendent helped keep the direction of the work clear.
- A significant element in the success of the pilot was the decision *not to score the portfolio*. The portfolio rubrics are descriptive of student work, going beyond the act of merely giving the student a grade and then moving on to

the next assignment. The school's portfolio or Descriptive Review approach to looking at student work focuses not on a grade but on using actual student achievement to plan the next instructional steps. New Standards and similar portfolio projects will help schools change their assessment practices, but they may not necessarily have a major impact on instruction if the focus is solely on scoring; finding a balance is essential.

- Teacher "buy-in" and accountability. Progress toward goals such as those of the portfolio project depends on *all* teachers' willing participation. Buy-in alone is not enough; teachers must be accountable for their work in forwarding the school's goal. Accountability takes the forms of monthly meetings, journals, and evidence of student achievement.
- The superintendent is key to supporting the work of the school and ensuring cohesion among schools in order to develop districtwide coherence. To achieve that goal, the district must protect schools from the tendency to adopt a new initiative each year or create competing priorities beyond those that develop in the normal course of any school year. As part of maintaining focus, the superintendent must help the board of education and community see the value of maintaining a steady course over time, including funding for ongoing staff development, use of consultants, and involvement in the pilot projects—in short, whatever is necessary to ensure that the work continues.

Portfolios have become an important part of Carrie E. Tompkins Elementary School's and the Croton-Harmon district's assessment profile. Together with standardized tests as well as traditional and authentic assessments, they provide a much richer picture of student achievement than any one measure can provide.

NOTE

1. New Standards is a joint project of the National Center on Education and the Economy and the Learning Research and Development Center at the University of Pittsburgh. Begun in 1990, its goal is to create a system of internationally benchmarked standards for student performance and an assessment system that will measure student performance against the standards.

8

Building a Culture of Inquiry
The School Quality Review Initiative

Debra R. Smith and David J. Ruff

Most school reform efforts have focused on general strategies to improve education, such as cooperative learning, block scheduling, interdisciplinary curriculum, portfolio assessment, shared decision making, and setting standards for learning. While all these approaches may contribute to creating enabling conditions, they do not necessarily lead to improved teaching and learning. This requires grappling directly with the specifics of teaching and learning through a careful look at student work and at students and teachers working. Because most teachers work in isolation, they rarely or never see colleagues' work or the work of students other than their own. For this reason, processes and tools for teachers' collaborative inquiry, reflection, and improvement of classroom practice must be developed.

The Southern Maine Partnership (SMP), a school–university collaboration, provides opportunities for individual teachers and schools to engage in critical dialogues about teaching and learning, examining practice in relation to research and research in light of the wisdom of practitioners. In this chapter, we describe the work of the Partnership in developing a School Quality Review Initiative (SQRI) as one element in a culture of inquiry in the southern Maine educational community.

Within an ongoing process of self-assessment and improvement, schools in the Partnership apply action research methods and some of the processes and protocols described in other chapters of this book. Some have chosen to host an SMP/SQRI visiting team review, an intensive review of teaching and learning in a school conducted by a group of "critical friends." Later, we describe the

SQRI process in a typical high school, with a particular focus on the visiting team review. Finally, we share some of what we've learned as a group about school-based collaborative inquiry and some of the actions that have resulted from the SQRI pilot.

RECOGNIZING THE NEED FOR COLLABORATIVE INQUIRY

Over the years, the Southern Maine Partnership's voluntary groups and projects have been the source of inspiration and active learning for many elementary and high school teachers and administrators in southern Maine. Through reflective practice groups, the Foxfire Network, the Assessment Mini Grant Program, and other endeavors, the Partnership has supported the work of individual educators and teams and has nurtured individual reflection and a culture in which teachers are valued as researchers, inventors, and consultants.

Some schools in the Partnership have become better able to respond to the needs of students. But in many schools, learner-centered change has been spotty or muddled, with multiple efforts and no alignment of goals that help the whole school move forward; in some cases, different efforts have actually contradicted one another. Very often, changes in practice or organization focused on the staff's implementation rather than on students' learning ("mistaking the plan for the product," as Allen puts it in the Introduction).

Over time, Partnership staff observed that in classrooms where changes in practice positively impacted learning, teachers' and students' work focused directly on learning, reflecting a high level of quality and engagement. Unfortunately, this focus was seldom shared schoolwide, and students could not be assured of a smooth educational journey. Rather, each school year was a brand-new experience with new rules and expectations. In schools making progress toward a more coherent educational experience for students, we saw a collegial professional culture in which rigorous dialogue, reflection, and action were ongoing (Wasley, Hampel, & Clark, 1997).

Early efforts to address these issues revealed their complexity. In one case, a monthly reflective practice group on assessment and curriculum had been running for 2 years, with attendance averaging 40 elementary, middle, and high school teachers at a meeting. Facilitated by SMP staff, the agenda was set by the group, and activities included reading articles; discussing concepts, ideas, and issues; and sharing strategies and examples of performance tasks, projects, rubrics, checklists, exhibitions, and portfolios.

The group decided to look at student work as a way of grappling with the question of setting standards, but at the meeting to which people were to bring examples of student work, attendance dropped from 40 to 17, and then only 2 brought anything. Even within a supportive community, teachers still found it very difficult to share the work of their students with colleagues, and even more difficult to use this information as a means to better understand the learning of students.

In examining the student work, the group realized that clearly stated standards drafted by adults sitting around a table can be quite ambiguous when applied to the real work of real students. Examples of student work often reveal more about the teacher than the learner. Teachers recognized that, in general, they tended to think and talk about what they do, not what learners achieve. The group noted that, as teachers, they didn't have ways to look at student work beyond the solo task of scoring or grading it.

Within reflective practice groups, teachers and SMP staff experimented with tools for focusing teacher dialogues around student work, including the Tuning Protocol, the California Protocol, the Prospect Center's Review of Children's Work, and Project Zero's Collaborative Assessment Conference. Teachers and Partnership staff began to understand more clearly the factors necessary for continuing and deepening this work, and providing the impetus to search for a framework that would support whole-school engagement with these processes.

We summarize our early lessons from our collaborative inquiry as follows:

- In order to affect learner-centered school change, the focus must switch from what teachers plan to what students do and learn.
- Schools do not improve teaching and learning in meaningful ways as a result of externally imposed mandates.
- Schools do not change because a few individuals do: Change requires collaboration of all members of the staff working together toward shared goals.
- Learner-centered school change requires in-depth, ongoing, purposeful collegial dialogue about the specifics of student work and learning. This is how learner-centered culture, shared meaning, and living standards are developed.
- New context-appropriate tools and processes are essential for effective change. People need to learn new skills, new roles, and new ways of relating to one another.
- An outside view is important to a school's perspective on itself. Schools working in isolation are less likely to keep moving than schools in partnership with others. Sharing resources, ideas, struggles, and successes is very powerful.

While we were meeting around these issues in southern Maine, David Green, a former member of Her Majesty's Inspectorate in Great Britain, was working with the New York Department of Education to adapt aspects of the British school inspection model to an American context. Green's ideas about knowing schools well through inquiry into teaching and learning and the model of review by a visiting team struck a chord. Partnership staff and educators from member districts began to discuss ways to incorporate these ideas into a model appropriate for our context.

THE SMP/SCHOOL QUALITY REVIEW INITIATIVE PROCESS

Partnership members used the 1994–1995 school year to develop a generative, iterative process that would help schools focus their improvement efforts on teaching and learning while developing a larger culture and capacity to sustain the work. Out of rich dialogue, periods of confusion, and insight from school-based educators, three key elements arose to undergird the SMP/SQRI design: (1) a set of common principles, (2) a process and inquiry tools that are adaptable to each school's unique context, and (3) a network of critical friends.

Common Principles

At an October 1994 gathering of Partnership members interested in the concept of a School Quality Review Initiative process, approximately 80 K–12 and university teachers, administrators, parents, students, and community members defined a set of principles for learner-centered schools. These three broad principles form the foundation for the Partnership's School Quality Review Initiative process (see Figure 8.1).

Participating schools commit to using these principles to guide their own inquiry and planning, and visiting teams use them to focus and organize their review of teaching and learning in a school. These common principles enable teachers to share a language and stance toward teaching and learning that provide opportunities from which deeper thinking and learning about the educational lives of children may derive.

A Process and Inquiry Tools

A design team of about a dozen volunteers began development of an implementation process. The design team struggled with the need to develop an ongoing process with a degree of uniformity that would promote understanding and collaboration while honoring the need for local adaptation based on each school's context.

After numerous drafts, a process for school engagement emerged. After initial whole-school agreement to participate, each school develops a focus question with an accompanying Inquiry Plan and commits to actions based on inquiry, evaluation of their work, and dissemination of their learning to their com-

FIGURE 8.1. The Southern Maine Partnership's Principles for Learner-Centered Schools

---

The Southern Maine Partnership believes that the school is a center for teaching and learning where students and teachers are actively engaged in learning.

Academic Focus

The school has a clear academic focus whereby teachers choose appropriately from a range of strategies to promote student learning. A core set of skills and knowledge for all students is clear and can be explicitly stated by teachers, students, parents, and community members. All teachers and students can answer the questions "What are you doing?" and "Why?"

Assessment and Accountability

The school holds itself accountable for ensuring that all students can demonstrate quality standards of literacy in all knowledge areas. It organizes and reorganizes itself accordingly. Appropriate forms of assessment that reflect high, public standards for learning are used to document student progress and achievement. The school uses multiple mechanisms for reporting frequently and publicly to parents, students, and the community on how well the school is meeting its stated outcomes.

Community

A sense of community permeates the school. Parents, teachers, students and other members of the school community are partners in learning. All members of the school community are treated with dignity and are valued, honored, encouraged, and supported in their development.

---

munities. Each school identifies a coordinating team (which may be an existing body, such as a school-improvement team) that includes teachers, administrators, support staff, at least one parent or community member, and students if appropriate to facilitate and document their school's work (see Figure 8.2). Below we briefly describe the elements of the inquiry process.

Focus Questions. The school coordinating team and faculty identify a focus question that, along with the Learner-Centered Principles, guides their self-assessment for a particular year. This question comes from the school's ongoing work and is developed from extensive faculty dialogue about what is most central to their work at this point in time. For example, one school's focus question was, "How does assessment drive our instruction?" Another asked, "How does student reflection inform our practice?"

FIGURE 8.2. Ongoing Self-Assessment for Continuous Improvement of Teaching and Learning

1. The school conducts its own ongoing inquiry and hosts a visiting review team every few years.
2. Includes:
   • exploring student work
   • observations
   • student shadowing
   • interviews
   • review of documents and policies
3. The *Annual School Profile* is a five- or six-page document that summarizes background information about the school, its mission and learner outcomes, progress towards its mission/outcomes, the SMP Learner-Centered Principles, and next steps.
4. Each school develops ways of reporting its progress to the community.
5. Tools and processes such as the Collaborative School Protocol, Tuning Protocol, Collaborative Assessment Conference, and Descriptive Review of Work may be used as appropriate for dialogues focused on teaching and learning.

Inquiry Plan. Based on their focus question, each school then develops an Inquiry Plan, defining how it will collect and analyze data about the focus question and how the Learner-Centered Principles are reflected in the school. As appropriate to their focus, schools use a variety of tools for this, such as:

- Exploring student work through use of processes and protocols, such as Descriptive Review
- Classroom observations
- Student shadowing (accompanying a student guide through his or her daily schedule)
- Interviews with faculty, parents, students, and/or community members
- Review of student performance data, documents, and policies
- A visiting team review (described in detail in the next section)

Inquiry Plans will change as the work progresses, but the initial plan serves as a year-long map for the inquiry process.

Action. As schools gather and analyze data relevant to the Learner-Centered Principles and their focus question, they can make decisions about teaching based on a solid understanding of the educational experiences of children. These actions are ongoing and intertwined with the inquiry process. They may take the form of small adjustments in teaching practice or larger decisions about programs and practices across the school.

Evaluation and Dissemination. Throughout the process of inquiry and action, the school engages in evaluating its own work. This evaluation both informs the ongoing process within the school and serves as a vehicle to communicate with the broader school community. This may take a variety of forms (some already in place), such as newsletters, reports, parent forums, presentations, and cable television shows.

In addition, each school conducts a summative evaluation via an annual School Profile to be presented to both internal and external audiences. While each school's self-assessment process is ongoing, developing the annual profile helps the school pause and take stock of its progress, to reflect on what has happened over the past year in improving teaching and learning, and to consider next steps. The School Profile is a brief (five to six pages) annual report including:

- Basic background information about the school, such as location, grade span, numbers of students and teachers, and other significant characteristics of the school and its community
- The school's vision and learner outcomes

- A description of the school's work and progress regarding its focus question, the SMP Learner-Centered Principles, and student achievement

A Network of Critical Friends

Realizing the complexity of this task, the design team also developed several support mechanisms for schools involved in the SMP/SQRI design, including an intensive week-long summer institute and a network of critical friends.

The summer institute provides school and visiting team members with an overview of SQRI, opportunities to explore the Learner-Centered Principles, practice using various inquiry methods and tools, and time for team planning. Institute facilitators are teachers and administrators who have been actively involved in developing the SQRI process and who have played leadership roles in schools and visiting team reviews.

During the first few days, everyone is engaged in the same activities together: looking for evidence of the Learner-Centered Principles in a description of a typical day for high school students; participating in a cultural simulation in which observers must try to figure out the "rules" of an unfamiliar culture; conducting observations of public settings and videotaped classroom segments; developing questions and conducting interviews; and exploring student work through various protocols. In the second half of the institute, school teams and visiting team groups split to work on planning specific to their future roles.

At the same time as they are learning and practicing inquiry processes, participants are forming a community of critical friends with strong commitment and trust. Throughout the year, this community develops as school teams share their work, problem solve together, and continue to practice using new inquiry tools in late-afternoon meetings every 4 to 6 weeks. Visiting team members are included in meetings as appropriate. In addition, teachers from the lead schools serve on visiting teams to other schools. The strength and safety of these connections enable teachers to share both successes and failures from their classrooms. This honest dialogue provides real learning opportunities for teachers, which, in turn, begin to impact the learning experiences of children.

SMP staff provides ongoing support for each school, including regular visits, posing questions, providing feedback, suggesting resources, and responding to schools' articulated needs.

THE VISITING TEAM REVIEW

A visiting team review provides the school with the opportunity to receive external critical feedback on the learning experience of its students. Schools involved in the process conduct a visiting team review as part of their inquiry plan every few years; all four pilot schools requested a review in 1995–1996.

Partnership staff coordinate the construction of visiting teams composed of educators (teachers, administrators, specialists), support staff, and, whenever possible, at least one parent/community member. Each team has a chair or co-chairs, depending on how the leaders choose to define the responsibilities for facilitating and managing the process. The size of the team depends on the size of the school, and the team's profile is matched with the school's focus question as closely as possible.

The visiting team spends a week exploring teaching and learning in the school through student shadowing (following a student for a day); classroom observations; interviews with teachers, students, parents, and other members of the school community; and examination of student work. The precise schedule of activities is developed by the school coordinating team and varies from school to school. The "week" may start on any day. Three of the four review visits conducted in the first year started on a Thursday.

At the end of each day, the visiting team meets to process what they learned that day. The team's understanding of the school deepens with each successive day as patterns, themes, and questions emerge. Data collection, analysis, and reporting are organized around the Learner-Centered Principles and the school's focus question.

By the fourth day, they are ready to begin drafting a report to the school. The team describes evidence and examples of the principles and focus question in operation and generates findings/statements from these. They deliberately do not make recommendations; rather, they pose questions that emerge from the review process for the school's consideration. Report highlights are presented orally to the entire staff and others the school invites on the fifth day. A final written report is prepared by the team, and a discussion with the school staff follows within a few weeks following the visit. In the next section, we briefly describe one of the pilot visiting team reviews.

THE SQRI PROCESS AT OCEAN VIEW HIGH SCHOOL

Ocean View High School (OVHS)[1] is a comprehensive grades 9–12 school with 72 faculty members serving approximately 1,000 students. The sole high school in the district, it has an experienced staff. Structured around content-area departments, the school has begun to explore various teaching strategies, including Critical Skills and Foxfire, and has incorporated student voice into school-wide decision making and worked to form greater ties with the community.

Development of the Inquiry Plan. The impetus for Ocean View High School's Inquiry Plan for the 1995–1996 school year actually began a year earlier. During the 1994–1995 school year the faculty collaborated on identifying six Common Beliefs on Effective Learning:

1. We respect diversity in learning and teaching styles.
2. Respect for ourselves and others is essential.
3. It is important to provide a physically, intellectually, and emotionally safe environment.
4. Education requires collaboration among school staff, students, parents, and community.
5. Learning requires perseverance, self-discipline, and hard work.
6. Intellectual curiosity and risk-taking sustain the learning process.

The faculty at OVHS was pleased that the Common Beliefs offered a shared vocabulary and marked a serious example of collaboration among the staff; however, validating the beliefs in classroom practice presented a problem. The school viewed SQRI as one means to investigate the validity of their beliefs. During the summer institute, the school settled on their final version of its focus question: "How are our Common Beliefs on Effective Learning evident in our school?"

The Inquiry Plan—Self-Study. Organizationally, the work at OVHS began with the School Improvement Team (SIT). Based on information from the summer institute, this group of teachers, students, administrators, and parents designated a smaller group with teachers, administrators, students, and a parent to coordinate schoolwide efforts to devise and implement the school's inquiry plan.

The OVHS Inquiry Plan originally included a series of voluntary events for the teachers to share various tools learned at the summer institute, such as the Tuning Protocol and the Collaborative Assessment Conference, to be followed by a visiting team review in the spring. The early sharing sessions were not very successful, either in attendance or in moving the school toward a deeper understanding of the focus question. These sessions were viewed by the faculty at large as additional work with little value, and so the groundwork for collegiality and understanding was not laid. The school leadership team was surprised, considering the heavy buy-in on the Common Beliefs, but recognized teachers' need to justify spending time and money.

Learning from this experience, the leadership team devised an alternative strategy focusing more heavily on gaining whole-school involvement via whole-school activities. This began with a series of written reflections by the staff. Teachers were asked to bring a written reflection to a staff meeting, detailing student work and students at work that displayed characteristics of the Common

Beliefs. These were shared in small groups, then collected to be analyzed by the leadership team. Several written examples were included in a newsletter, *The SQRI Press*, or, as it became known, *The Squirrel Press*. These written reflections provided a base for informal collegial conversations.

In addition, the leadership team incorporated the work of a community drug and alcohol awareness group, involving all students and faculty members at OVHS in five roundtable discussions looking at the climate at the school. The conversations, which focused on Common Belief numbers 3 and 4, provided the school faculty with additional data about their focus question.

The Visiting Team Review. In March 1996, OVHS hosted a visiting team review. The first 3 days of the review consisted of three basic activities: student shadowing, interviews with teachers and parents, and a review of student work displayed at an academic fair. The final 2 days were spent investigating loose ends and pulling together the oral and written reports (see Figure 8.3).

Student Shadowing. Visiting review team members were each assigned a student to "shadow" on the first and third days of the review. With the student serving as a guide, the team members followed the student's daily schedule. The students had been chosen by the leadership team with input from the entire faculty to represent a cross-section of the student body, and parents or guardians for all students were notified of their child's participation prior to the shadowing. Throughout the seven-period day, the reviewers were able to get a good sense of teacher–student interactions, student-to-student interactions, and the scope and complexity of student work expected from students at OVHS.

The classroom visits allowed reviewers to see student work and students working in real school contexts. The visits lacked authenticity at the beginning, but students, reviewers, and teachers quickly became comfortable with one another. The reviewers did not use any specific "protocol" during this time, nor were they silent observers; they conversed throughout the 2 days with students concerning their work and experiences. Reviewers consistently asked students to explain what they were doing and why it had value. These conversations around student work provided insights into the standards, values, and practices of the school based on evidence, not just words and intentions.

Interviews. The second day consisted of a tight schedule of interviews with teachers and parents followed by a visit to the academic fair. Using a protocol drawn up by the leadership and review teams, all but one adult who worked at the school was interviewed either on this day or on the fourth day of the review. Approximately 15 parents were also interviewed. Despite efforts by the school, almost all of these were parents of higher-achieving students; the team recognized that it was not getting a full range of parent opinion.

FIGURE 8.3. Visiting Schedule Template, Ocean View High School

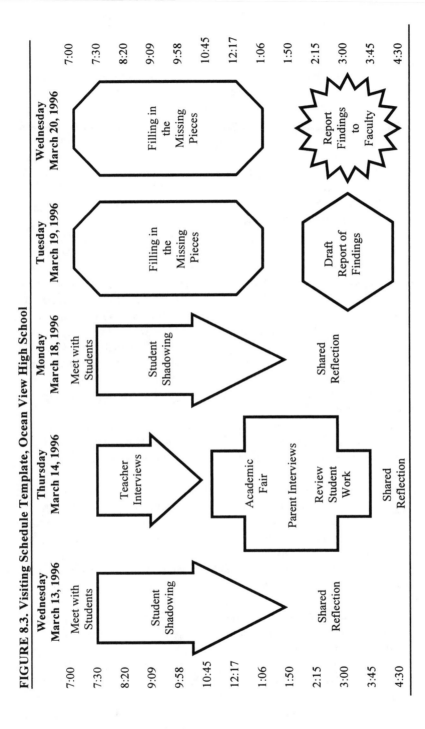

Interviews conducted with teachers in their classrooms provided another chance to discuss student work. However, these opportunities were limited by time and selection of work: In most cases, teachers had chosen to display on the walls only exemplary student work. As with the student shadowing, time to share student work had not been formalized. Even so, information and views from teachers supported by examples of student work made strong impressions on the review team. Comments and insights from teachers supported by examples of student work grounded the conversations and added to an understanding of teaching and learning at the school. Based on feedback from both OVHS faculty and the review team, future visiting team reviews will make student work a focal point for teacher interviews.

Exploring Student Work. The afternoon of the second day was spent at the academic fair, an event designed and intended as a showcase of student work to coincide with parent–teacher conferences. While some teachers chose to display a range of work, the majority of work tended to be exemplary "finished products" and so provided limited insight for the review team into the range of quality or the learning process behind the work. Reviewing the academic fair did provide the visiting team with some additional insights into student expectations at the school, and, in some cases, enlightening conversations arose among students, teachers, and reviewers. In one case, a student explained her English portfolio, based on the New Standards Project, in a form similar to a Tuning Protocol (see Chapter 4).

The review team felt that the observations and discussions of student work in context during the student shadowing and teacher interviews proved significantly more valuable than the out-of-context display at the academic fair.

Analysis and Reporting. The final 2 days were spent filling in missing pieces—visiting, interviewing, and observing across the school. The driving force for these 2 days came from the data analysis sessions that had occurred at the end of each of the first 3 days. In an almost undoable task, the team labored to make sense out of an overwhelming volume of data coming out of the student shadowing, review of student work, and interviews. Through this distilling of evidence, patterns began to emerge that were explored more deeply and confirmed or denied on ensuing days. At the end of the fourth day, the team moved to a hotel, where they worked late into the night, outlining their findings and questions and breaking into pairs to draft sections of the report that included supporting evidence and examples from the data.

On the afternoon of the final day, the entire faculty gathered in the school library for a presentation of the visiting team's findings. The team presented a series of statements correlating to the three Learner-Centered Principles of the Southern Maine Partnership and the six Common Beliefs of Ocean View High

School. Carefully worded without value judgments, these statements were based on interviews, observations, and the artifacts of student work. The final part of the presentation was a series of questions about the school and learning. These questions were not suggestions couched as questions, but concerns and questions that arose out of the shared reflections of the visiting review team.

Following are abbreviated examples of the report statements and evidence plus examples of the questions presented by the visiting team to Ocean View High School:

- The overwhelming majority of students at OVHS reported there was at least one adult to whom they could turn for help.
  —"If I had a problem, I could see _____ or _____. Some teachers want to get out of their class as quickly as possible." (student)
  —"The teachers are great. I went to see _____ at lunch and she put her sandwich down and we talked for 20 minutes." (student)
- In the advanced placement (AP) courses, teachers and students are able to articulate clearly the knowledge and skills expected of students.
  —"We know what we're supposed to know and we're motivated to learn it." (student)
  —"[AP] is about the only area where we know how we're held accountable." (teacher)
- In phase II to IV courses, the teachers' and students' abilities to articulate clearly the required knowledge and skills vary widely.
  —"I don't know what else to get out of this [class] besides the facts." (student)
  —*Student*: "I don't think you graded mine right. I rewrote this five times and got the same grade. What does 'vague' mean?"
  Teacher: "Try again; maybe you'll get a better grade."
- There is evidence that OVHS is attempting to expand the mechanisms used for reporting progress to parents and community.
  —"I call parents regularly. They like to know and the only way I can be sure they get it is to call." (teacher)
  —The Academic Fair is a way to show parents and the community the work students are doing.
  —The additional parent–teacher conference in the spring is an attempt to provide more information on student progress.

The visiting team co-chairs prepared a written report for the school during the following week, and 2 weeks later team members returned to the school for a discussion of the report.

In the weeks and months following the visit, OVHS faculty hotly debated some of the visiting team's findings. Of particular concern was the definition of "student-centered learning" and how teachers promote this ideal. The visiting team had noted the predominant teaching style to be "teacher-directed with few examples of student-centered or hands-on learning." This finding contradicted the school's own impression of its practice and prompted the staff to reconsider their earlier reflective writing.

The school's 1996–1997 focus question became "What is student-centered learning at Ocean View High School?" Based on this focus question, the school has sponsored a series of debates, forums, study groups, student work investigations, and presentations, which have included teachers, administration, parents, and students, to better understand student-centered learning and take action to align practice with what they explicitly value.

REFLECTION—LOOKING BACKWARD AND AHEAD

The work of Ocean View and the other pilot schools affirmed the power of the SQRI process to help schools focus their improvement efforts on teaching and learning and to develop a culture of learner-centered accountability within and among schools. It has also helped to identify several important challenges: (1) Looking at student work continues to be difficult; (2) schools need to develop more effective and meaningful ways to document, monitor, and report student achievement, and (3) the Partnership needs to sustain momentum and support for these schools while spreading these ideas across the Partnership.

Affirmations

Schools involved in the pilot process of the SMP School Quality Review Initiative have noted that the SQRI process has forced them to align all their improvement efforts with their focus question and the Learner-Centered principles; they no longer undertake multiple, disconnected projects.

The success of the SQRI is attributable in our view to several qualities affirmed in the pilot: (1) integration, (2) ownership, and (3) support. In the beginning of this initiative, many school people saw SQRI as yet another innovation that would add to their workload. It has been the SMP staff's explicit intent that this not be one more ill-fated intervention soon replaced or sidetracked by another, but a way for schools to integrate and focus what they were already doing and determine how that contributes to—or doesn't contribute to—their collectively agreed-upon focus. A year later we are hearing comments, such as "Now I see what this really means—we aren't working more, but working smarter."

From the beginning, Partnership members have been the developers and owners of the SQRI process. From the initial conversations through the design and piloting of the process, the SMP staff has continually asked, "Does this make sense? Will it add value to your school's work to improve teaching and learning? Is this sustainable in the daily life of schools?" The Learner-Centered Principles and the "tight–loose" properties of the SQRI design allow schools to work within a supportive framework while defining their own focus and activities. This has been essential to ownership of the work within schools and to the collective commitment of the group of schools and critical friends.

Through the summer institute and ongoing networking meetings, participants have developed new collaborative inquiry skills and tools for carrying out the schools' inquiry plans as well as a support network of critical friends. While it is possible for a school to undertake such a process alone, it is unlikely that a school working alone would have reached the depth of understanding realized by these schools working in collaboration. By working from common principles and a shared framework, and by training school teams and visiting team members together, participants have developed a strong sense of trust and community. The Learner-Centered Principles and the SQRI process serve as a set of agreements about what kinds of schools we are trying to become and about the kinds of evidence and examples visiting teams look for in reviewing teaching and learning in a school.

Focusing on Student Work

Schools in the Partnership have included various processes for exploring student work in their inquiry plans, but in practice they have not yet become central to their inquiry. The Tuning Protocol is used regularly in most of the schools, but often without being grounded in examples of student work. Focusing faculty dialogues around student work is the norm in a few of the elementary schools and is becoming more regular in others. In the second year, there is an increasing focus on student work, both informally and through the use of various protocols.

In addition, examining student work as part of the visiting team review has been problematic. As in the Academic Fair at Ocean View High School, we have encountered numerous problems concerning what work to explore during visiting team reviews and how to look at it. When asked to choose appropriate student work to explore, teachers analyze what work would be appropriate and then set out to collect it. But instead of choosing a range of samples to learn from, teachers may choose examples of what they want to show—a self-fulfilling prophecy. Many visiting team members also felt that student work removed from students working was not as revealing as exploring the work in the classroom context.

We are currently addressing these issues through two changes. Schools conducting a visiting team review now collect student work via a "vertical slice." In this process, a sample group of students collect all materials they work on during one typical school day. All of this student work is shared with the visiting team without a preliminary culling of the material. While this does not provide culminating work from each classroom, it reveals insight into teachers' everyday expectations and the nature and quality of students' work.

In a second innovation, interviews with students and teachers will be conducted using evidence of student work. This may result once again in primarily seeing exemplary pieces of student work, but it will ground the conversations. Taken together, these two changes will provide a better picture of the learning experience of children as seen through their work. Ultimately, this may lead to a deepening of the school's own examination and reflection on student work.

Documenting, Monitoring, and Reporting Student Achievement

Schools have had varied success in the reporting of student achievement. Within schools, teachers are beginning to ask one another difficult questions about student learning and teachers' and the school's responsibility for supporting all students. This requires building a school culture in which teachers feel collectively accountable for students' learning and feel supported in taking the risks involved in examining student work from one another's classes.

Moving outside the school has proven more difficult. Each of the schools involved has made public presentations to parents, school boards, and community members, but occasions of real interchange between schools and their communities around student achievement have been limited. Schools are currently exploring both what to share to develop a meaningful interchange and how to do so. We are seeing some hopeful activities, including broadcasting a weekly show on a local cable channels and increasing meaningful parent participation in various school committees.

We are also working with schools on defining what kinds of information communities want about the effectiveness and progress of schools in supporting students' learning, beyond traditionally accepted indicators such as standardized test scores, and ways to communicate this information. Moving from thinking about communicating to parents about their own children to communicating to the community about the collective performance and progress of the school is a task not completed quickly or easily, but it is becoming more central to the concerns of these schools.

Sustaining and Broadening SQRI's Work

During a project design session exploring dissemination of what we have learned, one member of the group commented, "This should not be about a small group of schools who are part of a project; this should be the way schools do business." We hope that as more educators learn about and use these collaborative inquiry tools and processes, it will indeed move students' work to the center of our school reform efforts and become integral to the way all schools do business. Our challenge during the 1996–1997 school year is to create systems for the ongoing support of the lead schools (the four pilot schools plus an additional middle school in the second year), while also integrating the tools and processes of SQRI with the wider work of the Partnership.

Some of the initiatives we've undertaken to develop the capacity for school-based inquiry across the Partnership include:

- *Providing open access—at multiple levels—to the SQRI tools and processes for all SMP schools.* Schools across the Partnership may participate in workshops, attend networking meetings, or send a team to the summer institute.
- *Supporting school coaching.* The Partnership has explored several school coaching models. One such model will have an outside coach work with both a critical friends group of grades 8–12 teachers to focus on practice and with the school leadership team. The work will be guided by a focus question of the school.
- *Creating learning histories.* Lead schools will pilot the development of histories of their change process. The overview and case studies that result from conducting interviews and collecting data will become tools for collaborative inquiry within the school and be published as part of the ELM World Wide Web site (see below).
- *Exploring connections to accreditation.* Ocean View High School is working with the New England Association of Schools and Colleges to incorporate its SQRI process into its self-study for accreditation.
- *Developing a high school collaborative.* Six high schools in the Partnership are currently exploring ways to integrate arts across the curriculum.
- *Developing an Electronic Learning Marketplace.* In collaboration with one Partnership member district, the Old Orchard Beach Schools, and the University of Southern Maine Department of Engineering, the Partnership will develop a World Wide Web site that will include sample assessments and curriculum, examples of student work, and links to relevant applications and Internet resources. The site will support educators, students, parents, and community members in examining student work and engaging in interactive dialogues about teaching and learning.

Before we actually implemented school-designed Inquiry Plans and conducted both internal and visiting team reviews, we didn't know if all schools would benefit from this intensive look at their work. We learned that schools that are quite sophisticated and reflective about their work are pushed to examine some provocative new questions, and schools that are less sophisticated in their reform efforts also find the experience and feedback enormously valuable in beginning to look at practices. By focusing on what children learn, not on what adults do, we are seeing increased learning opportunities for everybody in our schools.

NOTE

1. Ocean View High School is a created name for a real high school used here to protect the privacy of the school population.

REFERENCE

Wasley, P., Hampel, R., & Clark, R. (1997). *Kids and school reform.* San Francisco: Jossey-Bass.

9

A Richer Picture of Student Work
The Digital Portfolio

DAVID NIGUIDULA

In 1936, Reynold Johnson helped IBM produce a machine called the Markograph. This new device could read pencil marks to determine which circle a test-taker had filled in. The Markograph and its successors made the Scholastic Aptitude Test and other standardized tests possible, since the cost of scoring a test taken by thousands or hundreds of thousands of students was a fraction of what it would cost to score by hand.

Six decades later, students are still armed with No. 2 pencils and are told that "if you need to erase, make sure you erase your answer completely"—an instruction necessary because a machine, not a person, is going to do the scoring. The technology behind the Markograph has certainly proven to be durable; but the technology did not create America's predilection for standardized tests—of aptitude, achievement, intelligence—it simply facilitated it (Lemann, 1995a, b).

This chapter tells the story—or, at least, the beginning of the story—of a new application of technology called the "Digital Portfolio." It, too, is a tool designed to help assess students' abilities and to allow teachers (and others) to gain insights into students' skills and knowledge. Like the Markograph, the Digital Portfolio can be customized to accommodate different users for different purposes. The durability of the Digital Portfolio technology, however, will depend far less on the advancements in hardware and software than on how it is used by teachers and schools.

During the mid-1990s, the Coalition of Essential Schools and the Annenberg Institute for School Reform, both at Brown University, undertook a research project to study how schools adopt and use performance-assessment technology such as the Digital Portfolio. The project was sponsored by IBM and involved six schools from different parts of the country, serving different grade levels and different communities.[1]

From the outset, the study was a partnership of technologists, academics, administrators, teachers, and students. We have learned, together, that "what it takes" to develop Digital Portfolios is similar to what is required for many innovations and reforms in education: attention to the school as a complex system.

Later in this chapter, I consider some elements of the system affected by the introduction of the Digital Portfolio and their potential to support schools in learning from student work and performance. First, though, let me describe the Digital Portfolio and what it is supposed to do.

A RICHER PICTURE OF STUDENT WORK

The Digital Portfolio is a piece of multimedia software that allows students to organize, record, and reflect on their work. It grew out of a 1990–1993 research effort, the Exhibitions Project, conducted by the Coalition of Essential Schools and funded by IBM, which studied school-developed performance-assessment systems, or "exhibitions" (McDonald, 1996). Several of the schools in that study created portfolio-assessment systems.

Collections of student work, they discovered, can provide a much richer picture of a student's abilities than letter grades or test scores. Portfolios, however, also have drawbacks, including trying to figure out what to do with all of the material students collect over a school year or longer.

Enter technology. Computers are extraordinarily helpful tools for collecting, storing, and organizing information. Putting hundreds of pages of student writing (not to mention graphical, audio, or video material) on a hard drive or CD-ROM was very attractive to schools. The alternative seemed to be maintaining mind-boggling numbers of file cabinets. The technology here seemed to meet a very specific need.

Those involved in developing the Digital Portfolio, however, wanted to do more than automate the process of storing student work. Electronic archives may be helpful, but the Digital Portfolio was designed to help schools use the student work to inform their processes of reform. We drew on a school-change "strategy" from the Exhibitions Project called "planning backward" (McDonald, 1992), which encourages a school to articulate its vision of what students should know and be able to do upon graduation; establish exhibitions for students to demonstrate that they have that skills and knowledge; and then arrange the other systems in the school so that every student has the opportunity to complete those exhibitions and, thus, fulfill the school's vision of what a graduate should be.

We made three critical design decisions in developing the Digital Portfolio, based on the ideas of planning backward. First, *the vision should be the lens for looking at student work*. As we shall see in the next section, the Digital Portfolio's "main menu" consists of the school's goals for each student. When students store their work in a portfolio, they need to indicate what part of the school's vision they are demonstrating.

Second, *the student work itself must be prominent*. When a reader of the portfolio asks to see an example of a student's communication skills, the software shows actual student writing or oral presentations. Judgments the reader makes of the student's abilities needs to be based on seeing the actual work, rather than just a letter-grade proxy of it.

Third, *the student work must be presented in context*. Each of the schools in our study asked students to add some additional information to accompany the work in the portfolio. Contextual information varied from school to school. Most of the schools asked students to include the original assignment. All the schools asked students to include some kind of evaluation of the work. These included self-reflections, teacher evaluations and comments, and comments from third parties (for example, panelists at a student presentation).

A WALK THROUGH THE DIGITAL PORTFOLIO

In the research project, Michelle Riconscente and I developed a Digital Portfolio software prototype for each of the six schools in the project. Each school's portfolio was structured slightly differently, according to its visions and goals, but they shared a number of characteristics.

Each Digital Portfolio represents one student's work. The figures that follow show the portfolio of Evan, a senior at one of the high schools in the project. When you open the portfolio (see Figure 9.1), you see a photo of Evan and a set of buttons that invite you to learn more about the student in three ways:

- Who am I as a Communicator?
- Who am I as a Researcher?
- Who am I as a Problem Solver?

These three buttons correspond to the school's vision of what students should know and be able to do, across the disciplines. (The school actually thinks of these three questions as components of the larger question, "Who am I as a learner?") There is also a fourth button, labeled Individual, that allows

FIGURE 9.1. Main Menu of a Digital Student Portfolio

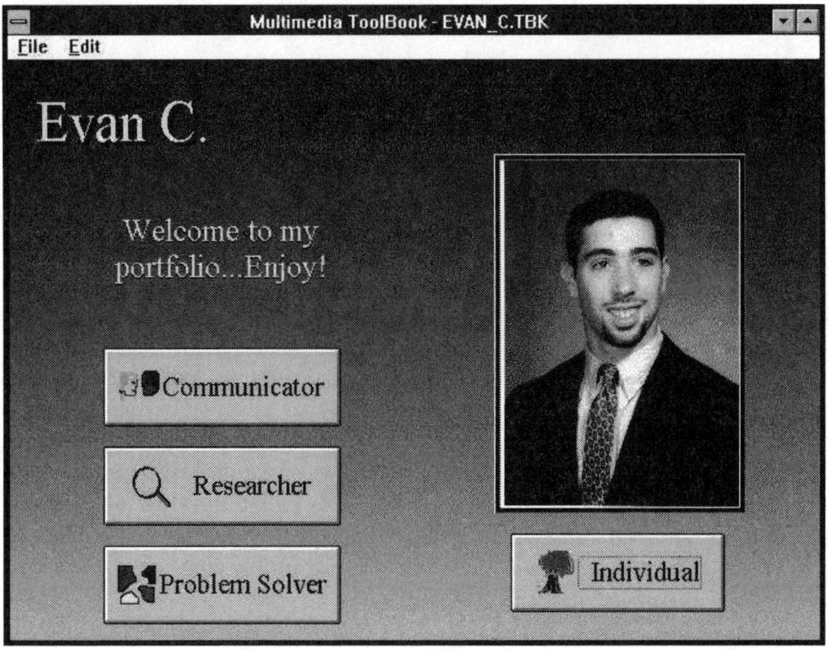

the student to display information about him- or herself that might not fit neatly in any of the categories above.

Clicking on any of the four buttons on the main menu screen takes you to a second menu (see Figure 9.2). This menu contains a list of student "entries" that show the student's abilities as a communicator, researcher, problem solver, or individual.

The entries can be sorted by curricular area. Selecting one of the checkboxes in the top right corner (labeled Humanities, Math/Science/Technology, Wellness/Health, and Fine Arts) shows only those entries that relate to that area. Figure 9.2, for example, shows entries that answer the question "Who am I as a Problem Solver?" The "M" next to an entry indicates that the work is from the Math/Science/Technology area.

The reader may click on the names of any of these entries to see the student work and its context. In Figure 9.3, we see a lab from a physics class. The screen contains several windows with components of the student work, which may be text, graphics, audio, or video. In this case, the components include a lab report describing an experiment dealing with the motion of pendulums, a set of calculations, a diagram showing how the experiment was set up, and a video containing the actual experiment.

FIGURE 9.2. List of Entries Demonstrating a Goal ("Who am I as a problem solver?")

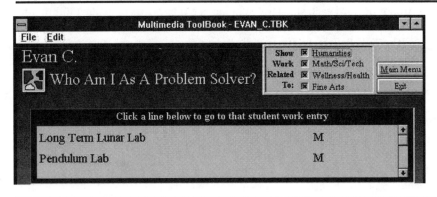

FIGURE 9.3. Sample Entry from a Digital Student Portfolio

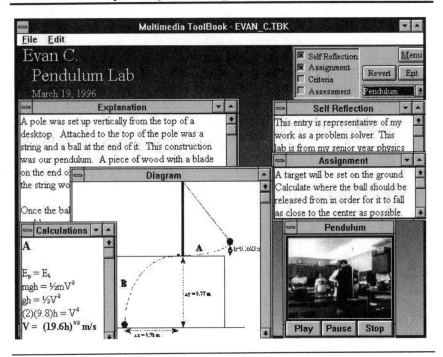

Additional windows provide information to help put the work in context. The design team of faculty and students that helped develop this school's Digital Portfolios decided each student would include four pieces of context information for each portfolio entry.

The *Self Reflection* allows the student to describe why this entry belongs in the portfolio and how this entry helps answer the question, "Who am I as a Communicator/Problem Solver/Researcher?" Usually this is a short written statement, although it could easily be a video or audio clip.

The *Assignment* describes what the student was asked to do. The information here might be the text of the assignment originally written by the teacher or a summary written by the student.

The *Criteria* lists the standards that are to be met by this particular exhibition. In taking the idea of "planning backward" seriously, the design team wanted a portfolio reader to know that each entry was assessed against a set of standards that were locally created and reflect the school's vision. (Of course, externally developed criteria could also be integrated, for example, from state curriculum frameworks or standards such as those developed by the National Council of Teachers of Mathematics.)

The *Assessment* contains assessments from teachers or other judges, such as peers or parents. In theory, other readers of the portfolio, such as a college admissions counselor, could add their own assessments.

VARIATIONS ON THE THEME

The Digital Portfolio was customized to support each school's assessment system. The variations in the software primarily occurred in two places: the main menu, which established the school's vision, and the kinds of information that helped to put the work in context.

The vision from the high school we've already looked at has two dimensions: the opening screen showed a set of skills (communication, problem solving, research) that extend across the school's curricular areas, as shown in Figure 9.2.

A second high school defined 19 goals, and a third had created a list of seven interdisciplinary domains. The project's other high school incorporated the list of goals and learning expectations determined by its state's education reform legislation. The middle school in the study listed eight skills, and the elementary school developed four "selves" (a "social" self, an "academic" self, an "artistic" self, and a "problem-solving" self).

The other primary variation among the Digital Portfolios was in the context-building information. For example, in Figure 9.3 we saw that students were asked to include the Assignment, a Self Reflection, the Assessments, and Criteria for each entry.

The high school that structured its portfolio around state-mandated goals asked students to indicate which of the 75 "learner expectations" each entry met. The technology thus allowed a single entry to be linked to any number of menu buttons corresponding to the school's goals. Schools that have tried to show the same cross-listing using paper portfolios end up with many duplicate copies of student work or a flurry of Post-it notes with cross-references.

All the schools had some area where a student could enter a self-assessment. In most cases, that meant the student explained why this particular entry belonged in the portfolio. At one school, students were asked to consider *all* the entries linked to a particular button on the main menu and one of the school's seven domains, and to write a cover letter describing how the *collection* of entries represented mastery of that domain. At the elementary school, students completed an "entry slip" that asked questions such as "Did you do this work alone or in a group?" and "What subject area does this entry represent?"

Other schools included different information. At one high school, for example, teachers were asked to assess each piece of work as above, at, or below grade level. At the middle school, each entry was linked to a skill and to one of eight "commonalties," for example, aesthetics. The commonalties were proposed by Ernest Boyer (1981) as themes around which interdisciplinary curriculum might be arranged.

Each school has continued to refine its notion of what should be included in the portfolio, reflecting the schools' evolving ideas of what they value in student work and what constitute good indicators of student progress. The software can then be modified to reflect the school's current thinking.

IMPLICATIONS: CHANGING A SCHOOL'S SYSTEMS

The Digital Portfolio, like most educational technologies, will not inherently change a school's systems. It might even act as a distraction from substantive change if it is adopted primarily for its technological dazzle. By creating a tool that allows a school to articulate its vision and allows students to demonstrate their progress towards meeting that vision, the Digital Portfolio could, instead, help schools learn from their students' work to enhance their own capacities for supporting student learning. The Digital Portfolio could also act as a kind of *provocation* for school change, that is, its development could raise questions and highlight important areas of a school's work for it to consider.

Digital Portfolios might easily be viewed as another technology project. However, schools that want to use it as a tool for change need to look beyond the technology and consider (at least) five areas of the school's operations:

- An articulation of the school's *vision* of what a graduate should know and be able to do

- The development of an *assessment* system that allows teachers and others to describe "good work" according to the school's vision and encourages students to demonstrate good work
- The *logistics* required to allow students, faculty, and others the time and space to work with the information in the portfolios
- The infrastructure, both in equipment and in people, to support the use of *technology*
- A school *culture* in which student work is regularly examined in order to improve the school's abilities to help all students meet the vision

The next sections briefly describe the five areas in turn; of course, in the daily life of a school they are not so easy to separate. For each, I include some of the questions for the schools raised—or underscored—in the process of developing the Digital Portfolio.

Vision

What should a student know and be able to do? The Digital Portfolio's main menu requires students to organize their work around the vision that the school has defined. This means that to use the Digital Portfolio well, the school has to articulate the vision in the first place. When students begin work with their own Digital Portfolios, they first see the main menu with a set of goals that they know they will have to fulfill and a number of empty slots that will eventually hold their work. As one student put it, "It's like an M&M without the chocolate."

The process of adding entries to the portfolio brings the vision to life. A student, with work in hand (or, more precisely, on disk), might start to enter the work into the portfolio but stop because of uncertainty about which of the school's goals were demonstrated by this particular entry. On a number of occasions, teachers at the research sites reported that helping students consider where an entry fit in the portfolio forced them (the teachers) to consider what the vision truly meant. Sometimes this meant clarifying the language of a particular goal; sometimes it led to a rethinking of the vision itself.

The Digital Portfolio gives schools a new way of looking at their vision and expectations. The tool also gives students a chance to interact with—and interpret—that vision by connecting their own work to this ideal of what a graduate should know and be able to do. This interaction contributes to understanding the vision as a "living document," affecting and responding to the work that students and teachers do.

Assessment

How can students demonstrate the vision? In the development of the Digital Portfolio, the research team asked each of the schools to consider what kinds of entries should be in the portfolio. Asked another way: How would students select entries that demonstrated the school's vision and goals?

In some of the schools, criteria for selecting entries were very clear; students and teachers often talked about what was expected of students and how their work tied to those expectations. In others, the criteria were often unclear. Students sensed that teachers were still grappling with the vision statement, which made it confusing for students to determine what entries belonged in the portfolio. For example, one school's students described a class in which almost all their work was done on worksheets, which students felt was not the kind of work they wanted to have in their portfolios.

Why do we collect student work? Portfolios are currently in vogue; in various forms, they have been associated with many of the school reform efforts of the 1980s and 1990s. Sometimes, however, schools adopt portfolios without being clear about the reasons for asking students to collect their work.

In one of the districts developing the Digital Portfolio, faculty provoked a discussion about portfolios as ways for students to celebrate their work *versus* ways to assess or evaluate it. Indeed, across the project schools, the Digital Portfolios were becoming places for students to demonstrate their accomplishments as *they* saw them, not necessarily places to demonstrate anyone else's evaluation of the work.

While most of the work entered had already been assessed by a teacher, the schools did not emphasize the evaluation side of the portfolio entry. Nor did they generally create new opportunities for readers of the portfolio to review and assess the work (although the technology supported adding new assessments at any time).

While this phenomenon indicated a need for more opportunities to celebrate, or "show off," student work, it also indicated that teachers were not yet prepared to use the Digital Portfolio as a tool for analyzing student work—both for strengths and weaknesses—as part of the school's improvement process.

What audiences are most important to us? The motivation for students to put together Digital Portfolios is often tied to the audience: Who is going to read this portfolio? We discovered that for a number of students the primary audience was themselves. Having a record of one's own accomplishments was motivation enough to put in the effort required to create a portfolio. They considered the portfolio to be their property and they could also show it to whomever they chose.

For other students and for many teachers, an external audience seemed to be necessary. They wanted to know that the portfolio would be used for something—a grade, a piece of a college application, a state requirement. At one high school, students volunteered to put together Digital Portfolios. While the majority of students began the project, only about 10% to 15% of the student body continued to enter work throughout the year on their own initiative. One reason for the fall-off was that no definite audience had been defined.

There are many potential audiences, including parents, next year's teachers, college admissions officers, and employers. The researchers have begun discussions with organizations representing some of these groups. As these audiences develop the capacity to review Digital Portfolios, the teachers' role may switch from being a recipient of the portfolio to being an editor, guiding students to reach other readers.

How do we know what's good? The Digital Portfolio, like most multimedia endeavors, can be very glitzy. Readers who first see a student's compilation of work are often impressed by how this information can be organized around a few button clicks and are thrilled to see student work containing video and audio clips. At this early stage, the actual completion of a Digital Portfolio is a significant accomplishment.

As the novelty wears off, we are left with the question of quality. What makes for a good portfolio? The quality of the original student work is obviously a major factor in determining the quality of an overall portfolio. Students are encouraged, and sometimes explicitly told, by teachers to include particular entries in their portfolios. In almost all cases, students' work was assessed by teachers before the student considered whether to include it in the portfolio; typically, entries with higher grades or more encouraging feedback were the ones the students selected.

But what makes a good portfolio distinct from a collection of good work? And is the distinction important?

The students who created portfolios noted a few components of portfolios that they thought were good: They showed effort (i.e., someone "put a lot of time into it"), they had a significant amount of material, and they used different media (graphics, audio, and video) to make the portfolio "more interesting."

Reading multimedia texts is a new skill, and portfolio authors and readers alike will need to learn the difference between a slick presentation and the actual substance of the student work.

In the future, schools may create "benchmarks" for Digital Portfolios, using earlier examples to illustrate (for other students) what can be done, what is minimally expected, and what would be considered excellent. As with all these questions, the school's vision should offer the primary guide. Digital Portfolios will surely become better-looking; it is important that they also tell us more and more about actual student learning.

Logistics

Who will select the work? As the study progressed, it became clear that many students wanted their Digital Portfolios to be personal records of their accomplishments. The portfolio was a reflection of who they were at that point in time, and thus the collection of work needed to represent them.

Students selected the work, but the influence of the teachers was also very clear. Students selected work that their teachers thought was "good" in the first place. The grade or the comments might be an indication that an item might belong in the portfolio. In those cases in which students were already putting together a portfolio for a particular class or subject area, these teachers provided general guidance on what kinds of work belonged in the portfolio and often guided students in making specific selections.

In several of the schools, students had an "adviser," whose role was to help them with their overall academic career. The advisers, who had gotten to know the students over time, provided help with the overall structure of the portfolio, helping the student to see what elements of his or her career should be represented.

By and large, students appreciated the relative autonomy of selecting pieces for their portfolios, but they also wanted guidance from adults. The balance between the two remains an important question for the schools.

When will information be digitized? Who will do it? If a Digital Portfolio is going to be a cumulative record of a student's work, schools must consider the time, space, and resources that will be necessary for all students to work on their portfolios.

The Digital Portfolio software assumes that the items to be entered have been digitized through some other program (a word processor, scanning software, etc.), which takes more time than it does to enter the information into the portfolio. Most students quickly realized that it would be easier if the original works were created on the computer in the first place.

All six schools in the project began their Digital Portfolio work with small pilot groups of students. Schools have told us that the best students for a pilot are those who can handle things when they go wrong. This has less to do with their actual abilities (real or perceived) than with the willingness to experiment and to deal with the "bugs" inevitable in each version of the software.

The schools needed to allocate time for students to digitize their work. This required developing structures that were often different from the regular school schedule.

At one of the larger high schools, for example, the computing coordinator established a class on Digital Portfolios. He made the analogy to the yearbook or the newspaper; students enrolled in this class would be responsible for helping the rest of the student body put together their Digital Portfolios. The students on the Digital Portfolio staff would learn enough about multimedia to help the other students in the building. Pairs of Digital Portfolio staffers were assigned to English classes, each of which had scheduled computer time at least once a week. The coordinator bought more time—and benefited from the enthusiasm of the students—by scheduling the Digital Portfolio class during the extended lunch period.

As schools become more serious about students collecting, organizing, and reflecting on their work, they will need to address how time, as well as space, is allocated, so that students can give their work the attention it deserves—and eat lunch, too.

Technology

What hardware, software, and networking will the school need? A school cannot begin to think seriously about Digital Portfolios until it has some technology to use. We developed the Digital Portfolio for computers that were on the high end at the time but have since been surpassed.[2]

While the software does not require special technology, we recognize that most schools do not have access to up-to-date equipment; according to one study, as of 1995 most schools were still using mid-1970s technology (Quality Education Data, 1995).

Given this reality, and the limited budgets that schools face, the specific kinds of hardware and software matter much less than the strategic thinking for deploying that equipment. One school in the project, for example, set aside a few computers as Digital Portfolio stations. In this relatively small school, placing those machines in a strategic location (in this case, a room off the library) made it easy for students working on portfolios to pop in as needed. In another school, students spent most of their day in a few rooms with a team of teachers; the machines in that school were distributed so that each team of about 80 students and four teachers had access to five or six computers in the team's classrooms.

We did not find a magic formula to determine how many computers a school needs to put together Digital Portfolios. Generally, the schools made more progress with implementing a Digital Portfolio system when they integrated the computing tools into the school's natural work patterns. Whoever needs to get to equipment should be able to get to it easily. Which leads to the next important question: Whose portfolio is it, anyway?

Who are the primary users of the equipment? Who is the author of the portfolio, and who are the readers? The assumptions about how Digital Portfolios will be created and examined help to determine how equipment will be used in the school.

All the schools in the project considered students as the primary creators of the Digital Portfolios. After all, the work central to the portfolio is the work created by students. Each of the schools decided that students would organize the work within the portfolio and use the software to create their portfolios.

Students developing portfolios need access to equipment to create portfolios—and so do teachers if they are to review them. If we add parents or other reviewers to the process, then schools not only have to rethink technology in classrooms but have to rethink how technology can link classrooms to the outside world. Some of the study schools arranged "drop-in" facilities in public spaces (such as the library), where students or teachers could work with the portfolios and where visitors could view them. Some also enhanced their networking throughout the building to encourage teacher usage.

Schools, then, need to consider their "wiring" when determining how students and teachers will work with Digital Portfolios. As McDonald (1996) points out, the discussion of physical wiring can point out the issues of a school's figurative wiring—the flows of information and processes of communication within the school. As the school addresses the question of who will use the equipment, it is also addressing the issue of who needs to communicate with whom and what information students and teachers, and others, need to access.

Who will support the system? The most critical link we observed in the development of the technological system is not the hardware or the software or the networking—it's the support. Two kinds of support are crucial: technical support to develop and maintain the machinery, and leadership to ensure that the resources are available to maintain the technical support.

The computing coordinator is often the one person in the building who knows the entire technology system. The coordinator will know not just where the machines are located and how they are connected, but also where to send them to be fixed or what support might be available from a district or regional office.

Like many computing coordinators (Sheingold & Hadley, 1990), those in the study schools were willing to experiment and learn on their own. They saw exciting possibilities for the use of the Digital Portfolio and also saw it as "leverage"—a way to get more students and/or teachers to become involved with technology.

Still, putting the Digital Portfolio technology together was no simple task: A single computer might need to be assembled from a dozen different components. Wiring the school required coordinators to string wires through crawl spaces or over drop ceilings—and to go back if the connection wasn't quite right.

What makes this effort more extraordinary is that it was done *on the side*. Of the original four coordinators in this effort, three had regular teaching loads, while the fourth had other administrative duties in multiple schools. (In the other two schools, a coordinator was brought in full-time, but essentially as a teacher's aide, not as a faculty member.) On paper, each could turn to a district or regional center for technical support, but in only one case could the computing coordinator steadily rely on this source for help.

With so much dependent on the computing coordinator, it is not a surprise that the relationship of the coordinator to the rest of the school became a critical link in the development of a technological method of examining student work. In a few cases, the Digital Portfolio became identified as the computer coordinator's exclusive project rather than something that involved all of the faculty.

This is where the other form of support comes in: administrative leadership. In the 20 years since the advent of the personal computer in the schools, millions, if not billions, of dollars have been spent on various educational technology projects that had very little impact beyond the teachers and students who were directly involved. When a technological innovation—or any innovation, for that matter—is limited to a particular teacher or department, it is unlikely to have any impact once that teacher leaves or the project ends. The principal, though, can help to connect the technological innovations to a school's overall mission and efforts for reform.

The administrative leadership finds and provides resources (equipment, money, personnel, etc.). Perhaps just as importantly, principals and superintendents provide visibility and political protection for a project. In one of the study districts, for example, the administrator continually brought updates and new versions of the portfolio to faculty and community meetings. These sessions served two purposes: to help the faculty and community understand what had been done thus far and to bring those groups into the conversation to help shape the next steps. Given the inevitable snafus in technological innovations, administrators need to help create an atmosphere of enthusiastic patience to allow the computer coordinator and others the room to create the necessary infrastructure.

CULTURE

How will the school discuss and reflect on student work? Who will be in the discussion? In an earlier section, I listed some of the potential audiences for the portfolios beyond the students and their teachers: parents, teachers from other schools, college admissions officers. If those audiences are to use the portfolios well, schools will need to develop structures that support examination of and reflection on the work in the portfolios.

All the schools have asked students to make some kind of presentation of their Digital Portfolios. At the middle school, for example, parents were invited to a special open house where all the students put their portfolios on display. At some of the high schools in the project, the students have presented their work to audiences of parents, community leaders, or school board members.

These presentations can also provide the opportunity for detailed feedback. At one of the high schools, the Digital Portfolio was used to demonstrate numerous students' work at the school's annual External Review, in which faculty members and invited guests discussed the school's goals and accomplishments. This session offered particular feedback on the Digital Portfolio—both on its structure and on the kinds of student work that was exhibited.

In one district, teachers from schools across the district took part in a Tuning Protocol (see Chapter 4) to share and critique the design for each school's Digital Portfolio. While the focus here was the design, it is easy to imagine such a session using mature Digital Portfolios to focus on questions of standards for student work and performance.

These sessions are early examples of how the Digital Portfolio can allow students and their teachers to benefit from other perspectives on student work. Such opportunities are likely to expand as schools support more and more public presentation of, and reflection on, student work. As the technology develops and students and teachers become more facile with its use, schools must struggle with the more difficult question of how to provide students and teachers with opportunities to examine and reflect on their work—alone and with others. The Digital Portfolio alone cannot make this happen, but it can contribute to a school culture where students' work is integral to the school's vision and change process.

NOTES

1. This research was funded primarily by IBM under the project title "Tools for Accountability." The company generously provided funds to Brown University for this research and grants of equipment to each of six schools to aid in the investigation: Eastern High School of Jefferson County, Kentucky; Thayer High School of Winchester, New Hampshire; University Heights High School of the Bronx, New York; and the three schools of the Croton-Harmon School District of Croton-on-Hudson, New York: Carrie E. Tompkins Elementary School, Pierre van Cortlandt Middle School, and Croton-Harmon High School.

An earlier version of the portfolio, showing an example from Eastern High School, is described in Niguidula (1993). Sample portfolios, plus descriptions of the school's processes in creating Digital Portfolios, are available on CD-ROM (Niguidula, 1997) from the Annenberg Institute for School Reform, Brown University.

2. The Digital Portfolio was written using Asymetrix Multimedia Toolbook for Windows 3.1; while the portfolio could be run on a machine with 8 megabytes of memory and a 386 processor, it was recommended that schools use machines with at least 16 MB of RAM and a 486 or Pentium processor.

REFERENCES

Boyer, E. (1981). *Quest for common learning.* New York: Carnegie Foundation.
Lemann, N. (1995a, September). The great sorting. *Atlantic Monthly,* pp. 84–100.

Lemann, N. (1995b, August). The structure of success in America. *Atlantic Monthly*, pp. 41–60.

McDonald, J. (1992). *Steps in planning backwards: Early lessons from the schools* (Studies on Exhibitions, No. 5). Providence, RI: Coalition of Essential Schools, Brown University.

McDonald, J. (1996). *Redesigning school: Lessons for the 21st century*. San Franciso: Jossey-Bass.

Niguidula, D. (1993). *The Digital Portfolio: A richer picture of student performance* (Studies on Exhibitions, No. 13). Providence, RI: Coalition of Essential Schools, Brown University.

Niguidula, D. (1997). *A Digital Portfolio sampler*. CD-ROM. Providence, RI: Annenberg Institute for School Reform, Brown University. See also the Annenberg Institute's Web site—www.aisr.brown.edu

Quality Education Data. (1995). World Wide Web site—www.qeddata.com

Sheingold, K., & Hadley, M. (1990). *Accomplished teachers: Integrating computers into classroom practice*. New York: Center for Technology in Education, Bank Street College of Education.

Afterword

What's in It for the Kids?

Helen Featherstone

At the beginning of Chapter 1, Steve Seidel recalls how uncertain he felt each time Elizabeth Parillo, one of the 10 teachers in the group using the Collaborative Assessment protocols, asked how the work she and her colleagues were doing with Seidel would benefit her third- and fourth-grade students:

> I always felt quite inadequate trying to provide an answer to her question. The truth was that I didn't know if sitting together for these many hours talking about specific pieces of writing would, in fact, translate into something positive for her students.

The essays in this book describe a variety of projects that put student work far closer to the center of the enterprise of schooling that it usually is; together they help us to see something about the ways in which collective inquiry that is centered around students' work and learning might alter schools and, with them, students' experience. They offer some answers to Parillo's question. They also help us to see what's hard about doing this sort of work.

CREATING AND EDUCATING AUDIENCES

In the classrooms in which most of today's teachers passed their school days, hardly anyone except a teacher—and occasionally a parent—ever read children's written work. A central insight of the Bay Area Writing Project and of related efforts to reform the teaching of writing in U.S. schools is that audience matters: Writing is a communicative act, and young people will enjoy and invest in their own writing more if they see others responding to it. Persuaded both by their own experiences in summer writing institutes and by the eloquence of writers such as Donald Graves and Lucy Calkins, many teachers have tried, in the past two decades, to expand audiences for their students' work. But creating new audiences is a complex undertaking: Many a teacher has listened in frustration as his or her elementary students, ignoring differences in genre, subject matter, and intent, addressed the same formulaic questions to each of a series of occupants of the classroom Author's Chair: "Where did you get the idea to write about _____?" "How did you decide to write a [poem/ story/play]?" These content-free questions provide the young authors with no evidence that their "listeners" had heard their words. It is hard to believe that such responses will propel writers to new heights or contribute to their confidence in their own efforts. Apparently audiences, like writers, need to learn some new skills in order to do their jobs well.

The essays in this book describe projects that reeducate existing audiences for student work and/or expand these audiences. Although audiences for children's writing have grown in the past 20 years, teachers are still the first and most important audience. Teachers read just about everything that students write in school (they sometimes even read texts not intended for their eyes—notes passed during math class, names inscribed lovingly in the margins of notebooks), and they almost always convey some sort of judgment of the quality of the work. Their questions and comments usually help to influence both the author's revisions and his own assessment of the value of the text. Their decisions often shape the way in which parents and other children see and respond to that work, determining, for example, whether a child will read a poem aloud to classmates and, if she does, the length and shape of the ensuing discussion. The Collaborative Assessment Conference is about the education of this critical audience: Through the conversations Seidel describes, 10 elementary teachers learned to look at children's poems, drawings, and stories with deeper interest and excitement and to respond to them with more astute and generative questions. They learned to appreciate important aspects of the writing task that had not been visible to them before.

The University Heights Roundtables (Chapter 6) create new—and important—audiences by bringing parents and community members into the school building for the purpose of reviewing portfolios. The Roundtables also create audiences by educating—and therefore changing and re-creating—this important audience of intimates: Over the course of the high school career of the senior who identifies herself pseudonymously as Anna, her mother and boyfriend get multiple chances to listen as others respond to her portfolio and presentations. On occasions of this sort, participants learn from one another what to focus on and how to describe their own responses to the work on the table.

In an important way the Roundtables shape what those present say—and probably what they learn to look for and at in the work of a high school student.

They may also influence the ways in which high school students see their own work. First of all, the norms of the event require students to go beyond the work on the table and to speak analytically about their learning and development by connecting these to the artifacts in the portfolio. In addition, the student listens as people who matter to her comment on a part of her life that they would not ordinarily see. A forum in which a high school girl presents her research project to a group of adults and hears her boyfriend declare publicly that she "has already had a major impact on our school community" and "will always be known as a role model here" has the potential to change the place of academic work in her life.

Because most of us reach out to our audiences, trying—either consciously or unconsciously—to provide them with work that will elicit the sort of positive response we crave (was it actually Gertrude Stein who said, "a writer needs three things: praise, praise, praise"?), the creation and education of audiences is critical to the development of student work.

In one of the early meetings of the Gloucester group described in Chapter 1, Cherylann Parker told Seidel: "I want them to move beyond simply saying 'I like this' or 'I don't like that.' I want them to look deeper, to think harder about why and what they like" (Seidel, 1995, p. 102).

Three years after the meetings described by Seidel, Parker elaborated on the way in which she had adapted the Collaborative Assessment Conference for use in her own classroom in order to help her fifth-graders respond more thoughtfully to one another's writing. Parker saw the protocols as a potential tool for enhancing classroom conversation about student work.

In fact, engaging students in close examination of one another's work affected the quality of that work profoundly. Her fifth-graders' polite, respectful questions "put pressure on [students] in a way that I could never put pressure as a teacher. Because the minute I put a grade on something, or said 'This isn't good enough, go back and redo it,' I'd get this incremental stuff—'What will she let me get by with?' Whereas when the kids would say, 'You might want to revise this to do such and such next time,' it was a completely different kind of conversation. And then they started competing to do revisions" (Featherstone, in press). Fifth-graders responded to serious sustained attention to their work with serious sustained effort.

Part of learning to see and appreciate—to be a good audience—is learning to wonder. Just as the opera buff asks questions about a performance of *Tosca* that do not occur to a first-time operagoer, the teacher who has spent countless Thursday afternoons examining a few drawings, poems, or stories and listening as colleagues describe and reflect on them has better questions than the teacher who has never had a chance to do this kind of collaborative work. "You are

FIGURE A.1. Cycle of Relationships

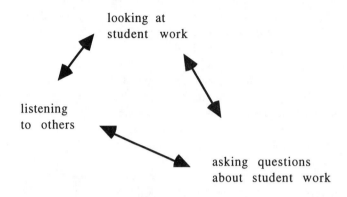

looking at
student work

listening
to others

asking questions
about student work

practicing your ability to wonder about children's work," Seidel told the Gloucester teachers. Reading the accounts of these structured conversations about children's work, we might posit a recursive, circular relationship between examining children's work, raising questions about the work, and listening to the ideas that others have as they describe and reflect on this work (see Figure A.1). Wondering, then, is both the fruit and the stuff of such conversations.

Locating Students' Strengths/Building Respect for Students' Work

All these protocols for close looking at students' work build teachers' respect for their students' strengths and accomplishments. Chapter 2, Beverly Falk's account of the Primary Language Record (PLR), provides multiple examples of the ways in which the PLR's emphasis on what children *are* learning, *can* do, and *do* know help teachers to discover their students' interests and to design instructional strategies that play to their strengths. She contrasts the PLR with more conventional assessments, quoting from 7-year-old Miguel's Individual Education Plan (IEP):

> Miguel does not demonstrate strong word-attack skills.
> Miguel does not read multisyllabic words.
> Miguel does not recognize content-related vocabulary.

After noticing that practically every sentence in the IEP contained the words "Miguel does not," Falk notes that Miguel's new special education teacher, Lucy Lopez, was not astonished to read in the last paragraph that "Miguel has a negative self-concept." The PLR helped Lopez to construct a very different portrait of Miguel's literacy learning:

> Miguel enjoys looking at books and can retell stories. He memorized most of his favorite nursery rhymes with intonation and sang some of them. When reading, he points to each word as he reads. He runs his fingers across the page when reading unfamiliar texts and uses picture clues to read unknown words. His sight vocabulary is developing through the use of "key words."

Lopez's observations helped her see the wide variety of ways in which Miguel's interests and activities support his literacy learning; not surprisingly, they also helped her to design successful lessons.

Discourse about schooling includes a lot of easy talk about the importance of respecting children. But as David Hawkins (1974) explains in his seminal essay on the critical role of subject matter in the relationship of teacher and child:

> To have respect for children is more than recognizing their potentialities in the abstract, it is also to seek out and value their accomplishments— however small these may be by the standards of adults. (p. 48)

Hawkins argues that robust substantive respect is possible only when teachers have opportunities to see a child engage with the world in ways that reveal what is unique and individual about a child's ideas and his or her approach to the world. The conversations that employ the Descriptive Review, the Collaborative Assessment Conference (CAC), and the Primary Language Record formats create a context in which teachers develop the skills needed to see what children reveal as they work.

After the Gloucester teachers' first CAC (Chapter 1), Julie Carter wrote, "It made me see a lot more than I would just sitting alone. And the more you looked, the more you saw." Looking back on the group's six meetings, Seidel was able to see the consequences of this New Seeing: "It seemed that the more the teachers saw in a piece of writing, the more they recognized the complexity of the child's effort and accomplishments." Working with the CAC had deepened the teachers' respect for children by sharpening their interest in children's work and hence their ability to see what children were achieving.

The Descriptive Review format that guides the work of the Philadelphia Teachers' Learning Cooperative (TLC; Chapter 3) focuses the attention of Lynne Strieb and her colleagues on the strengths of the child she is worried about—strengths that can fade into invisibility in the context of a reading lesson. As Strieb describes, answers questions, and passes around samples of Matthew's work, she and her colleagues see more and more clearly that Matthew is a child with extraordinary talent. "His work with markers is unbelievable!" exults one colleague; another connects Matthew's frustrations with reading to his intellectual and artistic gifts, recalling two of her own students: "They are drawers, thinkers, see-ers. They seem distressed by the discrepancy between their ability to grasp reading and their ability in other areas. . . . Kids who are good in art often have trouble learning to read if they are spirited, excited boys." A third teacher focuses on Matthew's extraordinary success with origami and suggests ways in which his reading instruction might build on his genius for working with step-by-step instructions. As we listen to the TLC teachers talk about Matthew, his abilities come into clearer and clearer focus, and their relevance to his literacy learning becomes more and more apparent. Along with the TLC, we construct a sturdy respect for Matthew as a learner.

CRAFTING MORE WORTHWHILE ASSIGNMENTS

Talking about their classroom work with descriptive processes, the Gloucester teachers linked portfolios to projects: "If you don't have projects," asked Parker, somewhat rhetorically, "what are you going to put in the portfolios? And if you have projects and no portfolios, where do you put the finished projects?" (Featherstone, in press). In fact, portfolios that hold only spelling quizzes and multiplication worksheets are all too common. However, as the essays in this volume make clear, thoughtful discussions of portfolios and the practice of portfolio assessment can provoke discussion of what makes a good assignment.

In Croton-Harmon, for example, teachers noticed that they and their students often selected different pieces as examples of "best work" for inclusion in portfolios: Teachers usually chose papers in which students demonstrated mastery of targeted skills, while students "tend[ed] to pick as their best work free-writing samples in which they [were] allowed to be more creative." According to King and Campbell-Allan (Chapter 7), this discovery led teachers to ask why their students found some assignments restrictive and unsatisfying; this exploration prompted them to think hard about assignments and to try to "balance the need for student choice and their need to have writing samples that demonstrate a range of language skills." David Niguidula (Chapter 9) reports that students in another school expressed reluctance to include worksheets in their portfolios—a preference that excluded just about all the work done for one of their classes; systematic omissions of this sort ought to provoke some soul-searching on the part of teachers.

The hour that the Gloucester teachers and Seidel (Chapter 1) spent examining and describing Jessica's poem "May is" deepened their appreciation of Jessica's accomplishment and their interest in her as a poet and an artist. Experiences of this sort encourage teachers to believe that their students will use open-ended assignments to work on problems that they have set for themselves. In doing so, they encourage teachers to reduce the proportion of assignments that prescribe the work too closely and rob students of the satisfactions they get from doing "best work."

THE SUSTENANCE OF THOUGHTFUL TEACHERS

"It is very hard to find a place to have a serious conversation about teaching that lasts more than a few minutes," observes Betsy Wice of the Philadelphia Teachers' Learning Cooperative (Chapter 3). Most of those seeking to change schools agree: Teachers, school reformers, and scholars all complain that schools and staffrooms provide little support for inquiry about teaching and learning, that teachers work in intellectual isolation from one another and manage teaching problems virtually alone. Teachers who try to initiate probing lunchtime discussions of teaching or subject matter may find themselves eating alone—or teased into a different topic (Little, 1982; Lord, 1994). Protocols for analysis and description of student work (the CAC, for example, or the PLR) shape a context for intellectual inquiry for which many teachers are hungry. This accomplishes several things: It provides the intellectual exhilaration of good conversation; it confirms the belief that teaching is intellectual work; it supports the development of communities of inquiry within the teaching profession.

Too many teachers leave teaching because they hunger for good conversation and a chance to think with other professionals about the central enigmas of their work. Most depart somewhat reluctantly—they enjoy their work with children, but they fear that they have stopped growing intellectually. They resist the simple answers that colleagues and administrators offer them when they raise questions about their students or their practice and long for the kind of thoughtful inquiry that acknowledges endemic uncertainties and tensions in the work of teaching. The conversations that grow within the confines of the Collaborative Assessment Conference, the Tuning Protocol, and the Descriptive Review acknowledge—and sometimes even celebrate—the ambiguity and complexity that is the bedrock of most teachers' daily experience. In Joel Kammer's account of a "Thursday Protocol" at Piner High School (Chapter 5) we see how rich such conversations can be—and how compelling they are to the teachers who seek them out.

These conversations do more than acknowledge that teachers have minds and that teaching is intellectual work. They ground this intellectual work in what matters most to teachers: the development and learning of individual students. These conversations are not about the long-term prospects of school reform or the role of industrialization in the development of the common school; they are about the daily stuff of classroom life, about the concrete and particular needs of students.

All teachers need help, resources, and support, but those who are trying to teach in new and ambitious ways (Cohen, 1988) are probably in particular need of settings that encourage conversations about the complexities of this work. We should not be surprised, though, that few find these in their staffroom. Teachers work on terms of involuntary intimacy, yet they have limited power either to choose their colleagues or to change them. Teachers in one building often disagree passionately about teaching practice. When people stand on opposing sides of important issues, when they must work side by side regardless of their feelings about one another, conversations about the core issues of teaching and learning can be risky. Rhoda Kanevsky's report (Chapter 3) on the success of efforts to do a Descriptive Review in a faculty with a troubled history is therefore particularly heartening:

> We did Descriptive Reviews in my school during a period when we were having difficulty talking about some hard issues. We did them two different times and everyone loved it. It was a moment when teachers spoke to each other in a different way and there was common ground in a different sense. The structure made it comfortable for everyone and put the focus back on concerns we all share.

Kanevsky leads us to hope that even teachers who disagree on matters of great moment can use protocols like the Collaborative Assessment Conference, the Descriptive Review, and the Tuning Protocol to build communities that sustain their intellectual lives.

The creation of such communities is critical to the success of current reform efforts. Changes in teaching and learning envisioned by groups such as the National Council of Teachers of Mathematics require that teachers rethink not only their pedagogy but also their roles in the development of curriculum and their conceptions of subject matter. This intellectual work cannot be accomplished in the sort of one-shot workshop that typically constitutes district-based professional development; many reformers argue that it can be done best in communities of teachers working together over time, conducting inquiries centered in their own practice (Ball & Cohen, 1995; Lord, 1994). Few such communities exist right now. However, the essays in this book provide reason to hope that rubrics to guide collaborative inquiry—such as the Collaborative Assessment Conference, the Tuning Protocol, and the Descriptive Review—can foster conversations within which intellectual communities such as the Philadelphia Teacher Learning Cooperative will grow.

BUT GETTING DEEPLY INTO STUDENT WORK IS DIFFICULT

However great the potential payoff of disciplined study of students' work, faculty groups that attempt this sort of inquiry encounter major difficulties. An account of the *first* CAC of the Gloucester group (Seidel, 1995) shows Seidel gently insisting that the teachers focus on what they see before them when they seem intent on doing almost anything else. "How old is the writer?" asks one teacher. "It's very creative and offbeat," approves another; "The drawing is more sophisticated than the writing," concludes a third. Over and over Seidel quietly urges the teachers to "describe what you see"; eventually the group focus shifts and a richly layered portrait of the picture and poem of 7-year-old Adam emerges. In Chapter 1, we see these same teachers investigating another palimpsest with persistence, curiosity, and insight. Clearly, however, this investigation was an accomplishment that required practice and self-discipline.

Similarly, Smith and Ruff (Chapter 8) report that when a reflective practice group whose monthly attendance averaged 40 decided to look at student work, more than half the regulars stayed home—and only 2 of the 17 teachers who did come brought any student work to the meeting. And Allen (Chapter 4) notes that while the Tuning Protocol helps educators to conduct focused conversations about *teachers'* work, it has succeeded less well in creating a context for discussion focused on *student* work. Clearly getting deeply into student work is hard. For one thing, as Ruff and Smith point out, student work reflects on the teacher; making that work public makes the teacher vulnerable to all sorts of judgments. In addition, few teachers have ever been asked to describe student work in the way that participants in the TLC or the Gloucester workshop do—yet most would feel that they *ought* to be able to do this sort of thing; just as most museum goers would beg off if asked to describe a Renoir painting, teachers may want to avoid an agenda that asks them to do publicly and for the first time something that looks easy and appears to be central to their work

The culture of schooling does not teach us to see wondering or describing as difficult and worthwhile labor or as skills worth cultivating. But both Seidel's Chapter 1 on the CAC and Allen's Chapter 4 on the Tuning Protocol help us to see how hard it actually is for teachers to dig deeply into student work. This difficulty should not surprise us: In relation to children's written work, the role of the teacher has always been to locate and mark errors and to analyze them diagnostically: What do children know? What are they unclear on? What must the teacher reteach? What must the student redo? Teachers learned from their own teachers that their job is to flag errors and assign a grade, not to wonder, to raise questions, to describe and respond. In addition, teachers must usually deal with student work in the aggregate—not one essay on Darwin but 90, 26 poems about the month of May instead of 1. The limited time available for response and evaluation, together with the external pressures for teaching mechanics, discourage careful attention to each individual piece.

THE WORK AHEAD: CONVINCING *STUDENTS* THAT THEIR WORK MATTERS

Important as is the respect of teachers for student work, convincing *students themselves* of the value of their work matters even more, for it is students, ultimately, who decide how much effort they will invest in academic endeavors and what goals and standards will shape their efforts. This book tells stories in which teachers, appropriately, play the lead roles, examining student work, talking to colleagues, considering dilemmas and ways to improve student learning. But, as the Gloucester teachers point out in their conversation about the CAC (Chapter 1), teachers' conversations about student work lay the foundation for new conversations between teacher and child, conversations that communicate to students "your work matters and you are on my mind and you exist in my mind when you are not with me."

"What you value, you talk about," a parent tells Vivian Paley (1979), rebuking educators for their reluctance to bring discussions of racial differences into their classrooms. The relationship between talk and valuing can sometimes be complex: As we talk with others about something, we hear their ideas and we think more about it. As we think more, we see it's value more clearly—as Julie Carter observed of the Collaborative Assessment Conference (Chapter 1), "The more you looked, the more you saw." Thus talking about student work helps us to see the complexity of what students are accomplishing. It also helps us to show students that we value their work, because, when we describe to a student what we see in his work, we show him that we have looked at it hard and thought about it. Like Cherylann Parker's fifth-graders, most of us respond to this sort of respectful attention to our work by investing more effort in it.

Portfolio assessment, and the attendant necessity of choosing student work to save in portfolios, creates possibilities for enhancing students' interest in their own work by creating occasions for talking with them about that work. And creating portfolio collections of school work can help students to value it in another way: Portfolios invite students to revisit work done in the past and to look for evidence of their own learning. The portfolio and its contents become not only a link to the past but also powerful evidence of growth that may have been invisible to the learner at the time it took place. At the elementary school I attended in the 1950s, teachers saved all student work across the year and sent it home in a spring binder on the last day of school. I remember how surprising these volumes always were to me: Over the course of the year I was very conscious of working many mathematical computations and memorizing vast numbers of names, dates, and rules, but I was not particularly aware that my skills were developing; each June I inspected the papers I had done in September and saw how simple the math problems were, how crude the handwriting seemed to be when I compared it to the stories and math problems done in May.

Remembering all this now, I am struck by the lack of sophistication with which my 10-year-old self inspected these school artifacts: Surely there was, in these collections of work, evidence that I had learned to do more than solve more cumbersome computations and hold my pencil with a steadier hand. But since no adult ever thought to talk with me about my learning, the response I remember probably should not surprise me. The experiences of teachers who have used portfolios as an opportunity to encourage children to think analytically about their own learning suggest, however, that both adults and children can learn a great deal from looking together at collections of student work. Vivian Wallace (1995) describes a project in Central Park East School in New York City in which children reviewed the contents of their portfolios (which contained work they had done in every grade) and talked with a teacher about what they saw and remembered. Wallace comments:

> What the children said about their work and their school was much richer and more detailed than we had imagined. They talked about their interests over time and their individual growth. They talked about the school, its culture and values, about being challenged and working hard. They talked about the way they learn and how they "know"; they talked about the ways teachers were teaching. They talked about solving problems and their uncertainties. They talked about their values and their standards and how these shaped their work habits and their work. (p. 6)

Wallace quotes some typical comments:

> I knew how to read but not that much, so I read that book over and over again; I probably read that book two hundred times, and you let me . . . (p. 6)

> When I read, I get ideas on ways to say things in my writing. When I talk to my friends about my writing I get ideas about more ways to set it up . . . (p. 6)

> . . . what taught me to draw was drawing. I copy other people's work. The more I see, the better I draw, the more I draw, the better I see . . . (p. 6)

When I was little, I designed a car with a fold-up mechanism, so you wouldn't have to look for a parking space. But solving problems is even harder, and takes longer when you are bigger. (p. 6)

I learned English by listening to the kids and watching what they were doing so I learned the meaning of the words. (p. 6)

The educators who are engaging students in this sort of reflection set an agenda for the rest of us: Let us try now to bring students into discussions of their own work—their poems and essays, lab reports and paintings—in ways that help them both to value the learning these efforts embody and to embrace new challenges for further work.

REFERENCES

Ball, D. L. & Cohen, D. K. (1995). *Developing practice, developing practitioners: Toward a practice-based theory of professional education.* Paper prepared for the National Commission on Teaching and America's Future, Teachers College, New York.

Cohen, D. K. (1988). Teaching practice: Plus que ca change . . . In P. W. Jackson (Ed.), *Contributing to educational change: Perspectives on research and practice* (pp. 27–84). Berkeley, CA: McCutchan.

Featherstone, H. (in press). Learning to look: Collaborative Assessment Conferences in the staffroom and the classroom. *Changing Minds, 13.*

Hawkins, D. (1974). I, thou, and it. In *The informed vision: Essays on learning and human nature* (p. 48). New York: Agathon.

Little, J. W. (1982). Norms of collegiality and experimentation: Workplace conditions of school success. *American Educational Research Journal, 19*(3), 325–340.

Lord, B. (1994). Teachers' professional development: Critical colleagueship and the role of professional communities. In N. Cobb (Ed.), *The future of education: Perspectives on national standards in America* (pp. 175–204). New York: College Entrance Examination Board.

Paley, V. (1979). *White teacher.* Cambridge, MA: Harvard University Press.

Seidel, S. (1995). To be the complete thing: A case study of teachers reading children's writing. Unpublished doctoral dissertation, Harvard Graduate School of Education, Cambridge, MA.

Wallace, V. (1995). Collections and recollection. In W. Cooper, M. Barr, & A. McKittrick (Eds.), *The Primary Language Record and the California Learning Record in use: Proceedings from the PLR/CLR International Seminar* (pp. 5–6). El Cajon, CA: Center for Language and Learning.

Appendix

Resources—Organizations and Publications

Organizations and publications that support teachers examining and reflecting on student work include:

Annenberg Institute for School Reform
Brown University
Box 1985
Providence, RI 02912
(401) 863-7990
www.aisr.brown.edu

Center for Collaborative Education
1573 Madison Avenue, Room 201
New York, NY 10029
(212) 348-7821
Publication: *Connections*

The Center for Language in Learning
10610 Quail Canyon Road
El Cajon, CA 92021
(619) 443-6320
clrecord@cll.org

Centre for Language in Primary Education
Webber Row
London SE1 8QW
England
www.rmplc.co.uk/orgs/clpe

Coalition of Essential Schools, Inc.
1814 Franklin St.
Suite 700
Oakland, CA 94612
www.essentialschools.org
Publication: *Horace*

Educational Extension Service
College of Education
116-1 Erickson Hall
Michigan State University
East Lansing, MI 48824
Publication: *Changing Minds*

Harvard Project Zero
Harvard Graduate School of Education
Longfellow Hall
Cambridge, MA 01238
(617) 495-4342
pzweb.harvard.edu

National Center for Restructuring Education, Schools and Teaching
(NCREST)
Box 110
Teachers College, Columbia University
525 West 120th Street
New York, NY 10027
(212) 678-3432
www.tc.columbia.edu/~ncrest
Publication: *Resources for Restructuring*

New York City Writing Project
Institute for Literacy Studies
Lehman College
Bedford Park Boulevard
Bronx, New York 10468
(718) 960-8758

Prospect Archive and Center for Education and Research
Box 326
North Bennington, VT 05257
Publication: *Review*

Southern Maine Partnership
University of Southern Maine
Bailey Hall
Gorham, ME 04038
(207) 780-5498

University Heights Middle School and High School
Bronx Community College
University Avenue & West 181st Street
Bronx, NY 10453
(718) 289-5300

Index

213

About the Contributors

David Allen (Editor) is a researcher at the Annenberg Institute for School Reform, Brown University. His work for the Coalition of Essential Schools focused on authentic assessment. He has taught English and ESL at the middle school, high school, and college levels. In 1996, he received a Fulbright research grant to study school reform in Poland.

Paul Allison is a teacher and the Coordinator of Curriculum and Assessment at University Heights Middle School and High School in the Bronx, where he's taught since 1987. He has been a teacher-consultant with the New York City Writing Project since 1986.

Lauren Campbell-Allan has been principal of the Carrie E. Tompkins Elementary School in Croton-on-Hudson, New York, since 1992. She has taught Spanish and Latin at the middle and high school levels and served as principal of a K–2 school.

Beverly Falk is the Associate Director of the National Center for Restructuring Education, Schools and Teaching (NCREST) at Teachers College, Columbia University. Her work focuses on supporting learner-centered teaching practices through authentic assessment development and research. She is the co-author of *Authentic Assessment in Action* (Teachers College Press).

Helen Featherstone is Associate Professor of Teacher Education at Michigan State University. She has served as the founding editor of two publications, *Changing Minds*, a bulletin on school reform, and *The Harvard Education Letter*. Her current research focuses on the teaching of elementary mathematics and on the efforts of experienced teachers to learn to teach math in new ways.

Howard Gardner is Professor of Education and Adjunct Professor of Psychology at Harvard University, Adjunct Professor of Neurology at the Boston University School of Medicine, and Co-Director of Harvard Project Zero. The recipient of many honors, including a MacArthur Prize Fellowship, he is the author of 18 books and several hundred articles. His latest book, *Extraordinary Minds,* was published in 1997.

Joel Kammer has taught in Santa Rosa, California, high schools since 1978. He has been department chair, district mentor teacher, and a regional fellow for the California Center for School Restructuring (CCSR). He has been a member of the Four Seasons national faculty and helped design the Annenberg Institute for School Reform's National School Reform Faculty program.

Sherry P. King is the Superintendent of the Mamaroneck, New York, Public Schools. Before coming to Mamaroneck, she served as high school principal and then superintendent of the Croton-Harmon School District (New York). She has been involved in New York State and national school reform efforts.

David Niguidula has worked in technology and school reform since the early 1980s. He has led the research on technology and authentic assessment at the Annenberg Institute for School Reform and the Coalition of Essential Schools, both at Brown University, and has taught in Brown University's Computer Science Department.

David J. Ruff is Associate Director of the Southern Maine Partnership, working closely with schools on issues of accountability for student achievement. Before coming to the Partnership, he taught high school English at Thornton Academy in Saco, Maine.

Steve Seidel began work with Harvard Project Zero's Arts Propel after 17 years of teaching high school. He is currently Principal Investigator on four projects. His numerous publications include a chapter in *With Portfolio in Hand* (Nona Lyons, Ed., Teachers College Press).

Debra R. Smith is Associate Director of the Southern Maine Partnership. Her work with teachers and schools over the past few years has focused on assessment and collaborative inquiry. An experienced teacher, researcher, and program evaluator, she is a doctoral candidate at Lesley College, Cambridge, MA.